Volume 7

THE G. STANLEY HALL LECTURE SERIES

Archives of the History of American Psychology, Akron, Ohio

G. STANLEY HALL, 1844–1924

Volume 7

THE G. STANLEY HALL LECTURE SERIES

Edited by
Vivian Parker Makosky

1986 HALL LECTURERS

Elizabeth Rice Allgeier
Elliot Aronson
Henry C. Ellis
Timothy B. Jay
Gary E. Schwartz

AMERICAN PSYCHOLOGICAL ASSOCIATION
WASHINGTON, D.C.

99982

Published by the American Psychological Association, Inc.
1200 Seventeenth Street, N.W., Washington, DC 20036
Copyright © 1987 by the American Psychological Association.
All rights reserved.

ISBN: 0-912704-70-5
ISSN: 8756-7865

Copies may be ordered from:
Order Department
American Psychological Association
P.O. Box 2710
Hyattsville, MD 20784

Printed in the United States of America

CONTENTS

PREFACE

Undergraduate students—particularly freshmen—are both the blessing and the curse of college faculty. For the most part they are bright, curious, and eager to launch into new learning. In psychology in particular, they are ready to learn new and wondrous things, facts that will be of both immediate and long-term relevance to their daily lives. Faculty members have the opportunity to captivate young minds and to convey to a new generation an enthusiasm for and love of their own discipline. The perennial popularity of introductory psychology provides an opportunity to touch the lives of the vast majority of the educated public, as well as to entice the best and brightest minds to further study of the field.

At the same time, traditional undergraduates are at a developmental stage either of wanting absolute truth, every answer clear and unassailable, or of believing that everything is simply a matter of opinion and that their own opinions are as good as any "expert" opinion. They can be scathingly critical of dull, outdated, or incomplete presentations of information. Although they are open to learning about the paradoxical and the bizarre, they are resistant to information that is counter to their own immediate experience, to what they "know" about human nature. From birth, they have been observing and attempting to understand, predict, and control the behavior of themselves and of others, and often they have learned a great deal that introductory psychology teachers must help them "unlearn," reframe, or understand in the context of exceptions and restrictions on generality.

The successful teacher of psychology is able to build on the positive attitude with which most students enter the class and is able to teach them to think critically and understand the value of empirical research. Success requires an understanding of the students' perspective and an ability to capture the attention of people exposed to years of MTV and rock videos. Teachers must invest a great deal of time and energy in developing the content, techniques, formats, approaches, and activities that will not only entice students to read their textbooks, but will also teach them something *in addition to* what they could learn from reading the text.

A major part of the challenge in teaching well is dealing with the massive amounts of information generated by today's scholars. More than 30,000 scholarly books and articles are published annually in psychology, all of them of potential relevance to the introductory course. Even the relatively small proportion of these materials readily available to most teachers constitutes an unmanageable load. In addition, such materials are seldom easily converted into an appropriate classroom presentation: Giving an imitation of a talking book is not only boring, it is also typically less informative than if the student read the more detailed and coherent written version.

Although there are many knowledgeable psychologists who can contribute to the scholarly literature, there are few who meet the needs of the G. Stanley Hall Lecture Series. Although lecturers must be specialists in the assigned areas, they must have the breadth of perspective to present the material in ways that are comprehensible to the non-specialist. Ideally, the lecturers are dynamic speakers who have a mastery of the relevant material, an aptitude for teaching undergraduates, and an understanding of the special problems inherent in teaching the introductory course. Each year, American Psychological Association (APA) Divisions as well as relevant boards and committees are asked to nominate outstanding psychologists for the next year's series, and it is from this pool of nominees that the lecturers are chosen.

This seventh volume of the Hall Series includes chapters based on the five lectures scheduled for the 1986 annual convention of the APA in Washington, DC. In fact, only four lectures were actually presented at the convention: Due to illness, Gary E. Schwartz was unable to make his presentation. However, his chapter is included in this volume. The authors and their topics are Elizabeth Rice Allgeier, coercive and consensual sexual interactions; Elliot Aronson, prejudice; Timothy B. Jay, computers and psychology; Gary E. Schwartz, personality and health; Henry C. Ellis, human memory. The chapters are presented in the order in which they were scheduled for presentation. Psychologists who are knowledgeable in each area and who are experienced teachers were asked to comment on drafts of the manuscripts. These comments were very helpful, both to the editor and to the authors. As anonymous readers, these people cannot be cited, but their assessments have shaped the descriptions that follow.

In the first chapter, Elizabeth Rice Allgeier presents a data-intensive overview of issues relating to coercive sexual interaction. Sexuality is an important concern for traditional undergraduate students, and violence and coercion in sexual behavior have recently become a topic for study by social and behavioral scientists. Allgeier discusses the beginning steps in the scientific study of a social issue. She outlines the difficulties and variations in definitions of violence and coercion. She presents rich descriptive data on characteristics of assailants, victims, and assault situations, along with caveats about the quality of and limitations on those data. Then she summarizes the evidence in support of formal hypotheses about the causes of coercion, and in summary, she outlines the conditions necessary for consensual sexual interactions.

Much of the data cited by Allgeier has been collected from college students or is directly relevant to students' lives in other ways. The information presented here can be of use to introductory psychology teachers even if the course does not include a separate section on sexuality: The material could be incorporated into discussions of aggression, sex roles, or research methodology.

In the second chapter, Elliot Aronson presents a significant social problem (prejudice) and then frames a solution (a teaching method). Reading the chapter *is* like the unraveling of a story. The organization as well as the content of the chapter should be quite helpful to any teacher of introductory psychology. The description of the jigsaw method is excellent, in part because it clearly demonstrates that experiments do not always operate as smoothly as desired, yet the results and the confirmatory research establish validity. Aronson shows that there are numerous strategies for promoting the success of school desegregation, and that there are numerous ways of operationally defining such success (e.g., reduction in prejudice, increased self-esteem of minority students, and improved school achievement).

Students enter introductory psychology expecting an easy course and find a difficult one, often because common sense interferes with learning the material. Aronson illustrates the advantages of using empirical research to generate answers to social issues. The creative and critical thinking of students will be sharpened by confronting the evidence that the science of psychology has answers to some social problems that are contrary to what the students thought they knew. The case presented is exceptionally versatile: It can be used as a single lecture or as a whole approach to social psychology, and it demonstrates a number of principles of social psychology. Aronson presents an excellent contrast between social theory and social research.

In chapter 3, Timothy B. Jay shows instructors of introductory psychology classes the role that computers can play. His paper is easily comprehensible for the novice. Although the material is organized as background for a lecture on computers, computer literacy, and the role of computers as tools across areas of psychology, Jay warns that instructors who have had no hands-on experience may not be able to present such a lecture effectively and may feel intimidated by the many students in the class familiar with a tool he or she is describing but has never used. If that is the case, the Jay chapter may well be what is needed to entice the reluctant teacher to the keyboard.

Jay makes it clear that computers and technology are an integral part of psychology, from the theoretical bench science areas to the applied testing and clinical areas. He discusses cognitive science, artificial intelligence and simulation, education, child development, human factors engineering, psychotherapy, evaluation and assessment, social processes and rehabilitation. He provides interesting examples, a good overall perspective, and challenging ideas.

In chapter 4, Gary E. Schwartz has organized his presentation around nine conclusions about personality and health. These are presented in a logical and coherent order, with separate headings throughout the chapter to allow you to select different parts of the manuscript for class presentation. The material presented here is a good complement to the typical introductory psychology book chapter on stress and adjustment or health psychology. In many instances, Schwartz presents a new perspective on an old topic (e.g., in viewing "disease" as feedback rather than as a disorder). In several instances, Schwartz has provided instructions for class demonstrations that can be done briefly, without highly specialized equipment, and with any number of students. In sum, he has achieved a balanced coverage of basic topics, with minimal overlap with the typical text, at a level of sophistication that will not alienate the instructor who is only minimally informed about the area of health psychology.

In the fifth chapter, Henry C. Ellis provides an excellent, up-to-date overview of the major topics in human memory. Not only is his presentation well organized, it is also conversational and free of unnecessary jargon. The introductory psychology teacher may begin reading with only the vaguest notion of such things as the episodic–semantic distinction and the ARESIDORI system, structural components of memory, subordinate and superordinate concepts, automatic and effortful processes, and elaboration and organization of memory. However, this chapter is an antidote to confusion and to an incomplete grasp of the issues. Ellis presents good examples to illustrate major points and clear definitions of terms. In addition, for those who wish to pursue the original sources, useful and important references are provided. But perhaps most important of all for the teacher, Ellis provides a clear pathway from interesting reading to interesting and informative classroom presentations. He provides good advice on how to approach topics, including specific demonstrations and classroom exercises. With the guidance provided in this chapter, you will be able to promote both discussion and understanding of human memory among your students.

Each year the contributions to the volume of the G. Stanley Hall Lecture Series differ not only in topic but also in style of presentation, amount of detail, and degree of focus on classroom techniques. At the same time, they are all superbly organized, well reasoned, scholarly, and well written. Each presentation contains facts, perspectives, and teaching techniques not readily available to the introductory psychology teacher in any other place. We strive to present something for everyone in this volume, and we believe that this has been a particularly successful year in that regard.

The committee charged with the selection of the G. Stanley Hall Lecturers whose papers appear in this volume included: Paul J. Lloyd, James A. Eison, Margaret A. Lloyd, Antonio E. Puente, and Elizabeth Scarborough. Their work is greatly appreciated. In addition, I would like to thank the colleagues who read earlier versions of the manuscripts and whose comments were valuable in clarifying and maintaining the perspective of introductory psychology teachers. Genevieve Whittemore, Anne Rogers, and Rhonda Washington provided much needed support in correspondence with authors and processing the paper flow. I also wish to thank Donna Stewart, who supervised this volume throughout the production process, and Kathryn Gutwillig, who was the technical editor for the manuscripts.

Vivian Parker Makosky

ELIZABETH RICE ALLGEIER

COERCIVE VERSUS CONSENSUAL SEXUAL INTERACTIONS

Elizabeth Rice Allgeier has been an Associate Professor of Psychology at Bowling Green State University since 1980. At the undergraduate level, Allgeier teaches introductory human sexuality, an advanced sex research seminar, and the psychology of gender. At the graduate level, she teaches clinical aspects of sex research, a sex research seminar, and theories of human sexual behavior. She received her BS from the University of Oregon in Community Service and Public Affairs in 1969, her MA from the State University of New York at Oswego in General Experimental Psychology in 1973, and her PhD from Purdue University in Social Psychology in 1976. She taught at the State University of New York at Fredonia from 1976 to 1980.

Allgeier became interested in the regulation of human sexual behavior while conducting sex research for a year with the *So*, a preliterate polygynous tribe in Uganda. She co-authored a two-volume ethnography on the *So* with Charles Laughlin in 1979. The experience with the *So* led to an interest in the relation between changing gender role norms and sexual interactions and she co-edited a book on that topic with Naomi McCormick in 1983. She is the co-author with Richard Allgeier of *Sexual Interactions*, a human sexuality text, the second edition of which will be available in late 1987.

Actively involved in The Society for the Scientific Study of Sex, Allgeier served as President of that organization from 1985 to 1986.

She was editor of *Research Notes* for the *Sex Information and Education Council of the United States* from 1981 to 1986 and is an Associate Editor for *The Journal of Sex Research*. She is also a Consulting and Contributing Editor for *Sexual Coercion and Assault* and for the *Journal of Psychology and Human Sexuality*.

COERCIVE VERSUS CONSENSUAL SEXUAL INTERACTIONS

Humans are blessed with a potential capacity for experiencing intense intimacy and connection, not to mention exquisite sensations, in the context of their sexual interactions with one another. Although I will be using the term consensual to refer to participation by fully informed adults who freely choose to engage in mutual sexual stimulation, the term *consensual* can also mean the ability humans have to be "sensual with" other humans. Unfortunately, however, many people also experience extreme physical pain and emotional trauma in the context of sexual interactions that are coerced.

I will devote most of this chapter to this latter kind of human experience, beginning with problems associated with operationally defining and determining the rates of sexual coercion. Hypotheses regarding the causes of sexual coercion will be described, and I will review the research on assailant and victim characteristics and on assaultive situations for their relevance to contemporary explanatory hypotheses. Finally, I will discuss methods to reduce some types of sexual coercion and will suggest some conditions that are necessary for consensual sexual interactions.

Definitions of Sexual Coercion

Many people have the following visual image of what is meant by the term *rape*. A menacing "creep in the bushes" leaps out at an unsuspecting, attractive, young woman, attacks her physically, threatens her with a weapon, knocks her to the ground, pulls down her pants, and forces his penis into her vagina. This is, in fact, one form of sexual coercion, but there are many other forms, and that is why I use the phrase *sexual coercion* rather than the term *rape,* or even the more currently respectable phrase, *sexual assault.*

In their annual *Uniform Crime Reports,* the Federal Bureau of Investigation (FBI) uses the phrase *forcible rape,* which seems to be redundant; strictly speaking, by using this definition, the FBI suggests that there is such a thing as consensual rape, or rape that was not forced. The FBI defines forcible rape as "the carnal knowledge of a female forcibly and against her will. Assaults or attempts to commit rape by force or threat of force are also included; however statutory rape (without force) and other sex offenses are excluded" (U.S. Department of Justice, 1985, p. 13). This definition implies that only women can be raped or sexually coerced. The behaviors that constitute "carnal knowledge," "force," or "threats of force" are not specified.

Most observers define the creep in the bushes scenario as a clear exemplar of rape, sexual assault, and sexual coercion. But what about the person who is asked by a teacher or employer to become sexually intimate and who complies, not because the sexual interest is mutual, but because of a desire to keep a job or pass a course? The victim does not want sexual contact, but decides that the alternative—being fired or flunked—is worse. Such behavior was not even recognized as coercive until the past decade; further, it is not called rape or sexual assault but is currently referred to as sexual harassment. What about the 12-year-old who complies with requests for sexual activity by an adult because for more than a decade the youth has been taught to respect and obey adults, and the youth is ignorant of the potential ramifications of sexual activity—pregnancy, sexually transmitted diseases, emotional dependency, and so forth? What about the graduate student in a high state of anxiety over the desire to be evaluated positively who is approached sexually by an attractive and more powerful faculty member? What about the adolescent female who protests against her boyfriend's attempt at sexual intimacy, but who ultimately complies or "consents," in fear that he will reject her if she does not?

In addition to variations in roles and forms of power used in sexual coercion, several other factors are controversial among researchers studying sexual assault. What specific acts constitute sexual coercion, and what parts of the body must be involved? Box (1983) pointed out that there is broad legal agreement in definitions of rape among the states that "reflects a male fetish with one female orifice and one instrument for its violation" (p. 121).

Box has described these and other definitional problems very well, and I recommend his book, *Power, Crime, and Mystification* (1983). He points out that the law emphasizes the absence of consent in defining sexual coercion, but it is difficult to establish what is meant by consent. The difficulties of determining consent are exacerbated, according to Box:

> by the law taking into account the offender's "honest and reasonable" beliefs about consent. . . . But by making lack of consent the distinguishing feature of rape, the law misses an obvious point. It is not so much the absence of consent, although that has to exist, but the presence of coercion which makes rape fundamentally different from normal acts of intercourse. In a situation where the female's choice is severely restricted by the male being able to impose sanctions for refusal, the question of her consent should become secondary to his ability to coerce. (p. 123)

In agreement with Box, my research colleagues and I at Bowling Green State University define all of the scenarios I mentioned previously, involving children, graduate students, and so forth, as examples of sexual coercion because of the absence of freedom to give consent and the presence of the assailant's ability to coerce. In our research surveys and experiments, we use the following definition of sexual coercion: "the use of physical violence, threats of bodily harm, or psychological, economic, or evaluative pressure to force you, or to attempt to force you, into engaging in sexual intercourse, oral sex, or anal sex." We agree with Box (1983) that the absence of the victim's ability or desire to consent and the presence of coercive behavior and threats are important criteria, so we include a further statement in our questionnaires: "The essential feature of sexual coercion is that it involves forcing you or attempting to force you to have sex against your will," and we provide several examples including an attack by a stranger, being told by a date to "put out" or walk home, and having intercourse with a professor who has implied that otherwise a failing grade in his course will result.

Clearly, this definition is more inclusive than that used by the FBI, and it differs from that used in victimization surveys. Unfortunately, there is no agreement on definitions of sexual coercion among those doing victimization surveys, which makes comparisons among studies difficult. For example, Koss and her colleagues (Koss, 1983, 1985; Koss, Leonard, Beezley, & Oros, 1985; Koss & Oros, 1982) distinguished between (a) *acknowledged victims*—women whose assault met the legal definition of rape and who indicated that they consider that they have been raped; (b) *unacknowledged victims*—women whose assault met the legal definition of rape but who did not consider the episode to have been rape; (c) *moderately victimized*—women who experienced attempted but not completed sexual intercourse through the use of physical force or threat of force; (d) *low victimized*—women who had sexual intercourse when they did not want it as a result of extreme verbal coercion, false promises, or threats to end the relationship. For these researchers then, the term *coercion*—which literally means force—is only used to refer to verbal attempts to pressure a woman into sex. Notice also that an *attempt* to obtain sex through physical force or threat of force is rated as involving a greater extent of victimization (i.e., moderate victimization) than is *completed* nonconsensual intercourse through the use of verbal coercion (i.e., low victimization).

In contrast to Koss and colleagues, Mahoney, Shively, and Traw (1986) asked respondents to indicate whether they had experienced any of 19 coerced (defined as "against will") acts ranging from hand holding to the use of a weapon to obtain sex. Respondents then received a total coercive sexual experience score that measured how many of the different sexually coercive behaviors they had ever experienced. The severity or intrusiveness of the behavior was not differentially weighted in their categorization scheme, so that it would have been possible for one woman to get a score of 2 because she reported two episodes of forced intercourse, one in which the assailant used a weapon and one in which the assailant threatened to use a weapon, whereas another woman would get a score of 4 because she reported nonconsensual hand holding, kissing, breast touching, and knee touching.

In a third study on sexual coercion, Ageton (1983) employed a nationally representative sample of male and female adolescents from 1976 to 1981 who were 11–17 years of age at the beginning of the study. Sexual assault victims and offenders were selected for inclusion in the assault sample on the basis of their responses to two series of questions: Initially, they were asked how many times in the last year they had (1) tried to have sexual relations with someone against their will, (2) pressured or pushed someone such as a date or friend to do more sexually than they wanted to do, (3) physically hurt or threatened to hurt someone to get them to have sex, (4) been sexually attacked or raped or had an attempt made to do so, (5) been pressured or pushed by someone such as a date or friend to do more sexually than they wanted (Ageton, 1983, p. 9). Interviewers then read a general description of the situation that Ageton defined as sexual assault to adolescents who were potential victims or offenders:

The following set of questions is related to the event you reported earlier in the interview of having been pressured by someone to do more sexually than you wanted to do. For purposes of this interview, we are interested in the sexual situation in which someone pressured you into contact with the private parts of your body or theirs. (p. 10)

Thus sexual coercion is defined differently by Koss and colleagues, Mahoney et al. (1986), and Ageton (1983). It is relatively easy to criticize definitions used in research on coercion until one begins to look at the variety of experiences reported by respondents and the self-reported effects of coercive episodes on victims. The point of this discussion is to demonstrate that the task of understanding the prevalence, incidence, causes, and correlates of sexual coercion is made more difficult by the fact that coercion is defined differently by different research groups. As Ageton (1983) graciously pointed out in discussing the different sexual assault incidence rates provided by the *Uniform Crime Reports* (UCR), the *National Crime Surveys* (NCS), and her Sexual Assault Project (SAP), the assault rates from each can be valuable depending on whether one is interested in arrest rates (UCR), self-reported sexual victimization (NCS), or in being able to generalize self-reported coercive behavior or victimization from a representative U.S. sample of female and male adolescents (SAP).

Incidence and Prevalence Rates Based on Uniform Crime Reports (FBI) Statistics

With these definitional problems in mind, I will now examine the incidence and prevalence rates from several sources beginning with the data base yielding the most conservative estimate. According to the FBI, there were 84,233 reported assaults in 1984, an increase of 6.7% over the number reported for 1983 (U.S. Department of Justice, 1985). Thus 69 out of every 100,000 women in the United States reported an assault to police that the police considered to be founded and that ultimately resulted in the arrest of the alleged rapist. A naive observer of this statistic would not worry much about being a victim of sexual assault, as the apparent risk is only .00069. This statistic, however, really provides a better indicator of the extremely low risk faced by rapists of being reported and arrested than it does of the risk of being sexually coerced. As is acknowledged in the *Uniform Crime Reports* (U.S. Department of Justice, 1985), forcible rape is "one of the most underreported of all Index crimes" (p. 14), thus their figures represent a minimum estimate.

Table 1
Adolescence Sexual Assault Rates From Three National Samples in 1976

Source	Population sampled	Rate per 100,000
Uniform Crime Reports (UCR)	Arrest records of males aged 12–19	50
National Crime Survey (NCS)	Survey of victims	120
Sexual Assault Project (SAP)	Interviews with both genders aged 13–19	5,000–16,000

Note. UCR data from the U.S. Department of Justice (1985). NCS data from the U.S. Department of Justice (1980a). SAP data from Ageton (1983).

Incidence and Prevalence Rates Based on Victimization Surveys

Examination of the prevalence rates from victimization surveys of representative samples in the U.S. suggests that sexual assault is far more common than the FBI statistics indicate. However, the prevalence rate varies widely among different victimization studies. A comparison of the rates of sexual assaults involving adolescents from three different national sources in 1978 demonstrates the difficulty in determining the "true" sexual assault rate. As shown in Table 1, the rate per 100,000 adolescents ranged from 50 to 16,000, depending on the source of the estimate. Ageton (1983), who obtained her estimate by interviewing a representative national sample of adolescent men and women ranging in age from 11 to 17 at the start of the 5-year project in 1976, concluded that, because of the problem of nonreporting, the upper end of this estimate is probably the most accurate. In her sample, about 10% of the women studied each year were assaulted.

In a victimization survey of women of all ages, Russell (1984) interviewed 930 women from a sample of households in San Francisco. She found that 24% of women aged 18 or older had experienced at least one completed rape, and 31% had experienced at least one attempted rape. Altogether, 44% had experienced at least one attempted or completed rape. Only 8% of these attempted or completed rapes were reported to the police.

In most other studies yielding incidence and prevalence rates the samples have been of more restricted populations, such as adolescents and college students. Hall and Flannery (1985) used a random digit dialing technique to obtain a random sample of women and men aged 14–17, who were living in Milwaukee, 56% of whom were interviewed after parental consent had been obtained. Twelve percent of the women and 2% of the men reported that a man had used physical

Table 2
Coercive Sexuality Reported by Samples of College Women

Source	Definition of coercion	Sample	Reporting period	% reporting coercion
Kanin, 1957	Offensive and displeasing sexual aggression	First-year college women	Year before entering college	62%
Kanin & Parcell, 1977	Offensive and displeasing sexual aggression	282 college women	Year of study	51%
Kanin & Parcell, 1977	Offensive and displeasing sexual aggression	282 college women	Year of study, plus high school experiences	83%
Nelson, 1979	Sexually offensive situations	380 college women	Lifetime	75%
Korman & Leslie, 1982	Male sexual aggression	400 college women	During or since high school	63%
Korman & Leslie, 1982	Male sexual aggression	400 college women	Year of study	38%
Koss, 1985	Sexual aggression	2,016 college women	Lifetime	55%
Mynatt & Allgeier, 1985, 1987	Sexual coercion	125 college women	Lifetime	42%

force or threats to make them have sex (or do something sexual, in the case of men) against their will.

Studies of college students have yielded particularly high incidence and prevalence rates, partially because the definition of coercion is broader than that used by the FBI. In the earliest published study of sexual coercion in dating relationships, Kanin (1957) found that 62% of a sample of first-year college women reported that they had experienced "offensive and displeasing" sexual aggression from a man in the year before they entered college, and other samples have yielded similarly high rates (see Table 2).

Students in my classes frequently ask if the women anonymously reporting sexual victimization in these surveys are really telling the truth or if they could be reinterpreting an event that they later regretted. That is certainly possible in some cases, but the data from several studies in which men were asked to report their sexually coercive behaviors provide some validity to the anonymous reports by women. For instance, in Kanin's (1969) random sample of 400 college men, 22% reported having attempted to have sexual intercourse with a woman by using force in a total of 181 different episodes. More recently, Rapaport and Burkhart (1984) found that 28% of their sample of 190 college men reported having used a directly coercive method at least once, and 15% of the subjects reported having forced a woman to have intercourse at least once. Only 39% of the sample denied any coercive sexual involvement.

Clearly, then, experience with sexual coercion is far more common than would be suggested by official government statistics. As will be seen later, these assaults almost always involve acquaintances, and when the assailant and victim know one another, the victim rarely reports the assault to police or other authorities.

The Problem of Nonreporting of Sexual Assault

The underreporting of sexual assault poses several problems for sexual assault researchers. First, there is the already-noted difficulty of determining prevalence rates. Second, researchers who wish to understand the dynamics and causes of sexual assault face major generalization problems. If incarcerated rapists and victims who reported sexual assault to authorities did not differ systematically from the much larger population of nonidentified rapists and nonreporting victims, then making generalizations on the basis of information from convicted rapists and reporting victims would not be a problem. However, there are a number of reasons to believe that incarcerated rapists and reporting victims do not represent the typical rapist or victim.

The percentage of all rapists who are reported is not known, but Koss (1985) estimated that as few as 10% of assaults are reported to authorities. In her study of 2,016 college women, 37% described assaults that met the legal definition of rape or attempted rape. If the assailant was an acquaintance, however, none of the victims reported it to the police, a crisis center, or a hospital emergency room. Only 4% of the entire sample of victims reported to police.

Based on the population of those rapes that are reported, Schram (1978) concluded that only 5% of alleged assailants are arrested and less than 3% are convicted. I think that in all likelihood, the percentage of rapists who are incarcerated (and thus available for researchers to study) is well under 1% of all rapists, because the overwhelming majority of victims do not report their sexual assaults.

Why do most victims of sexual assault fail to report the crime to authorities? To try to obtain an answer to this question, Feldman-

Summers and Norris (1984) used notices in clinics and public service announcements to recruit women who had been assaulted. They obtained responses from 179 female rape victims, 48 of whom reported to the police only, 8 reported to a social service agency only, 73 reported to both the police and an agency, and 50 reported to neither. Compared with those who did not report to police, those who did indicated stronger social pressures from family or friends to report and were more likely to believe that reporting to the police would result in being treated in a positive way and less likely to believe that reporting would result in a trial in which the victim would have to testify. Two situational variables also differed significantly for reporters of assault and nonreporters of assault: About 74% of the reporters (versus 44% of the nonreporters) suffered cuts or bruises requiring medical attention. In addition, prior social contact with the assailant (versus no prior contact) was strongly related to the decision to report. Of those who reported, only 36% had had prior social contact, whereas 61% of the nonreporters had had social contact with the assailant prior to the assault.

This finding is consistent with the results of our surveys at Bowling Green State University in which half of the women who had been victims of strangers reported the assault to authorities, compared with only 2% of those who knew their assailant (Mynatt & Allgeier, 1987; see also Koss, 1985). These findings are not surprising given previous research indicating that women who have no observable injuries or who are assaulted by an acquaintance are less likely to be believed than are women who are physically injured and are raped by a stranger (Feldman-Summers & Palmer, 1980).

The victim of an acquaintance may be less likely to report than the victim of a stranger due to the victim's (misguided) nurturance: The victim may want to avoid getting someone she or he knows in trouble. This hypothesis needs to be tested. Another motive for nonreporting by victims of acquaintances is self-blame. In Byers's (1979) random sample of 720 college women, only 4 of the assaults were reported to the police, and charges resulted in only 2 of the assaults. The primary reasons the victims gave for not reporting the assault were that it was a private matter and that the victim felt herself partially to blame. Over 75% of these assaults involved an acquaintance. Janoff-Bulman (1979) found that victims engage in behavioral self-blame for the assault, and Mynatt and I (Mynatt & Allgeier, 1987) found that the greater the degree of prior social contact between a victim and her assailant, the more likely the victim was to attribute some responsibility for the assault to herself.

In a very interesting series of experimental studies investigating what they called the "hindsight effect," Janoff-Bulman, Timko, and Carli (1985) asked college students to read one of three date scenarios which differed only in outcome. In these scenarios, a woman was described as having been either raped, beaten, or taken home after a date. After reading one of the scenarios including the outcome, people were asked to indicate what they thought their prediction of the outcome would have been prior to reading the outcome. The students overestimated the likelihood of the outcome that they had read. In a second study, Janoff-Bulman et al. (1985) had half the volunteers read the date scenario in which the woman was raped, whereas the other half read the scenario in which she was simply taken home. Those who read the rape scenario attributed greater behavioral blame to the woman for the outcome than did those who read the version in which the woman was taken home, a finding suggesting that observers engage in the same kind of attribution of blame that victims do to themselves. Most people have experienced this hindsight effect in which they blame themselves for a tragedy: "Oh, if only I had done such-and-such!" Such self-blame and blaming by observers might be expected to lessen the extent to which victims would be encouraged by others to report the crime (as found by Feldman-Summers & Norris, 1984). In a third experiment, Janoff-Bulman et al. (1985) attempted to determine how readily the hindsight effect of blaming the victim could be undone by providing observers with multiple outcomes for an event. After reading either the rape or "taken home" scenario, readers were asked to write reasons why an outcome different from the one they read could have occurred. Serious consideration of an alternative outcome had no effect on blaming the rape victim, and the authors concluded that the victim-blaming bias produced by the hindsight effect is very difficult to reverse. Providing students with scenarios from the Janoff-Bulman et al. (1985) study and asking for student attributions of responsibility can provide an effective class demonstration of the blame-the-victim phenomenon so prevalent in our society.

Earlier, I noted that Feldman-Summers and Norris (1984) found that positive expectations of police response to the reporting of an assault was associated with the decision to report. Several other studies have focused on the role of the victim's expectations of police response. Dukes and Mattley (1977) interviewed 45 recent victims of rape to try to explain why some victims report the offense to police whereas others do not. Results of open- and closed-ended questions indicated that the extent of fear immediately after the rapist left was statistically related to perceived police consideration in the handling of rape cases. When victims were afraid, they reported to police if the police were perceived as providing a haven.

Forrest (1979) studied the relation of victim characteristics and crime circumstances to victims' perceptions of treatment by criminal justice personnel by administering questionnaires to 146 female victims of forcible rape. The majority of significant results involved the circumstances of the crime prior to the rape. Victims who had consumed alcohol prior to the assault reported less empathetic treatment from the prosecutor than those who did not; victims who had used drugs other than alcohol prior to the assault reported less empathy from the detective than those who did not. Victims who met the offender in a bar reported less empathetic treatment from both the detective and prosecutor, and victims who met the offender hitchhiking reported that the patrol officer was less empathetic. Finally, victims acquainted with the offender reported less empathy from the patrol officer and the detective than those unacquainted with the offender. Forrest concluded that a victim's perception of the treatment she received was most influenced by the variables associated with the victim's prerape behavior.

Beyond the factors of victim self-blame, lack of support from others to report the assault, and negative expectations of police response to the victim in a victim's decision not to report, there is the problem of the victim's definition of an assault. For example, of those women who reported experiences that met the legal definition of rape in Koss's (1985) study, 57% described themselves as having been raped, but 43% were "unacknowledged,"—that is, they did not define the events as rape (see also Zellman & Goodchilds, 1983). Parcell and Kanin (1976) found that, particularly if the assailant is an acquaintance or date, victims fail to perceive the episode as "rape" although they will anonymously report that they had intercourse against their will and that they pleaded, kicked, screamed, and tried to get away; only 11% of these women defined their episode as "rape" (S.R. Parcell, personal communication, July 30, 1980). Men who acknowledge that they have engaged in coercive sexual behavior anonymously report such behaviors in their partners as well. Based on a review of the reasons 440 women used to decide to report their rape to police, Cartwright and the Sexual Assault Study Group (1986) concluded that an assailant's use of a weapon was the factor most highly related with the decision to report. It can be hypothesized that the use of a weapon makes it more likely that victims will perceive themselves as having been raped, and less likely that they will blame themselves for the assault, thus increasing the likelihood that they will report the crime. Among adolescents who do define an incident as rape, they may not report it because they do not want their parents to know, due to their fear of being blamed or having their activities restricted (Belden, 1979; Krasner, Meyer, & Carroll, 1976).

From this review, it can be concluded that sexual coercion is widespread in our society, that most victims fail to report the crime, particularly if they know the assailant, and that they avoid doing so because of self-blame, fear of blame or nonbelief by others, and fear of negative responses by legal authorities. Despite the attribution of responsibility for the crime to the victim by observers and by the victim, few scholars suggest that sexual coercion is caused by the victim.

What does cause rape? I have asked students in my classes to write down their explanation of the cause of the crime, and their responses mirror the diversity of hypotheses within the sexual assault research community.

Factors Proposed As Causes of Sexual Coercion

Scientists differ in their beliefs regarding the underlying dynamics of sexual assault, and some of these differences appear to be tied to the rapist's and the victim's formal and informal views of the world, or, in Kelly's (1955) terms, one's "constructions," of the purpose of sex, the nature of men and women, and appropriate role relations between men and women. Whether people are trying to understand the phenomenon of sexual coercion or some other kind of human relationship, they construct models in an attempt to understand, and potentially to predict, what causes certain events (Kelly, 1955). Different individuals have different perspectives and thus may develop different constructions of the same sequence of behaviors.

For example, a young woman wearing shorts and a t-shirt went jogging early one evening near Bowling Green State University where she was a student. She was attacked by a young man who had a knife and attempted to rape her. At the outset, the way in which the woman construed the episode was probably quite different from the way it was construed by the man. The report of the assault in the college paper was followed by letters from students who attributed a variety of causes to the episode. Many of these letters focused on the attire of the woman as causal in the attack, although they did not suggest alternative modes of dress for jogging. They also suggested that by jogging in the early evening, she was asking for trouble.

There followed a second series of letters attacking the assumptions or constructions of the first series. These later writers construed the motives of the authors of the first group of letters as trying to deny women freedom of activity and movement and to promote fearfulness and submissiveness in women.

The factors used to explain sexual coercion that I describe are not necessarily mutually exclusive, but for the sake of simplicity, I discuss each in isolation. Russell (1984) has developed a four-factor model based on Finkelhor's (1984) analysis of the conditions that increase the likelihood of child abuse. I am employing Russell's model, with modifications based on the review of sociological theories of rape causation by Deming and Eppy (1981), as well as those provided in some other studies. I enumerate five broad factor groups: (1) factors creating a predisposition to use sexual coercion, (2) factors reducing internal inhibitions against sexual coercion, (3) factors reducing social

inhibitions against sexual coercion, (4) factors increasing a potential victim's vulnerability to sexual coercion, and (5) factors that interact to increase the likelihood of sexual coercion.

1. Factors Creating a Predisposition To Use Sexual Coercion

The following have been proposed as factors that contribute to a pre-disposition to use sexual coercion.

• *The biological capacity and desire of men to rape.* In her classic book *Against Our Will* Brownmiller asserted that

> Man's discovery that his genitalia could serve as a weapon to gen-erate fear must rank as one of the most important discoveries of prehistoric times, along with the use of fire, and the first crude stone axe. From prehistoric times to the present, I believe, rape has played a critical function. It is nothing more or less than a conscious process of intimidation by which *all men* keep *all women* in a state of fear (1975, p. 5, emphasis in original).

Russell (1984) emphasized another, more critical, biological dif-ference between men and women: men's superior physical strength. However, Russell pointed out that possession of superior strength does not determine whether or not most men want to use sexual coer-cion against women or whether rape is motivated by sexual desire or by the desire to control and dominate (as Brownmiller suggested).

• *Childhood sexual abuse histories of assailants.* Some researchers have suggested that rapists have been sexually abused themselves as children and adolescents and have learned a pattern of sexual coer-cion in their relationships with others.

• *Male gender-role socialization.* Weis and Borges (1973) defined rape as an outcome of a socialization process in which men are ex-pected to be the initiators of sexual activity. They asserted that men who are insecure may use aggression to intimidate and dominate women. Chodorow (1978) argued that in the process of developing a masculine identity, boys are taken care of by their mothers with rela-tively little input from their fathers. This process may emphasize avoiding feminine attitudes, traits, and behavior, and a correlated de-valuing of women.

• *Effects of exposure to violent erotica or aggressive media.* Russell (1984) and other researchers have hypothesized that exposure to ma-terial that depicts women in a degrading or humiliating fashion, that explicitly portrays eroticized versions of coercive sexual relationships, or that portrays sexually aggressive acts against independent women may condition men to link aggressive behavior with sexual arousal.

• *Rape as a means of social control.* Brownmiller has asserted that the fact "that *some* men rape provides a sufficient threat to keep all women in a constant state of intimidation" (1975, p. 229, emphasis in original). A generalized fear of rape, she suggested, restricts women's freedom of movement.

2. Factors Reducing Internal Inhibitions Against Sexual Coercion.

The following factors have been suggested as contributing to reduced internal inhibitions against sexual coercion.
   • *Cultural values that encourage sexual coercion.* There may be attitudes that encourage or condone sexual coercion widely held in our culture. These include perceptions of women as objects or private property and of female sexuality as a commodity (Clark & Lewis, 1977). Other cultural values that may exist are the beliefs that women secretly want to be raped, that they say "no" when they mean yes, that they frequently precipitate their victimization by being reluctant to have sex, and that sexual aggression by men is normal.
   • *Subcultural support for sexual coercion.* Assailants may have peer groups or family members who are more supportive of the use of sexual coercion and who pressure young men to be sexually active.
   • *Irresistible impulse.* Men cannot control their behavior once they are sexually aroused.
   • *Psychopathology.* Rapists are mentally disordered.
   • *Intoxication.* Intoxication by alcohol or drugs reduce a person's inhibitions against using sexual coercion.

3. Factors Reducing Social Inhibitions Against Sexual Coercion.

Certain factors may reduce social inhibitions against sexual coercion.
   • *The power disparity between men and women.* Clark and Lewis (1977) proposed that in all unequal power relationships the powerful member relies on violence or the threat of violence to maintain his or her position.
   • *Male dominance and a culture of violence.* Russell's (1984) two-factor explanation was based on Sanday's (1979) analysis of a number of tribal societies. Sanday described 17% of the 186 societies she studied as "rape prone." In these rape-prone groups, men had greater power and authority than women and expressed contempt for women, and these groups glorified violence by men.
   • *Ineffectiveness of the institutions of social control.* The frequency of sexual assault may be a result of the ineffectiveness of our legal and social systems in responding to the crime. Data have clearly demonstrated the low incidence of rapists being reported, arrested, and convicted.

4. Factors Increasing a Potential Victim's Vulnerability to Sexual Coercion.

A potential victim's vulnerability to sexual coercion may increase due to the following factors.

• *Socialization of women as victims.* The traditional socialization of women to be passive, weak, submissive, nurturant, obedient, and so forth may reduce the effectiveness with which they can thwart or escape a would-be rapist. Russell (1984) propounded, in contrast, that women who adopt a more independent and less "feminine" approach to life may engage in behaviors that place them at a greater risk for assault (e.g., living alone, going out without a man, or hitchhiking).

• *Victim precipitation.* Schlafly stated that "sexual harassment on the job is not a problem for the virtuous woman, except in the rarest of cases. . . . Men hardly ever ask sexual favors of women from whom the certain answer is no. . . . Virtuous women are seldom accosted by unwelcome sexual propositions or familiarities" (1981, p. 400). Based on his study of rape cases in Philadelphia, Amir (1971) concluded that 19% of the women studied had precipitated their own assaults through their behavior before, during, or after an assault. Amir defined the event as victim-precipitated if the police wrote that " 'she behaved provocatively, seems she was seductive.' . . . 'she was irresponsible and endangered herself.' . . . 'known as a prostitute,' or 'known in the neighborhood as a bad character' " (p. 266). The victim-precipitation factor is in considerable disrepute among scientists (although it continues to be widely accepted by many laypeople).

• *Victim vulnerability risk factors.* Koss (1985) hypothesized that some women may have increased vulnerability to coercion by engaging in risky behaviors or because of passivity, submissiveness, or insensitivity to situational conditions. Russell (1984) listed some other risk factors, including ineffective resistance in the face of attempted coercion by someone a woman knows and trusts, living alone, having a variety of sex partners, intoxication by drugs or alcohol, and being poor and thus having limited access to resources such as a car or apartment with good security measures. Another source of victim vulnerability may be the fear that the rapist will murder. Some researchers (e.g., Sales, Baum, & Shore, 1984) have attempted to make sure that readers understand that their research focused on victim *reaction* factors rather than victim *selection* factors so that their research will not be used to contribute to the "blame the victim" model (Allgeier, in press).

5. Factors That Interact to Increase the Likelihood of Sexual Coercion.

Can the interaction of factors just mentioned increase the likelihood of sexual coercion? For example, is coercion more likely because many men are socialized to be aggressive and dominant, and many women are simultaneously socialized to be passive and submissive?

• *Miscommunication and sexual scripts.* Communication patterns between men and women may be conducive to misperception and sexual coercion. That is, women are traditionally socialized to display disinterest in sexual activity and to resist or to attempt to delay the onset of sexual intimacy in a relationship (sometimes, in spite of their own feelings) because of their expected role of gatekeeper (Mc-Cormick & Jesser, 1983; Weis & Borges, 1973).

In one script, a man who "scores" on a first date is a "stud"; the woman who allows him to do so is a "slut." One of my students told me that his sister had gone out with a young man to whom she was highly attracted. After they returned from their date, they began necking and petting, and ended up making love. The man then asked her if she always went to bed on a first date. She said, "No, but you were so 'easy'!" Part of the humor of this story may lie in its reversal of the expected gender role behavior in sexual situations.

Characteristics of Assailants

What do researchers know about people who coerce others to engage in sexual contact? As noted earlier, the bulk of current research does not reveal the extent to which the results from the small samples of incarcerated rapists who have been scientifically studied can be generalized to the enormously larger population of sexually coercive men who have not been reported, located, arrested, tried, convicted, and imprisoned. In this review of the knowledge about sexual assailants, then, I will attempt to distinguish between information about arrested assailants and information about nonidentified assailants.

Demographics

The largest proportion of those arrested for sexual assault are men aged 20–24 (U.S. Department of Justice, 1980b). Other studies have found that the majority of rapists are in the 15–24 age range (Amir, 1971; Katz & Mazur, 1979; MacDonald, 1971; Mulvihill, Tumin, & Curtis, 1969; Russell, 1984). Most arrested rapists are White, heterosexual men in their late adolescence or early adulthood, but even women, gay men, and young boys have been convicted of rape.

In Smithyman's (1979) sample of 50 nonidentified rapists, 72% had never been arrested, and only 6% had been arrested on a sex charge. High school diplomas had been obtained by 84%, 58% had entered college, 42% were in white collar jobs, and 26% were married. In Ageton's (1983) study, there were no differences in race, social class, or place-of-residence between adolescent assailants and nonassailants, a finding consistent with those from other studies of nonidentified assailants (Kanin, 1967; Polk et al., 1981).

Relationship to Victim

Official FBI reports have concluded that from one third to one half of all arrested rapists knew their victims (U.S. Department of Justice, 1980b), but studies of self-identified rapists suggest that the proportion of rapes involving acquaintances is much higher than that involving strangers. Kanin (1985) studied 71 self-identified rapists, all White, unmarried undergraduate volunteers from university classes and campus organizations. Kanin used the legal criterion of rape as penetration of a "nonconsenting female by employing or threatening force" (p. 221). All the cases involved date rape and the majority had had from two to five dates together prior to the rape; most of the pairs had sexually interacted on a prior date(s). Studies with victims, which I review later in the chapter, also support the conclusion that the overwhelming majority of rapes occur between people who know one another to a greater (e.g., spouses, lovers, etc.) or lesser (casual acquaintances) extent.

Forms of Coercion

The use of a weapon during sexual assault is common among identified rapists (Katz & Mazur, 1979). Hursch and Selkin (1974) reported that weapons were used in 59% of the completed and 48% of the attempted assaults in their study. In 75% of cases, physical force is also used (Hursch, 1977; Schram, 1978).

The proportion of men in various nonarrested samples who report having used force to attempt to have sexual intercourse has varied. It appears that the use of weapons and physical force by nonincarcerated rapists is less common than use by those whose sexual assault results in reporting, apprehension, trial, and conviction.

In Koss and Oros's (1982) survey of college students, 53% of the men reported having been misunderstood as to the level of sexual intimacy they desired, and 23% reported having been so sexually aroused that they could not stop themselves even though the woman did not want to have sexual intercourse. Using physical force to make a woman engage in kissing or petting, however, was reported by only 6.4% of the men. Also, 2.4% unsuccessfully and 2.7% successfully used physical force to engage in intercourse. Threats of physical

Table 3
Forms of Coercion Used on Dates by Undergraduate Male Rapists

Forms of coercion	Rapists	Controls
Falsely professing love	86%	25%
Attempts to intoxicate a woman with alcohol	76%	23%
Falsely promising "pinning," engagement, marriage	46%	6%
Threats to terminate the relationship	31%	7%
Attempts to intoxicate with marijuana	28%	19%
Threats to leave woman stranded	9%	0%

Note. Data from Kanin (1985).

force to have sex were reported by 1.9% to be successful and by 2% to be unsuccessful.

Rapaport and Burkhart (1984) found that 43% of 201 college men reported on a questionnaire that they had used a sexually coercive method at least once or twice, and 15% reported forced intercourse. The use of physical restraint to have sexual intercourse was reported by 12% of the men, but none of the men reported having used a weapon to coerce a woman for sexual contact. The most common sexual strategy was to persuade the woman through verbal means—33% reported using this method once or twice, 20% reported doing so several times, and 17% reported doing so often. Ignoring the woman's protests was also a relatively common strategy (26%, once or twice; 8%, several times; 1%, often). Over one third of their sample of 190 reported having engaged in this behavior. The use of threat, restraint, or assaultive behavior was reported by a much smaller proportion of the sample.

Kanin (1967) surveyed 254 male college students, and 26% of them reported having used force to attempt to have intercourse which they perceived to be offensive and disagreeable to the woman. In a subsequent study, Kanin (1985) found a conspicuous absence of the use of weapons and fists by self-identified rapists, but described the rapists' quests for intercourse as bordering on a "no-holds-barred contest" (p. 223). For comparison purposes, Kanin used a control group of 227 White, undergraduate, unmarried men, from which he excluded 36 men because they had attempted or succeeded in sexual assault. He concluded from his data that these undergraduate male rapists were most likely to use lying, drugs, extortion, and fraud for sexual coercion (see Table 3). Kanin concluded that the infliction of punishment or suffering during the rape was "incidental in the vast majority of cases and, at best, served a secondary function. There is very little evidence here that violence functioned as a sexual stimulant for these men" (p. 230).

The overwhelming proportion of the adolescent male offenders in Ageton's (1983) sample also relied on verbal forms of coercion (68% in 1978, 83% in 1979, and 71% in 1980). The second most frequently used form of coercion was taking the victim by surprise, which was reported by 29% of the offenders in a single year. The use of alcohol or drugs was the third most frequently used form of coercion, with 22% being the highest proportion of men reporting this strategy in a single year. Less than 13% of the offenders in any single year reported using any kind of physical force or weapon to coerce their victims, and no one in the sample reported injuring the victim with a weapon. An interesting finding in light of Brownmiller's (1975) assertions regarding the importance of men's superior strength was the perception of male offenders that their size and strength had intimidated the victim: This was reported by 4% to 12% of the offenders in the 3 years for which Ageton reports data.

Forms of Victim Resistance Reported by Rapists

Not surprisingly, women are more likely to resist an unarmed rapist than one who has a weapon (Katz & Mazur, 1979). Based on data from clinical observations of rapists, all of whom were strangers to their victims, Selkin (1975) suggested that active resistance is most effective when used at the beginning of an assault. One third of 915 cases of assault in Denver in the early 1970s were avoided by the victim's use of active resistance strategies including running away, fighting and resisting physically, and screaming for help.

The majority of the undergraduate male rapists in Kanin's (1985) sample agreed with the statement that the woman's rejection of coitus after rather intensive sexual interaction is "primarily the expression of her need to stabilize intimacy for personal reasons, and not to exploit or to be fashionably provocative" (p. 229). Kanin concluded that at the time of the coercion, however, the man didn't recognize this, but focused instead on whether her rejection was genuine or a reflection of the adequacy of his sexual powers. Some of the men in Kanin's sample reported that they had exerted greater efforts on dates with other women, but had been clearly rebuffed; some of the men also expressed surprise that their partners were so easily intimidated.

Although there was considerable variation in sexual coercion "success rates" across the 3 years in Ageton's (1983) study (39% in 1978, 70% in 1979, and 59% in 1980), in all 3 years men reported that the primary reason for not completing an assault was victim resistance. The only other reason for "failure" by men was their own guilt or fright (20%).

Early Experiences and Socialization

A relatively high proportion of convicted rapists were themselves victims of violent sexual abuse, physical assault, or neglect during their preschool, childhood, and adolescent years (Blount & Chandler, 1979; Sack & Mason, 1980). Groth (1979) found that about one third of the offenders he studied were sexually victimized during childhood and adolescence. In comparison, only about one tenth of adult male nonoffenders reported histories of being sexually assaulted. Many adult sex offenders also reported patterns of having sexually victimized others during their childhood and adolescence (Lewis, Shanok, & Pincus, 1979). Half the adults studied by Groth (1979) reported that they had committed sex crimes between the ages of 8 and 16. In 1977, 53 boys aged 10 or under were arrested for rape ("Three boys," 1981), a statistic that some may find surprising because boys of that age do not typically ejaculate. This fact, however, does not imply that they lack sexual or aggressive motives.

One of the major contributions of Ageton's (1983) study is that because of the use of interviews with male and female adolescents over a 5-year period, she has both prospective and retrospective information. Some men who had not engaged in sexual coercion at the beginning of the study had done so by the time later interviews were conducted. In presenting her data comparing background variables between assailants and nonassailants, she took the conservative position that only differences that appeared in 2 or more years were likely to reflect real distinctions between assailants and nonassailants. Variables that consistently distinguished the offenders and nonoffenders both prospectively and retrospectively were the number of family crises reported, such as divorce or prolonged unemployment of family members, and their scores on measures of Family Normlessness and Perceived Negative Labeling by Family. Offenders were also more likely to report "that one has to violate school norms and rules in order to achieve academically" (p. 112).

Peer Group Relations

In Ageton's (1983) study, one of the strongest correlates (and predictors) of assailant versus nonassailant status was involvement with delinquent peers and participation in delinquent behavior and physical assaults. Furthermore, the peers of the offenders were more approving of both sexual intercourse in general, and forced sex in particular, than were the peers of the nonoffenders. Comparison of future offenders with future nonoffenders indicated that the offenders-to-be were significantly more tolerant of deviant behavior and had peer groups who were perceived as more approving of delinquent behavior than characterized the nonoffenders. Two years prior to their self-reported sexual assaults, future assailants were substantially more committed to a delinquent peer group than were the nonassailants.

Kanin (1985) hypothesized that the erotic subculture of rapists labels four types of women as legitimate targets of sexual coercion. Essentially, the "pick-up," the "loose woman," the "teaser," and the "economic exploiter" were viewed as violating sexual expectations after "flaunting, advertising, and promising sexual accessibility" (p. 225). Kanin noted that the undergraduate male rapists in his sample were aware that frequent encounters with "rough sex" would evoke suspicion of derangement, even from their close friends, and only about 25% would tell their friends about such encounters.

An additional concern of the rapists was that frequent use of assaultive methods could detract from their status by suggesting their "sexual failure and the inability to succeed by more sophisticated means" (p. 226). Thus their friends were not perceived as rewarding violence, per se; instead, the rapists felt it was acceptable to coerce these types of women because of their provocative behavior. To gauge the extent to which the students' peer groups would condone aggressive and offensive sexual efforts, Kanin asked respondents what they thought would be the reputational consequences in the eyes of their best friends "if they found out that you offended a woman by *trying* to force her to have sexual intercourse, during the course of which you used physical force and/or threats" (p. 225).

Consistent with Ageton's (1983) findings, Kanin (1985) found that positive reputational consequences from their peers were expected by 54% of the rapists versus 16% of the controls for coercive behavior with a bar "pick-up." For a woman with a "loose" reputation, positive consequences were expected by 27% versus 10% of the two groups. Coercion of a known "teaser" was thought to bring positive consequences by 81% of the rapists versus 40% of the controls, and for an "economic exploiter," 73% of the rapists versus 39% of the controls expected positive consequences. Coercion of a more or less regular date, however, was expected to bring positive reputational consequences by only 9% of the rapists and 7% of the controls.

Kanin (1985) also asked the men, "What degree of pressure do your best friends exert on you to seek sexual encounters?" Forty percent of the rapists versus 9% of the control group reported either a great deal or considerable pressure. Moderate pressure was reported by 45% of the rapists and 28% of the controls, and little or none was reported by 15% of the rapists and 63% of the controls. Kanin concluded that the rapists had a differential association with close friends who encourage and reward sexual experience and who also support sexual coercion of certain women. He also found that 93% of the rapists who indicated they were recipients of great, considerable, or moderate peer group pressure for sexual activity indicated that rape can be justified, versus 45% of the rapists who reported that their peers exerted little or no pressure for sexual activity. Of the rapists, 93%, compared with 37% of the controls, said that their best friends would definitely approve of the use of drugs, lying, extortion, and fraud as tactics for certain women. Such procedures were seriously suggested to 91% of the rapists versus 32% of the controls by their best friends as functional for sexual success.

When he inquired about the behavior of these men in high school, Kanin (1985) found the same peer group phenomenon operating, only in an exaggerated fashion. For example, 85% of the rapists (versus 26% of controls) reported high school friendships in which pressure for heterosexual expression was "great and considerable." The rapists were much more likely to have a history of collaborative sex. Involvement in a "gang-bang" or a sequential sexual sharing of a woman with a male friend was reported by 41% of the rapists versus 7% of the controls. Furthermore, over 67% of the rapists (vs. 13% of controls) had had intercourse with a woman whom a friend had recommended as sexually congenial. The first female-genital contact (manual, oral, or coital) was the result of having been "fixed up" by a friend for 21% of the rapists and 6% of the controls.

Personality Characteristics

Psychological tests of convicted rapists provide profiles of hostile, resentful, self-centered men who impulsively seek immediate gratification of their desires, choosing their victims on the basis of immediate availability (Panton, 1978). Rapists possess greater interpersonal hostility and alienation than do nonrapist offender control subjects, and the modal psychiatric diagnosis for rapists is antisocial personality disorder (Armentrout & Hauer, 1978; Groth, 1979; Rada, 1978; Rader, 1977). However, Abel, Becker, and Skinner (1980) concluded that less than 5% of men were psychotic when they committed rape. Some have suggested that convicted rapists are mentally deficient, but research has not established that rapists have lower IQs than men convicted of nonsexual crimes (Karacan, Williams, Guerrero, & Salis, 1974; Ruff, Templer, & Ayers, 1976; Vera, Bernard, & Holzed, 1979; Wolfe & Baker, 1980).

In a sample of college students, Mahoney et al. (1986) found that the higher the hypermasculinity scores of college men, the greater the number of coercive sexual behaviors they reported. The Hypermasculinity Scale (Mosher & Sirkin, 1984) contains 30 pairs of forced choice items such as

A. I like fast cars and fast women.
B. I like dependable cars and faithful women.

    A. You have to screw some women before they know who is boss.

    B. You have to love some women before they know you don't
       want to be boss

(This scale could be administered to undergraduate psychology students, along with the Attraction to Hypermasculine Males Scale, which is described later.) Consistent with Mahoney et al.'s (1986) results, Tieger (1981) found that men who reported a high likelihood to rape if they were sure they would not get caught were more masculine in their gender role identification (as measured by Bem, 1974) than were men reporting no likelihood of raping.

The degree of involvement in sexually coercive behaviors by Rapaport and Burkhart's (1984) male college students was negatively related to scores on the responsibility and socialization scales of the California Psychological Inventory (CPI). That is, the more coercive the men were, the less responsible and the less socially conscientious they were. Despite the search for psychopathic characteristics of incarcerated and self-identified rapists by a number of researchers, relatively little evidence exists to suggest that rapists are more psychiatrically disturbed than are nonrapists (Scully & Marolla, 1984, 1985).

Sexual Characteristics

Responses to depiction of sexual activity. Convicted rapists are highly aroused by depictions of both consenting and nonconsenting sexual stimuli, whereas nonrapist controls show high arousal only to the consenting depictions (Abel, Barlow, Blanchard, & Guild, 1977). In their work with college samples, Malamuth and his colleagues (Malamuth, Haber, & Feshbach, 1980; Malamuth, Heim, & Feshbach, 1980) found that men who reported some likelihood of raping (LR) if sure of not getting caught responded with more arousal to depictions of coerced sexual intercourse than did those who indicated no LR. Briere and Malamuth (1983) found that those men indicating some LR *and* some likelihood to use force (LF) to have sex had more sexual experience than did those indicating LR, but no LF. Other findings regarding sexual arousal of LR men are reported in the section on attitudes that follows.

Sexual relations with others. The number of coercive behaviors reported by the men in Mahoney et al.'s (1986) study was positively correlated with the number of coital experiences, coital partners, years of sexual activity, and coital partners per year. Based on his work with self-identified rapists, Kanin (1985) advanced the controversial hypothesis that rape is motivated by sexual drives rather than by a desire for aggression or domination. He suggested that rapists may perceive themselves as sexually deprived compared with the self-perceptions of nonrapists. The rapists in his sample had considerably more heterosexual experience, had engaged in a more persistent quest for heterosexual encounters, and used more exploitative techniques to gain sexual access. All of the rapists (versus 59% of controls) reported having had consensual coitus in the past (and prior to committing rape). Heterosexual orgasms resulting from coitus, fellatio, and masturbation averaged 6 times a month for the rapists, versus 0.8 for controls. When asked the frequency with which they attempted to seduce a new date, 62% of the rapists, versus 19% of the controls, responded "most of the time." The rapists, despite their more extensive experience, were more likely to report dissatisfaction with their frequency of sexual activity in the past year than were the controls, 79% and 32% respectively. When asked, "how many orgasms (ejaculations) per week, from any source, do you think you would require in order to give you sexual satisfaction?" the rapists reported a mean of 4.5 versus 2.8 for controls. Kanin concluded that the rapists experience "relative deprivation in that dissatisfaction largely stems from their inability to achieve ambitious goals" (p. 229).

Sexual dysfunctions and prior sexual relations with victims. Based on their interviews with convicted rapists, Scully and Marolla (1985) found that many of the rapists both denied their crime and argued that their victims had enjoyed themselves despite the use of weapons and the infliction of serious injury, including death. Many of them believed that they were helping the victim to realize a fantasy. Interviews by Groth and Burgess (1977) with 170 convicted rapists, however, indicated that sexual dysfunctions were very common during the rape. Only a quarter of the rapists reported no problems with erection or ejaculation during the assault. The proportion of men reporting retarded ejaculation (15%) during the assault is higher than that generally found in other nonrapist samples. For instance, Masters and Johnson (1970) reported that only about 1 in 700 men experiences retarded ejaculation. Erectile dysfunction was reported by 16% of the men in the Groth and Burgess (1977) study. Practically none of the convicted rapists reported similar dysfunctions in their sexual relations with consenting partners. Selkin (1975) also found that vaginal intercourse occurred in less than half the rape cases investigated.

In his sample of White, unmarried, undergraduate men, Kanin (1985) found that the majority of the rapists had had two to five dates with their victim prior to the rape and most of the pairs had sexually interacted on a prior date. Every case of rape followed a fairly extensive bout of sex play with the most common activity being oral–genital sex. Only six of the men were reported to the police, and in every case, charges were dropped. In Ageton's (1983) study, 40% or more of the assaultive men believed that factors that led them to commit assault were the victim's physical build, her teasing and flirting, and their own sexual excitement.

Evidence of Antisocial Behavior

In Amir's (1971) study of cases of forcible rape, 49% of those rapists who were arrested had previous arrest records, most frequently for crimes against property. Most convicted rapists have been found to be sociopathic (Littner, 1973; Rada, 1978) or generally violent and amoral (Gebhard, Gagnon, Pomeroy, & Christenson, 1965). Among the 114 convicted rapists interviewed by Scully and Marolla (1985), 39% also had convictions for burglary or robbery, 29% for abduction, 25% for sodomy, 11% for first or second degree murder, and 12% for previous rapes. The majority of these men had previous criminal histories. Their self-reported motivation for committing the rape frequently included revenge against or punishment of the victim or another woman. That is, the victim, as a member of a particular category—women—was a substitute for another woman whom the rapist wanted to punish. For example, in one case, the rapist had fought with his wife over what later turned out to be her misdiagnosed case of a sexually transmitted disease, which she accused him of having given to her. He then drove around and picked up a stranger whose car had broken down. When she attempted to resist his sexual overtures, he flew into a rage and beat her. He stated: "I have never felt that much anger before. If she had resisted, I would have killed her. . . . The rape was for revenge. I didn't have an orgasm. She was there to get my hostile feelings off on" (p. 255).

Evidence of delinquent and antisocial behavior also appears in the research with nonidentified rapists, as noted earlier in the section on peer group relations. In Ageton's (1983) study, both prospective and retrospective links were found between adolescent involvement with delinquent peers and behaviors and their likelihood of committing sexual assault. In addition, Kanin's (1985) research supports the hypothesis that assailants' peers approve of the use of coercive tactics with particular types of women.

Attitudes

Among 352 male college students, Briere and Malamuth (1983) found that self-reported levels of sexual aggression were correlated with beliefs that victims are responsible for their rapes, rape reports are manipulations, male dominance is justified, and women enjoy sexual violence. Sexually aggressive men also scored higher on the

Adversarial Sexual Beliefs Scale (Burt, 1980) and had higher accept-ance of domestic violence.

Gender roles. Students who report a likelihood of raping (LR) if they are sure of not getting caught have attitudes similar to those of convicted rapists (Malamuth, 1981). A pattern of disinhibitory beliefs about the sexual nature of rape, the responsibility of the rape victim, and sex role stereotyping are more characteristic of men who report high LR than those who report low LR (Tieger, 1981). Kanin (1969) found that men who reported having committed at least one sexually aggressive act viewed the interaction as centering on female provoc-ativeness and tended to justify their behavior by focusing on the wom-an's bad-girl behavior and by categorically deindividualizing her. Sim-ilarly, in Mosher's (1970) study of sexual callousness toward women, 36% of the men agreed with the statement, "You have to fuck some women before they know who is boss" (p. 321). Approximately 86% of the rapists (versus 19% of controls) in Kanin's (1985) study believed that rape could be justified under certain conditions.

Although the findings just described suggest that attitudes sup-portive of traditional gender role norms should be correlated with the likelihood of men to be sexually coercive, direct tests of this hy-pothesis have yielded mixed results. Ageton (1983) found no relation between gender role attitudes for assault versus nonassault status among the male adolescents in her sample. Similarly, Rapaport and Burkhart (1984) found that none of their general sex role attitude measures (e.g., Own Sex Role Satisfaction, Sex Role Stereotyping, Sexual Conservatism, Burt, 1980; Attitudes Toward Women, Spence & Helmreich, 1978) predicted degree of involvement in sexually coercive behavior.

On the other hand, Check and Malamuth (1983) found that col-lege students with high scores on the Sex Role Stereotyping Scale were similar to rapists in their self-reported arousal to rape depic-tions; that is they reported equal arousal to depictions of rape and consenting sexual interactions, whereas those low in sex role stereo-typing reported less arousal to rape than to consensual depictions. Also, men who were high in sex role stereotyping reported greater likelihood of raping than men low in sex role stereotyping. Costin (1985) found that men's beliefs in rape myths was correlated with holding traditional attitudes toward gender role. In addition, signifi-cant correlations were obtained by Rapaport and Burkhart (1984) be-tween degree of involvement in sexually coercive behavior and scores on Burt's (1980) Adversarial Sexual Beliefs Scale and Attitudes To-ward Interpersonal Violence Scale. The Endorsement of Force Scale, developed by Rapaport and Burkhart (1984), also correlated with self-reported coercion. Rapaport and Burkhart (1984) concluded that sexually coercive men act on a system of values in which women are perceived as adversaries, and that this value system is potentiated by the characterological dimensions of irresponsibility and poor socialization. In general, then, traditional versus egalitarian attitudes toward gender roles is probably insufficient in and of itself to predict likelihood of engaging in sexual coercion. Instead, such attitudes probably interact with other factors such as acceptance of violence and perceptions of men and women as adversaries to increase the potential for sexually coercive behavior.

Exposure to violent erotica. A final topic on rapist attitudes is exposure to violent erotica. Many people are uncomfortable with the eroticized depictions of rape in which women are portrayed as ultimately enjoying their own victimization. Such depictions are parallel to the beliefs of some incarcerated rapists that victims secretly desire the assailant's sexual coerciveness (Scully & Marolla, 1985). Furthermore, people do not see portrayals of the victims of other crimes (robbery, assault, mugging, etc.) enjoying their victimization. After holding hearings in a number of cities on the effects of exposure to pornography, the Presidential Commission on Pornography concluded in 1986 that exposure to materials in which women are sexually victimized causes men to be sexually aggressive. It should be noted that several members of the Commission—notably, Becker (1986), who has done extensive research with incarcerated rapists—dissented from the majority conclusion. In order to instruct a class to evaluate this conclusion, it is useful to ask students what kinds of research findings would be needed to support the Commission's conclusion. So far, no one has been able to design a study that would be ethically acceptable to test the hypothesis that exposure to erotica that depicts the sexual victimization of women is sufficient to impel men to rape. For instance, it is not financially or ethically feasible to expose one group of men to eroticized rape films and another group to neutral films and then follow them to see if the first group commits a greater number of rapes than the second group does.

Mosher, a psychologist who has studied the assault phenomenon and calloused attitudes toward women, cogently pointed out the flaws in their review procedures when he testified before the Commission (Mosher, 1986). I think that his testimony should be required reading for students in any course concerned with the evaluation of scientific findings in determining public policy decisions. Essentially, Mosher suggested that Edwin Meese and most of the other members of the Commission began their hearings with the presupposition that pornography causes rape, and they did not adhere to scientific rules of evidence in reaching their conclusions. Given the importance of the issue, it is unfortunate that the Commission generally took an advocacy stance (advocating the elimination of erotica) rather than conducting a scientific inquiry. Their conclusions can be used by those who advocate censorship to support their position or, alternatively, can be criticized by those who advocate freedom of speech to dismiss the Commission's conclusions on the basis of their nonscientific procedures.

Based on the available research, I don't think that either stance is warranted. Two of the most active researchers in this area, Malamuth and Donnerstein, and their colleagues have conducted numerous studies attempting to understand the effects of exposure to aggressive pornography (Malamuth & Donnerstein, 1984). Most of their research has focused on changes in attitudes toward women and rape following exposure to various depictions of violent erotica. They have also examined changes in levels of aggressiveness, as measured by willingness to administer shock in lab settings. Essentially, this body of research indicated that exposure to eroticized depictions of the sexual coercion of women produces arousal in male observers and leads to increased acceptance of rape myths (e.g., women secretly desire rape). Stock (1982) found that eroticized depictions also increased women's arousal, but when women in her study were exposed to realistic depictions of rape, they were not aroused; this casts doubt on the idea that women secretly desire rape.

Donnerstein and Berkowitz (1981) have also found differences in both levels of arousal and levels of aggressiveness in men as a function of the depiction of the victim's response to sexual coercion. After having a female confederate insult the male subjects or treat them neutrally, they were exposed to one of four films—a neutral film, one involving consensual sex, one involving rape in which the victim had a negative reaction, and a rape film in which the victim responded positively. After viewing the films, the men were given an opportunity to shock the female confederate. For those men who had previously been insulted, exposure to both the positive and negative rape films increased their aggressiveness toward the female confederate. Even the noninsulted men became more aggressive following exposure to the rape film showing a positive reaction in the victim. In another study, Malamuth (1981) found that men who report some likelihood to rape if they could be sure of not being caught report more arousing fantasies in response to violent erotica than to consensual erotica, whereas the reverse is true for men who report no likelihood of raping.

These findings suggest, then, that exposure to violent erotica is not harmless, but it does not tell us if these men will subsequently leave the lab to seek a rape victim. Due to concern about this possibility and in an attempt to determine the effectiveness of debriefing observers after exposure to violent erotica, Malamuth and Check (1984; see also Check & Malamuth, 1984) gave observers a debriefing that emphasized the horror of rape and the inaccuracy of rape myths. In response to a seemingly unconnected "public survey," administered about 10 days later, men exposed to the violent erotica and subsequently debriefed were less accepting of certain rape myths than those men exposed to consensual erotica.

Thus increased educational programs about the realities of rape may be helpful in dispelling beliefs that women enjoy rape. In this regard, Fischer (1986) compared the responses to a date rape vignette presented at both the beginning and end of the semester to students who were enrolled in either introductory psychology or human sexuality classes (in which rape was covered as part of the course material) in two successive years. She found the greatest rejection of the men's assaultive behavior in the responses of students in the sexuality class at the end of the semester. However, in the first year of the research, the rape lecture was confrontational in nature in one of the sexuality classes. For this group, the men's responses became *more* accepting of the male assailant's behavior, suggesting that confrontational approaches are not effective in changing attitudes toward date rape.

The Recidivism Issue

Among the 114 convicted rapists interviewed by Scully and Marolla (1985), 25% had previously been convicted of sodomy, 26% had prior convictions for sex offenses, and 12% had been convicted of more than one rape. Among self-identified rapists, only 8% of the 71 undergraduate men in Kanin's (1985) study reported that they were recidivists, and of these only one admitted to having committed a prior rape under comparable circumstances. Although only 2% of the men in Rapaport and Burkhart's (1984) sample reported that they had forced a woman to have sexual intercourse against her will "several times" and none of them reported that they had "often" done so, less invasive forms of coercion were reported by higher percentages of the sample. Forced breast touching (18%), forced thigh or crotch touching (16%), and forced unfastening of outer clothing (13%) was reported as having happened several times. The recidivism rates reported from studies are probably underestimates due to the fact that men may fail to perceive an episode as coercive when women initially resist, men may persist, and the couple may end up having sex when, in fact, the woman did not wish to do so. More research is needed—probably using interview methods—to obtain an accurate picture of the recidivism rate among self-identified assailants.

Characteristics of Victims

Although researchers know a little more about victims than they do about assailants, with victims, they also face a generalization problem, and they need to distinguish between victims who report to authorities and those who do not report, but who will anonymously acknowledge having been sexually coerced in response to victimization surveys.

Demographics

A consistent finding with victims who report assault to authorities and with those who only report anonymously on questionnaires and in interviews is that females are at greatest risk during their adolescence and early 20s (Katz & Mazur, 1979; Russell, 1984). In the Philadelphia Assault Victim Study of women who went to emergency rooms after being assaulted (McCahill, Meyer, & Fischman, 1979), the proportion of victims aged 0–11 was 16%; 12–15, 23%; 16–20, 24.7%; and 21 and older, 35.8%. Adolescents between the ages of 13–17 constituted 30% of Hayman, Stewart, Lewis, and Grant's (1968) sample of 451 cases of sexual assault that were reported to the District of Columbia police department; their rate was the highest of any age group in proportion to the population. Amir (1971) and MacDonald (1971) found that 15–19 year olds accounted for approximately 25% of rapes and the rate increased to 44–47% when the age range was expanded to include the years 10–19 (Amir, 1971).

Victims in McCahill et al.'s (1979) study were primarily Black, lower class, and poor (see also McDermott, 1979). In Hayman et al.'s (1968) study, the sexual assault rate for non-Whites was higher than the rate for Whites, particularly among adolescents. McCahill et al. (1979) concluded that women in lower income groups were much more likely to report rape than were those in higher income brackets. Research with women who report their assaults may overrepresent minority group members and the poor. Victims who can afford it may seek treatment from private sources to avoid reporting to police and attendant publicity (Hall & Flannery, 1985). In support of this possibility, Ageton (1983) found no relation between socioeconomic status and likelihood of being victimized, and Russell (1984) found that income was unrelated to being sexually coerced.

In terms of marital status, in McCahill et al.'s (1979) study, 78.2% of the victims were single, 8.7% were currently married, and 13.2% were separated, widowed, or divorced. Findings regarding the marital status of nonreporting victims were consistent with that from those who report. In Russell's (1984) study, 85% of the victims were single at the time of the assault. The relation between single status and victimization may be partially due to the greater likelihood of being assaulted during adolescence than at later ages.

Relationship to Assailant

In their report of research with 408 crisis center clients, Ruch and Chandler (1982) found that among the adult women, 53% had been assaulted by strangers, 33% were acquaintances, 9% were friends or dates, and 5% reported other victim–rapist preassault relationships. Bart (1981) reported that 71% of the victims in her sample were assaulted by strangers. Resick, Calhoun, Atkeson, and Ellis (1981) found that 57% of the women in their sample were raped by complete strangers, versus 21% who were dating the offender, and 5% who were raped by relatives, ex-boyfriends, and boyfriends. Assault by acquaintances was more common among adolescents than adults, and less likely to be known to parents or reported to the police (Hayman et al., 1968). In McCahill et al.'s (1979) study, 45.6% of the rapes involved a total stranger, 13% involved a relative stranger (a person whom the victim had seen before, but had never spoken to). A casual acquaintance or friend was involved in 36.4% of the rapes, and nuclear or extended family members were involved in 5% of the rapes. Similarly, in McDermott's (1979) study, most of the rape reports involved a stranger. These findings, however, overrepresent the occurrence of rape by strangers due to the relative underreporting of acquaintance assault.

In Russell's (1984) probability sample of 930 women in the San Francisco Bay Area, 91% of assault victims knew their assailant. College student victimization surveys also indicate that the overwhelming majority of women knew their assailant. Undergraduate women were assaulted by acquaintances in 96% of Skelton's (1984) sample, 86% of Byers, Eastman, Nilson, and Roehl's (1977) sample, and 99% of Parcell and Kanin's (1976) sample. In our research at Bowling Green State University, 92% of the victims knew their assailants (Mynatt & Allgeier, 1987).

In Kanin's (1957) survey, the proportion of offensive episodes reported involving necking and petting above the waist was distributed relatively equally among levels of relationship (first date, occasional date, regular date, pinned, or engaged). Petting below the waist, attempted intercourse, and attempted intercourse with physical violence occurred more frequently in more committed relationships. Male sexual aggression, without preceding consensual sexual activity, was more common in the more casual relationships. In Kanin and Parcell's (1977) study two decades later, however, this pattern had changed. Breast and genital fondling, and all efforts at intercourse were concentrated among casual rather than involved couples. Offensive aggression was less likely to be preceded by consensual sexual intimacy, and the more sexually aggressive the level of offense, the less likely it was to be preceded by consensual sexual intimacy. They speculated that by the 1970s, advanced sexual activity was normative among involved couples and was therefore not considered offensive.

Koss (1985) classified relationships according to their superficial appropriateness for sexual interaction. Relationships between victims and offenders who were dating or were formally or informally engaged were classified as appropriate relationships. "Inappropriate relationships" involved victims and offenders who were strangers, relatives, neighbors, or nonromantic friends. She found that acknowledged rape occurred in "appropriate social relationships" more often than did low-sexual victimization or unacknowledged rape. Unacknowledged rape victims reported greater prior intimacy than did moderately victimized or acknowledged rape victims.

Forms of Coercion

McDermott (1979) found that nonstranger rapes were less likely to involve a weapon and less likely to involve physical injury in addition to the rape. In McCahill et al.'s (1979) study, a majority (64%) of the victims reported being pushed or held during the assault. Slapping (17%), brutal beatings (22%), and choking (20%) were also reported by victims. Various kinds of nonphysical force were also reported by 84% of the victims. Coercion or the threatening of bodily harm was reported for 56% of the rapes. The offender made threatening statements or gestures with an object or weapon in 36% of the cases, or without an object or weapon in 20% of the cases. Similarly, in Nelson's (1979) study, physical coercion was the most prominent type of force used, followed by covert threats.

Fisher (1979) examined data from 814 cases of rape and attempted rape to try to predict the amount of physical injury to the rape victim. Multiple regression accounted for 29% of the variance in victim injury, using 10 independent variables. Five of the variables were characteristic of the victim–offender interaction, and 5 were predispositional characteristics—2 of the victim and 3 of the offender. Possession of a knife by an offender and victim resistance together accounted for half of the explained variance.

Among nonreporting victims, in Koss's (1985) study, acknowledged rape victims experienced more forms of verbal pressure than low-victimized women. The low-victimized women by definition reported fewer types of force, more moderate force, and a lower intensity of violence than all other groups. These women appear to have been victimized via the use of the kinds of tactics described by the men in Kanin's (1985) sample—refer back to Table 3. Acknowledged rape victims reported an intensity of violence that was significantly greater than that experienced by low- and moderately sexually victimized women.

Assaulted female adolescents in Ageton's (1983) study were coerced primarily through verbal persuasion (58–65%) or were intimidated by the size and strength of their assailants (39–66%). The third most common form of coercion was pushing, slapping, and mild roughness, reported by 27–40% of the victims over the three years.

Successful and Unsuccessful Resistance Strategies

The kind of resistance employed by a (potential) victim appears to be related to whether or not she or he is able to escape, as will be described below. In Nelson's (1979) study, victims dealt with offensive sexual aggression by talking, getting away from, or struggling with the offender. Anger was the most frequent reaction of the victim to the situation, shame was the least frequent reaction. Fear was likely to be reported when the respondent was not in a dating situation with the male offender and when a threat to personal safety was involved. Victims in Nelson's (1979) study seldom told parents of the offense and even less frequently reported it to authorities or discussed it with a counselor. Byers (1979) found that victims reported using a variety of verbal and physical responses: fighting, crying, yelling, and pushing the man away.

The extent of resistance appears to be related to the kind of coercion used by the assailant and the perception of the episode by the victim. Among Koss's (1985) sample, the low-victimized women reported using fewer forms of resistance and were less certain about the clarity of their nonconsent than were all other victimized groups. The highest intensity of resistance was reported by moderately victimized women and by acknowledged rape victims.

Most victims in Ageton's (1983) study used several strategies in trying to resist the assault. In each of 3 years, the forms of resistance reported by the largest proportion of victims were reasoning with the assailant (43–48%), becoming hostile and angry (32–45%), and physically resisting (28–39%). Only about 5% of the victims reported having offered no resistance at all. Nonresistance was a result of the fear of intimidation due to a relationship with the offender. In all 3 years, the majority of victims were successful in escaping the assault, with the completed assault rate ranging from 20–33%.

Bart (1981) distributed self-report questionnaires to 94 women, obtained via advertisements, press releases, flyers, and public service announcements, in an attempt to identify differentiating characteristics between attacks in which women were raped and attacks in which women successfully resisted. Thirteen of the women had been raped once and had also successfully resisted once. Bart studied these 13 women because each woman served as her own control: Her background factors, except for the assault, were the same in both instances. Through interviews, Bart found that when women successfully resisted rape, they were more likely to have used several strategies (e.g., struggling, screaming, talking) than women who were raped (who relied primarily on talking). Bart also found that women who were concerned mainly with avoiding death and mutilation were more likely to be raped than women who were concerned mainly with not being raped. Women were more likely to be raped if force or the threat of force was used, if they knew their assailant, and if they had had a prior sexual relationship with the assailant. Finally, women were more likely to escape an assailant if the event occurred outside.

In their Denver Rape Prevention Research Project, Hursch and Selkin (1974) found that 79% of 165 successful resisters of attempted rape escaped by means of active resistance, such as screaming, fighting, and running. Only 16 of the women resisted by talking only. Hursch and Selkin (1974) compared the personality characteristics of rape victims and rape resisters and found that rape resisters were more dominant and more confident in coping with social situations than rape victims were. Selkin (1978) compared victims with women who successfully escaped assault attempts and found that the latter were higher on the dominance, social presence, sociability, and communality subscales of the CPI.

A comparison of victims of attempted versus completed rape by Javorek (1979) indicated that whether the potential victim screamed for help or not was the most useful predictor of rape avoidance. Burt (1980) found that fleeing or attempting to flee was associated with the highest rate of rape avoidance: Of the women using this escape strategy, 81% avoided being raped. However, Koss's (1985) data indicated that successful escape may be influenced by both resistance strategies and by offender characteristics. Moderately victimized women in her study reported fewer forms of physical force and violence from the assailant than did highly victimized women, but the degree of resistance reported by the two groups of women was equivalent. Koss suggested that some men, although willing to engage in sexually aggressive behavior, may stop at lower levels of violence in response to the victim's resistance, whereas other men may persist and become even more aggressive in response to resistance. Based on Kanin's (1985) research with assailants, very active resistance on the part of potential victims seems like the most effective strategy—at least with acquaintances.

Early Experiences and Socialization

In Hall and Flannery's (1985) survey, the percentage of women who had been raped did not differ as a function of racial or ethnic membership, parental education, or neighborhood. Young women living with both parents were significantly less likely to be raped than those in other living situations. Among the young women in father-absent homes, those living with the mother and a stepfather were equally likely to be raped as those living with the mother only. Sexual assault was not significantly related to whether or not the mother was employed. Being brought up in a religion and having a current religious preference were both negatively related to rape victimization.

Peer Group Relations

Adolescent women who identified with a delinquent peer group were more likely to be (or to become) victims of sexual assault than were women who didn't identify with delinquents in Ageton's (1983) sample. In Hall and Flannery's (1985) survey, the sexual climate of the peer group was also related to having been sexually assaulted. Of those women aged 14–17 who said that none of the five girls they knew best had had sex, 6% had been raped. Of those who said that three to five of their girlfriends had had sex, 22% had been raped. Hall and Flannery suggest that it might be hypothesized that if a young woman is part of a peer group who are known to be sexually active and perhaps is sexually active herself, men are likely to perceive her as interested in sex and to have "led them on." Thus the rapists might feel more justified in forcing sex on her in a dating situation. DeLamater and MacCorquodale (1979) found that sexual experience in adolescents was correlated to being a member of a sexually active peer group.

Personality Characteristics

Of the victims interviewed by McCahill et al. (1979), 26.8% had previously had some kind of private or publicly funded mental health counseling, including psychiatric, psychological, or other psychotherapy. It is not known, however, if a greater proportion of this sample had received treatment than characterizes the general population of women. Most studies investigating general personality characteristics of victims versus those of nonvictims have found very few differences (Koss, 1985; Rapaport & Burkhart, 1984).

In their work with college women who have been victimized, Burkhart and Stanton (1987) suggest that adherence to the feminine role of being nurturant may have reduced the ability of one of the victims in their sample to resist her assailant. This woman was with her date at a fraternity party. Burkhart and Stanton report that her date had obviously planned the assault and had feigned illness. Out of concern, she accompanied him to his bedroom where he forced her to have sex. When the authors interviewed her, they asked how the assailant had responded to her resistance and what had happened when she cried out. She said:

> Even as I say this now, it sounds crazy to me, after what he did to me . . . but I didn't scream, not because I didn't think to scream. I remember thinking about screaming as I tried to fight him off, but I decided not to scream. . . . I can't believe I even thought this. . . . I decided not to scream because I didn't want to embarrass him (Burkhart & Stanton, in press).

When asked to rate adjectives describing their ideal man, victims in Koss's (1985) study were more likely than nonvictims to select "aggressive" men, but less likely to see "sexual inexperience" and "suggestibility" as desirable characteristics in men than were the nonvictims. This finding is consistent with the results of a subsequent study by Mahoney et al. (1986) in which they modified Mosher and Sirkin's (1984) Hypermasculinity Scale to create an Attraction to Hypermasculine Males Scale that could be administered to women. Attraction to hypermasculine males by the undergraduate women in their sample was positively correlated with the number of sexually coercive experiences the women reported.

Sexual Behavior

Among those studies that have examined the sexual behavior of victims and nonvictims, the victimized group is consistently more sexually active, suggesting that this variable may be related to the victim's vulnerability to sexual assault.

Sexual relations with others. Among the 2,016 college women surveyed by Koss (1985), the acknowledged victims had significantly more sexual partners (12) than did nonvictims (4), but the average ages of acknowledged victims (15.97) and nonvictims (17.35) at first intercourse was not significantly different because of considerable within-group variation. Acknowledged victims' first sexual partners were more likely to be strangers, casual dates, or married men, and less often a steady boyfriend or fiancé, than was true of nonvictims. Victims also had sex for the first time for different reasons than did nonvictims. Nonvictims did so because of desire or wanting to please their partners; victims were more likely to report having felt coerced (although for the majority, first coitus did not involve assault, per se), or obligated, or that there was nothing that they could do about it. Victims were less likely to report that they believed that their first intercourse experience would lead to marriage and they were less likely to have been steadily dating their first coital partner at the time of the act.

Koss (1985) indicated that her findings may support a sexual exposure dimension in that women who are exposed at an earlier age to a greater variety of partners, by virtue of more liberal premarital sexual values, may be statistically more likely to be victimized. Some researchers (e.g., Tsai, Feldman-Summers, & Edgar, 1979) have described the correlates of childhood sexual abuse, and their findings are consistent with the hypothesis that sexual victimization may alter sexual standards and behavior.

Prior sexual relations with assailant. In Byers's (1979) study, many of the victims reported having engaged in sexual activity with the assailant willingly or unwillingly on an occasion previous to the assault. In her representative sample of adolescents in the U.S., Ageton (1983) found that the assailant in the majority of assaults was a date or boyfriend of the victim and concluded that the "dating situation provided the setting in which most female adolescents were sexually assaulted in the late 1970s" (p. 41).

Evidence of Antisocial Behavior

In McCahill et al. (1979), almost one-fifth of the victims (19%) reported incidents of truancy and fighting. During childhood and adolescence, 12% of the sample were runaways, and 15% had had some previous trouble with police, either during adolescence or adulthood. Ageton's (1983) research, which employed a control group, is even more convincing of the relationship between involvement in antisocial behavior and vulnerability to sexual assault. Compared with the control group, victims were more involved in a wide variety of delinquent behaviors, including serious offenses, and they were far more tolerant of deviant behaviors than were the controls.

Attitudes

Nelson (1979) found that gender role attitudes were not related to reactions to offensive sexual behaviors. Although Costin (1985) found that women's beliefs in rape myths were associated with holding traditional attitudes toward gender roles, Ageton (1983) found that assault status was not related to traditional versus egalitarian gender role attitudes.

Koss (1985) found that acknowledged victims had more liberal premarital sexual values than did nonvictimized women. Acknowledged victims did not differ from nonvictims in acceptance of sexual aggression, conservative attitudes toward female sexuality, rejection of rape myths, unacceptability of aggression, attitudes toward women, or rape attitudes. Both nonvictims and acknowledged victims were more likely to view heterosexual relations as gameplaying than were the other three groups.

Recidivism Issue

Although the issue of victim's repeated experience with sexual coercion—the victim recidivism rate—has not been given a great deal of publicity, perhaps partially due to fears that such publicity will fuel the "blame-the-victim" attitudes that permeate our society, studies that have asked victims about their number of prior sexual coercion episodes have been quite consistent in showing that once victimized, a woman is likely to experience further sexual coercion.

In McCahill et al.'s (1979) study of women who reported to an emergency room for treatment following an assault, 20% of the victims had been sexually assaulted by the same or another offender at least once before the present rape. Data from women who do not report their assaults to authorities, however, show considerably higher recidivism rates. Thirty years ago, Kirkpatrick and Kanin (1957) found that of the women in their sample who had experienced sexual assault, there was a mean of 6.3 different assaults per woman. College women who reported having been assaulted in Korman and Leslie's (1982) sample reported an average of 5.7 episodes since their senior year of high school, and 74% of the victims had experienced more than one assault. Kanin and Parcell (1977) found that half of the undergraduate women in their sample had experienced offensive and displeasing sexual aggression during the academic year; these women reported a total of 725 assaults, for an average of 5.1 offensive episodes per woman. And in an intriguing finding from Kanin and Parcell's study, the total number of offensive episodes reported by those who had been assaulted in the past year—"current victims"— was compared with those who had not been assaulted in the past year—"non-current victims." The former reported having experienced a life-time total of 22.5 episodes of coercion, compared with 8.5 for the non-current group.

In her study of 263 college women, 46% of whom had been sexually coerced, Skelton (1984) found that the greater the number of sexual assaults experienced by each woman, the lower her self-esteem and assertiveness. Prospective research is clearly needed on this issue to determine if low self-esteem and assertiveness contributes to the inability to escape coercive situations, or if repeated experience with coercion lowers one's self-esteem and assertiveness, and our research group at Bowling Green State University has planned such a project. However, finding an appropriate sample of victims and nonvictims in an undergraduate population is not as easy as it might seem.

Hrabowy and I (Allgeier & Hrabowy, 1987; Hrabowy, 1987) studied the long-term correlates of coercive sexual experiences during childhood, and we included questions regarding unwanted sexual experiences before and after the age of 16. We administered the questionnaire to a large random sample of undergraduate women, 383 (61%) of whom completed and returned the questionnaires. The majority of the women had experienced a number of unwanted sexual experiences before the age of 16, but the statistic that we found most dismaying was the percentage of women who fell into the following four groups:

No unwanted sexual experiences: 64 (17%);

Unwanted sexual experiences before, but not after the age of 16: 23 (6%);

Unwanted sexual experiences after, but not before the age of 16: 131 (34%); and

Unwanted sexual experiences before *and* after the age of 16: 165 (43%).

Our data suggested that repeated unwanted sexual experiences were normative in our sample. Why were all these repeated sexually coercive experiences occurring? Longitudinal prospective research is badly needed to address this question.

Most research has tended to focus on attributes of the perpetrator or the victim, but a small number of studies has examined the situations in which sexual coercion occurs, which is my next topic.

Characteristics of Assault Situations

Many people have engaged in behavior that they later regretted because of various aspects of the situation they were in. For example, after having a few drinks, one may have decided to tell someone what he or she *really* thinks of the person, or one may have become more sexually intimate with someone than he or she would have done, had one been sober. Alcohol ingestion is common in rape situations for both the assailant and the victim. The majority of incarcerated rapists were either drinking or drunk at the time of the assault (Wolfe & Baker, 1980). The National Commission on the Causes and Prevention of Violence (Eisenhower, 1969) concluded that victims, offenders, or both, are likely to be drinking prior to sexual assault, and Russell (1984) concluded that female alcoholics may be particularly vulnerable to assault because they may be in no condition to defend themselves once they have started drinking. Among the nonidentified rapists in Ageton's (1983) study, offenders reported a greater percentage of drug use than did nonoffenders, and 64%–83% indicated that they were drunk or high during the assault. Victims in Ageton's study also reported more trouble from drinking and drug use than did the nonvictim controls.

In contrast to the "creep in the bushes" and "dark alley" scenarios, most assaults occur in locations that are familiar to the assailant, the victim, or both. In McCahill et al.'s (1979) study, 42% of the rapes took place in either the victim's or the assailant's home. More than half of the rapes (59.1%) in McCahill et al.'s (1979) study took place when it was dark, and weekends were slightly more likely to be times of assault than were weekdays. Ageton (1983) found that approximately three quarters of the assaults in her sample occurred in one of three locations: a vehicle, the assailant's home, or the victim's home, with no single dominant location. The remaining 25% occurred in motel rooms, schools or other public buildings, and out of doors. Hall and Flannery (1985) found that a victim's hitchhiking was significantly related to rape in their sample. Only seven of the young women said that they had accepted a ride from a stranger within the past two weeks, but of those seven, four (57%) had been sexually assaulted. However, none of the women in Ageton's (1983) study had been hitchhiking prior to the assault.

Summary of the Knowledge About Sexual Coercion

Earlier, I described five major models and their corresponding hypotheses regarding the causes of sexual coercion. In summarizing the empirical data on assault, it may be helpful to review these hypotheses.

Factors Creating a Predisposition to Be Sexually Coercive

Among the five hypotheses subsumed under this explanation, the first concerned the biological capacity and desire of men to rape. Clearly, *perceptions* of the capacity of men to overpower women do intimidate some women's attempts at resistance. Interestingly, a greater proportion of women reported feeling intimidated by their assailants' superior strength than was believed by assailants to be the basis on which they coerced their victims. It should be noted, however, that anyone with a source of power (physical, use of weapons, evaluative, economic, etc.) can coerce another person to engage in unwanted behaviors. It is difficult to test the extent to which men have an inherent "desire to rape." Although about a third of men in numerous studies have indicated some likelihood that they would rape if they could be sure of not getting caught, it is important to remember that two thirds indicate no likelihood of raping even if sure that they wouldn't be caught. At the moment, there is no evidence that men are innately predisposed to rape.

Assailants are more likely than nonassailants to have experienced sexual coercion during childhood and adolescence, and, in turn, to be sexually coercive at a young age. They also tend to have more disruptive family lives and to feel that they are negatively perceived by their families and teachers.

Masculine gender role socialization has been hypothesized to encourage sexual coercion, but it is likely that it is exaggerated forms of such socialization rather than training to be "instrumental" and "independent," per se, that is related to coercive behavior. Although traditional gender role attitudes are related to acceptance of rape myths in men, coercive behavior itself is primarily related to association with delinquent peers, approval by peers of high levels of sexual activity and of coercion of certain "types" of women, endorsement of hypermasculine characteristics, and engaging in delinquent and antisocial activities.

Exposure to violent erotica increases negative attitudes toward women, rape myth acceptance, and aggression expressed in laboratory settings. It is not yet clear if, or the extent to which, such attitudes are translated into behavior outside the lab, or if there is a direct link between seeing sexually aggressive depictions and engaging in sexual coercion.

The hypothesis that rape is used by some men as a means of socially controlling some women is supported somewhat by the fact that men reported having been motivated by desires to dominate or punish their victims. This motivational pattern appears to be more common among incarcerated rapists than nonidentified rapists of acquaintances. Date rape may involve more sexual than aggressive motivation, although some of these nonidentified assailants do view certain women as deviating from appropriate behavior and thus being acceptable targets for assault. In summary, there is mixed support for this model.

Factors Reducing Internal Inhibitions Against Sexual Coercion

Both cultural and subcultural values are hypothesized under this model to facilitate the likelihood that men will employ sexual coercion, and both of these hypotheses have received considerable support. Sexually aggressive men are more accepting of adversarial sexual relations, interpersonal violence, and domestic violence. The subcultural support for the sexual coercion hypothesis receives particularly strong support through several studies using very different methodologies. Assailants identify with delinquent peers who approve of high levels of sexual activity and the use of coercion against specific types of "bad" women.

The hypotheses of irresistible impulse and psychopathology under this model are not supported by research indicating that many assailants (particularly with acquaintances) respond to the level of resistance given by the potential victims and that they do not differ in levels of psychopathology from nonassailants. They do appear to be sociopathic, but receive support for coercive behavior under some circumstances from their peers.

Intoxication with alcohol or drugs appears to be present, and may play a role in reducing internal inhibitions, in a large proportion of rapes. Given the large percentage of rapes that occur in social and dating situations, in which intoxicants are also commonly used, more research needs to be done to determine if alcohol and drugs are primarily correlative or causative in their relation to sexual coercion.

Factors Reducing Social Inhibitions Against Sexual Coercion

Under this model, it is hypothesized that male–female power disparities, culturally condoned violence, and the ineffectiveness of institutions of social control reduce inhibitions against sexual coercion. Regarding the latter hypothesis, the statistics on the likelihood of being reported, arrested, tried, and convicted amply demonstrate the inadequate responses by victims and the criminal justice system to sexual assault. Therefore, it is unsettling that approximately one third of men anonymously indicate that there would be some likelihood that they would rape if they could be sure of not getting caught. I administered Malamuth's Likelihood to Rape Scale (Malamuth, Haber, & Feshbach, 1980; Malamuth, Heim, & Feshbach, 1980) in the middle of the semester to my large human sexuality class for demonstration purposes and was astounded to get the same general percentage. I do not believe that most young men are aware of the relative impunity with which they can commit rape, nor is it clear whether or not they think of possible legal consequences. Furthermore, many men do not construe their sexually coercive behavior as "rape" per se. However, for the third of men who indicate some likelihood of raping if they could be sure of not getting caught, increasing their awareness of the very low risk of being held accountable for the crime might have some unfortunate consequences.

The hypotheses of male dominance and power disparities between men and women as being causative in reducing inhibitions against sexual coercion are somewhat more complicated. Although there is little that one can do faced with an assailant yielding a lethal weapon, in most cases of sexual assault weapons are not used, and strong resistance appears to deter attempts at sexual coercion in a large percentage of cases. Women may feel more intimidated than necessary in many cases; this suggests that educational approaches encouraging and supporting women for taking active strategies to escape sexual assault attempts may be effective in reducing the prevalence of sexual coercion. In other words, the widely held belief that women lack power may reduce their effectiveness to a greater extent than do actual disparities in the extent of power held by men and women.

Factors Increasing a Potential Victim's Vulnerability to Sexual Coercion

The most controversial (and least supported) hypothesis under this model is the belief that people precipitate or provoke their own sexual victimization. There is no evidence to suggest that people want to be raped any more than they want to be mugged, beaten, or otherwise assaulted. On the other hand, factors associated with increased vulnerability to sexual coercion have been identified, such as sexual activity (e.g., age at first intercourse, number of partners, motivations for engaging in sex, etc.). Additional factors, such as living alone, going out without male escorts, or going to bars, are also associated with an increased risk of assault. Although these have been collectively labeled as "exposure" factors, I will be suggesting some strategies in the next section that may potentially allow women freedom of choice with respect to social and sexual activities without increasing their risk of victimization beyond that shared by all women in the culture.

The hypothesis that traditional gender role socialization increases risk to sexual assault does not receive consistent support in the literature. On the other hand, active rather than passive responses to coercion attempts may be related to the likelihood of escaping assault attempts.

Factors That Interact to Increase the Likelihood of Sexual Coercion

The major hypothesis advanced under this model is the idea that differing gender roles in sexual scripts and miscommunication may increase the likelihood of coercion. Although men are expected to press and women are expected to limit the extent of sexual interaction in our culture, it is probably not *mis*communication, but *under-*

communication of their disinclination to have sex that is related to sexual assault, at least among acquaintances. The more strategies that are used by women to escape coercion attempts, the more likely they are to be successful in avoiding rape.

Most assailants and victims are in their adolescence or early 20s, and victims tend to be slightly younger than assailants. The assailant and victim generally know one another and in many cases are dating. In assault by a stranger, the use of weapons is common, but among acquaintances, physical restraint and psychological coercion are the "weapons" used to induce compliance. Strong and active resistance to coercion attempts appears to reduce the likelihood that assault will be successful among acquaintances.

Data from several recent studies suggests that assailants (e.g., hypermasculine men) may be attracted to the specific "types" of women whom they perceive to be legitimate targets of sexual coercion. In turn, victims of sexual coercion are more attracted to hypermasculine men than are women who have not been sexually coerced.

I have been focusing on a dismal topic, and I initially intended to end this chapter with a discussion of assault prevention strategies. However, I have argued elsewhere (Allgeier, 1985) that it may be more helpful to focus on the conditions under which sex is appropriate rather than using the "don't do it" caveat. Similarly, it may be more useful to discuss approaches to negotiating consensual sexual intimacy than to advise (as some might argue that the data indicate) "Don't have sex early, severely restrict your number of partners, stay away from highly masculine men, and avoid being independent!" What can we do as educators, as parents, and as potential sexual partners to increase the likelihood that sexual contacts will involve mutual consent and pleasure?

Conditions Necessary for Consensual Sexual Interactions

In conducting research, scientists are now required to obtain the "informed consent" of subjects, and this concept plus some associated ethical issues in the research process may be useful in exploring the conditions that are necessary for truly consensual sexual intimacy. The concept of informed consent includes the requirement that research participants be fully informed about the research in which they are invited to participate prior to giving their consent. In addition, their consent must be freely given; specifically, if inducements are offered, such as credit toward a course grade, other means must be available (e.g., reading research reports, etc.) to obtain the rewards. In submitting research proposals and informed consent forms to ethics boards, researchers must describe how they will protect research participants from harm, and how the benefits to be derived from the research outweigh any potential physical and psychological risks.

In our culture, it is common for parents to serve as "ethical review boards," particularly for daughters, regarding the conditions under which sexual intimacy is acceptable. Unfortunately, most parents give very little useful information about the process of negotiations between people who are considering becoming sexually intimate. Some parents confine themselves to the proscriptive "Don't!" or "Don't do it until you're married." The meaning of "it" (kissing? hugging? breast caressing? genital stimulation? vaginal penetration? oral sex?) is typically left undefined. Thus young people are given no practical guidelines for decision making and the negotiation of their sexual relationships.

A number of societal and individual problems (assault, unwanted pregnancy, sexually transmitted diseases, feelings of guilt or exploitation) might be reduced by socializing our adolescents to ask for and give informed consent to one another in their relationships. Parrot (1983) gives an entertaining and potentially very helpful demonstration of one aspect of this process. In conducting a modified version of her demonstration in my human sexuality course, I ask for a male volunteer from the class, brief him, obtain his informed consent to participate in the role-play, and he and I go through an approximation of the following conversation between two people who know one another from a class and have just begun a conversation in the student union:

Betsy: Oh, hi, Bill. I noticed that you weren't in class last time, and I wondered if you were sick or something.

Bill: Yeah, I had a bout with the flu, and so I've been looking for you to see if I could borrow your lecture notes. I also wanted to see if you wanted to go out for dinner and to a movie Saturday night. If you did, I thought I could get the notes when I pick you up.

Betsy: Oh, sure, you can borrow my notes. What movie did you have in mind?

Bill: Well, (name of recent movie) is playing in town. Would you like to see that?

Betsy: Gee, I've already seen that. Have you seen (name of another recent movie)?

Bill: No, and that's one I want to see, too. Do you have any preferences about where we go for dinner?

Betsy: Well, I like almost anything. How about Mexican?

Bill: Oh, well, I'm doing Mexican Friday night with a bunch of the guys. How about Chinese?

Betsy: Yeah, I like Chinese, too. Listen, Bill, after the movie, you can come up to my apartment for awhile if you like. My roommate is having a party that will probably go pretty late. But I want you to know that I don't kiss open-mouthed on the first date, and I don't want any breast-fondling until I get to know you pretty well . . . maybe in a month or so. Depending on how things are going, mutual manual genital stimulation might be acceptable in a couple of months. Are you okay with all this, and are you still interested in going out Saturday night?

I have never figured out whether the hysterical laughter of students in my class is because of the discrepancy in age between the student volunteer and me or because of the blatency with which I have laid out the acceptability of the various forms of sexual intimacy. After the students stop laughing, I ask them what they found so funny. They generally say that they can't imagine just saying stuff like that—that it would take the spontaneity out of it all. I ask how they feel about the negotiations regarding the specific movie and kind of food, and they don't have any problem with that; it is the negotiations over sex that seem weird. I point out that becoming sexually intimate is surely a more serious decision than the choice of a movie or restaurant and try to suggest that negotiations regarding the conditions under which *that* is acceptable are much more important than whether Bill eats Mexican food two nights in a row, or Betsy sees the same movie twice.

There are several other common objections by my students to the woman's stipulation of the conditions under which she will engage in various forms of sexual intimacy. They question the appropriateness of talking about such limits in public before Bill has even made an attempt at intimacy. They also ask, "What if she changes her mind?" I suggest that an early, public discussion of these issues potentially reduces the risk of coercion: Bill is unlikely to attempt sexual intimacy in public, and if they are in a private setting, Betsy has less protection from coercion in the event that he is not interested in the conditions under which she finds intimacy acceptable. Regarding the latter issue, of course, I point out that agreements are always open to renegotiation if either of them changes his or her mind.

One other aspect of the students' reactions interests me. Obviously, I have given them a sexist, one-sided model of the negotiation of sexual intimacy, but no one has ever commented on it, perhaps because it happens to fit in with their stereotypes of the woman as limit-setter. But the next time I do it, I think I will let Bill's intentions and values be portrayed regarding the conditions under which *he* finds intimacy acceptable or not acceptable, just as he had input on the restaurant and movie.

While in a public setting dealing with issues of sexual intimacy,

Bill and Betsy could also discuss the importance and means of reducing their risk of unplanned pregnancy or exposure to sexually transmitted diseases. Another important topic for them to consider (still in a public setting) is the meaning of sexual intimacy with one another. What do each of them want from this relationship? Do they want recreation, friendship, approval and reassurance that they are sexually desirable, or long-term emotional commitment potentially leading to marriage? If there are differences in their goals, one or both of them might want to reconsider their interest in sexual intimacy.

To be able to engage in such a dialogue requires that both people know their sexual and relationship policies, are able to talk about them openly, and value themselves enough to negotiate a satisfying relationship or to decide that a particular relationship is not likely to lead to mutual pleasure and enhancement. That is where I think that we, as educators and parents, and where our students, as potential future parents, can provide some help. Travis, Gaulier, and I have begun pilot work with college students attempting to determine their sexual policies. Specifically, we have asked them to assume that they are very attracted to someone, and to describe what conditions would lead them to act on their attraction versus choosing to experience their feelings without acting on them. They had a difficult time with this exercise: The concept of a sexual policy was foreign to almost all of them, and they asked numerous questions trying to understand the task. The task is to reduce the prevalence of sexual coercion and to increase the extent to which both people in a sexual interaction are "positive in their desires—rather than the female feeling obliged or socially coerced into physical acts that do not reflect her desire" as Box (1983, p. 124) put it. Men, too, can feel coerced to "come on" sexually to prove their manhood.

Accordingly, the concept and legitimacy of developing sexual policies—the conditions under which one will and will not behaviorally express his or her sexual arousal with another person can be introduced. We can discuss with our students and children the pain and trauma of feeling exploitative or exploited and the conditions under which that can occur. We can also positively affirm the reality that under conditions of mutual consent, respect, and equality, sexual and emotional intimacy can enrich our lives and our sense of connection to one another.

References

Abel, G. G., Barlow, D. H., Blanchard, E. B., & Guild, D. (1977). The components of rapists' sexual arousal. *Archives of General Psychiatry, 34,* 895–903.

Abel, G. G., Becker, J., & Skinner, L. (1980). Aggressive behavior and sex. *Psychiatric Clinics of North America, 3*, 133–151.

Ageton, S. S. (1983). *Sexual assault among adolescents*. Lexington, MA: Heath.

Allgeier, E. R. (1985). Are you ready for sex? Informed consent for sexual intimacy. *SIECUS Reports, 13*(6), 8–9.

Allgeier, E. R. (in press). Reducing victim vulnerability. *Sexual Coercion and Assault*.

Allgeier, E. R., & Hrabowy, I. (1987). Sexual coercion recidivism rates among victims from childhood through college. Manuscript in preparation.

Amir, M. (1971). *Patterns in forcible rape*. Chicago: University of Chicago Press.

Armentrout, J. A., & Hauer, A. L. (1978). MMPIs of rapists of adults, rapists of children, and nonrapist sex offenders. *Journal of Clinical Psychology, 34*, 330–332.

Bart, P. B. (1981). A study of women who were both raped and avoided rape. *Journal of Social Issues, 37*, 123–137.

Becker, J. (1986, November). *The Presidential Commission on Pornography: Politics, process, and product*. Plenary session presented at the annual meeting of the Society for the Scientific Study of Sex, St. Louis.

Belden, L. (1979). *Why women do not report sexual assault*. Portland, OR: Portland Women's Crisis Line.

Bem, S. L. (1974). The measurement of psychological androgyny. *Journal of Consulting and Clinical Psychology, 42*, 155–162.

Blount, H. B., & Chandler, T. A. (1979). Relationship between childhood abuse and assaultive behavior in adolescent male psychiatric patients. *Psychological Reports, 44*, 1126.

Box, S. (1983). *Power, crime, and mystification*. London: Tavistock.

Briere, J., & Malamuth, N. M. (1983). Self-reported likelihood of sexually aggressive behavior: Attitudinal versus sexual explanations. *Journal of Research in Personality, 17*, 315–323.

Brownmiller, S. (1975). *Against our will: Men, women and rape*. New York: Simon & Schuster.

Burkhart, B. R., & Stanton, A. L. (in press). Sexual aggression in acquaintance relationships. In G. Russell (Ed.), *Violence in intimate relationships*. Great Neck, NY: PMA Publishing.

Burt, M. R. (1980). Cultural myths and supports for rape. *Journal of Personality and Social Psychology, 38*, 217–230.

Byers, E. S. (1979, June). Characteristics of unreported sexual assaults among college women. Paper presented at the meeting of the Canadian Psychological Association, Quebec.

Byers, E. S., Eastman, A. M., Nilson, B. G., & Roehl, C. E. (1977, August). Relationship between degree of sexual assault, antecedent conditions, and victim–offender relationship. Paper presented at the convention of the American Psychological Association, San Francisco.

Cartwright, P., & The Sexual Assault Study Group (1986). Reported sexual assault in Nashville-Davidson County, TN, 1980 to 1982. *American Journal of Obstetrics and Gynecology, 154*, 1064–1068.

Check, J. V. P., & Malamuth, N. M. (1983). Sex role stereotyping and reactions to depictions of stranger versus acquaintance rape. *Journal of Personality and Social Psychology, 45*, 344–356.

Check, J. V. P., & Malamuth, N. M. (1984). Can there be positive effects of participation in pornography experiments? *The Journal of Sex Research, 20,* 14–31.

Chodorow, N. (1978). *The reproduction of mothering: Psychoanalysis and the sociology of gender.* Berkeley and Los Angeles: University of California Press.

Clark, L., & Lewis, D. (1977). *Rape: The price of coercive sexuality.* Toronto, Canada: Women's Press.

Costin, F. (1985). Beliefs about rape and women's social roles. *Archives of Sexual Behavior, 14,* 319–325.

DeLamater, J. D., & MacCorquodale, P. (1979). *Premarital sexuality: Attitudes, relationships, behavior.* Madison: University of Wisconsin Press.

Deming, M. P., & Eppy, A. (1981). The sociology of rape. *Sociology and Social Research, 65,* 357–380.

Donnerstein, E., & Berkowitz, L. (1981). Victim reactions in aggressive erotic films as a factor in violence against women. *Journal of Personality and Social Psychology, 41,* 710–724.

Dukes, R. L., & Mattley, C. L. (1977). Predicting rape victim reportage. *Sociology and Social Research, 62,* 63–84.

Eisenhower, M. S. (1969). *To establish justice, to insure domestic tranquility.* Final report of the National Commission on Causes and Prevention of Violence. Washington, DC: U.S. Government Printing Office.

Feldman-Summers, S., & Norris, J. (1984). Differences between rape victims who report and those who do not report to a public agency. *Journal of Applied Social Psychology, 14,* 562–573.

Feldman-Summers, S., & Palmer, G. (1980). Rape as viewed by judges, prosecutors, and police officers. *Criminal Justice and Behavior, 7,* 19–40.

Finkelhor, D. (1984). *Child sexual abuse: New theory and research.* New York: Free Press.

Fischer, G. L. (1986). College student attitudes toward forcible date rape: Changes after taking a human sexuality course. *Journal of Sex Education and Therapy, 15,* 42–46.

Fisher, W. S. (1979). Predictability of victim injury in incidents of rape. *Dissertation Abstracts International, 40*(5), 2912-A. (University Microfilms No. 7923724, 205)

Forrest, L. M. (1979). Rape victim characteristics and crime circumstances: Their relationship to the victim's perception of the treatment received from criminal justice personnel. *Dissertation Abstracts International, 40*(7), 4245-A. (University Microfilms No. 7927783, 144)

Gebhard, P. H., Gagnon, J. H., Pomeroy, W. B., & Christenson, C. V. (1965). *Sex offenders.* New York: Harper & Row.

Groth, A. N. (1979). *Men who rape: The psychology of the offender.* New York: Plenum Press.

Groth, A. N., & Burgess, A. (1977). Sexual dysfunction during rape. *The New England Journal of Medicine, 297,* 764–766.

Hall, E. R., & Flannery, P. J. (1985). Prevalence and correlates of sexual assault experiences in adolescents. *Victimology: An International Journal, 9,* 398–406.

Hayman, C. R., Stewart, W. F., Lewis, F. R., & Grant, M. (1968). Sexual assault on women and children in the District of Columbia. *Public Health Reports, 83,* 1021–1028.

Herdt, G. H. (1981). *Guardians of the flutes: Idioms of masculinity, a study of ritualized homosexual behavior.* New York: McGraw-Hill.

Hrabowy, I. (1987). Self-reported long-term correlates of child sexual abuse. Unpublished master's thesis, Bowling Green State University, OH.

Hursch, C. J. (1977). *The trouble with rape.* Chicago: Nelson-Hall Publishers.

Hursch, C. J., & Selkin, J. (1974). *Rape prevention research project.* Mimeographed annual report of the Violence Research Unit, Division of Psychiatric Service, Department of Health and Hospitals, Denver.

Janoff-Bulman, R. (1979). Characterological versus behavioral self-blame: Inquiries into depression and rape. *Journal of Personality and Social Psychology, 37,* 1798–1809.

Janoff-Bulman, R., Timko, C., & Carli, L. L. (1985). Cognitive biases in blaming the victim. *Journal of Experimental Social Psychology, 21,* 161–177.

Javorek, F. J. (1979). When rape is not inevitable: Discriminating between completed and attempted rape cases for non-sleeping targets. Denver: Violence Research Unit.

Kanin, E. J. (1957). Male aggression in dating-courtship relations. *American Journal of Sociology, 63,* 197–204.

Kanin, E. J. (1967). Reference groups and sex conduct norm violation. *Sociological Quarterly, 8,* 495–504.

Kanin, E. J. (1969). Selected dyadic aspects of male sex aggression. *The Journal of Sex Research, 5,* 12–28.

Kanin, E. J. (1985). Date rapists: Differential sexual socialization and relative deprivation. *Archives of Sexual Behavior, 14,* 219–231.

Kanin, E. J. & Parcell, S. R. (1977). Sexual aggression: A second look at the offended female. *Archives of Sexual Behavior, 6,* 67–76.

Karacan, I., Williams, R. L., Guerrero, M. W., & Salis, P. J. (1974). Nocturnal penile tumescence and sleep of convicted rapists and other prisoners. *Archives of Sexual Behavior, 3,* 19–25.

Katz, S., & Mazur, M. A. (1979). *Understanding the rape victim: A synthesis of research findings.* New York: Wiley.

Kelly, G. A. (1955). *The psychology of personal constructs* (Vols. 1–2). New York: Norton.

Kirkpatrick, C., & Kanin, E. (1957). Male sex aggression on a university campus. *American Sociological Review, 22,* 52–58.

Korman, S. K., & Leslie, G. R. (1982). The relationship of feminist ideology and date expense sharing to perception of sexual aggression in dating. *The Journal of Sex Research, 18,* 114–129.

Koss, M. P. (1983). The scope of rape: Implications for the clinical treatment of victims. *The Clinical Psychologist, 36,* 88–91.

Koss, M. P. (1985). The hidden rape victim: Personality, attitudinal, and situational characteristics. *Psychology of Women Quarterly, 9,* 193–212.

Koss, M. P., Leonard, K. E., Beezley, D. A., & Oros, C. J. (1985). Nonstranger sexual aggression: A discriminant analysis of the psychological characteristics of undetected offenders. *Sex Roles, 12,* 981–992.

Koss, M. P., & Oros, C. J. (1982). Sexual experiences survey: A research instrument investigating sexual aggression and victimization. *Journal of Consulting and Clinical Psychology, 50,* 455–457.

Krasner, W., Meyer, L. C., & Carroll, N. E. (1976). *Victims of rape.* Washington,

DC: United States Department of Health, Education, and Welfare. (DHEW Publication No. Adm-477-485)

Lewis, D. O., Shanok, S. S., & Pincus, J. H. (1979). Juvenile male sexual assaulters. *American Journal of Psychiatry, 136*, 1194–1196.

Littner, N. (1973). The psychology of the sex offender: Causes, treatment, prognosis. *Police Law Quarterly, 3*(2), 5–31.

MacDonald, J. (1971). *Rape: Offenders and their victims.* Springfield, IL: Charles C Thomas.

Mahoney, E. R., Shively, M. D., & Traw, M. (1986). Sexual coercion and assault: Male socialization and female risk. *Sexual Coercion & Assault, 1,* 2–8.

Malamuth, N. M. (1981). Rape proclivity among males. *Journal of Social Issues, 37,* 138–157.

Malamuth, N. M., & Check, J. V. P. (1984). Debriefing effectiveness following exposure to pornographic rape depictions. *The Journal of Sex Research, 20,* 1–13.

Malamuth, N. M., & Donnerstein, E. (1984). *Pornography and sexual aggression.* Orlando, FL: Academic Press.

Malamuth, N. M., Haber, S., & Feshbach, S. (1980). Testing hypotheses regarding rape: Exposure to sexual violence, sex differences, and the "normality" of rapists. *Journal of Research in Personality, 14,* 121–137.

Malamuth, N. M., Heim, M., & Feshbach, S. (1980). Sexual responsiveness of college students to rape depictions: Inhibitory and disinhibitory effects. *Journal of Personality and Social Psychology, 36,* 399–408.

Masters, W. H., & Johnson, V. E. (1970). *Human sexual inadequacy.* Boston: Little, Brown.

McCahill, T. W., Meyer, L. C., & Fischman, A. M. (1979). *The aftermath of rape.* Lexington, MA: Lexington Books.

McCormick, N. B., & Jesser, C. J. (1983). The courtship game: Power in the sexual encounter. In E. R. Allgeier & N. B. McCormick (Eds.), *Changing boundaries: Gender roles and sexual behavior* (pp. 64–86). Palo Alto, CA: Mayfield Publishing Co.

McDermott, M. J. (1979). *Rape victimization in 26 American cities.* U.S. Department of Justice, LEAA, Criminal Justice Center, Analytic Report SD-VAD-6. Washington, DC: U.S. Government Printing Office. (Stock No. 027-000-00809-7)

Mosher, D. L. (1970). Sex callousness toward women. *Technical Report of the Commission on Obscenity and Pornography, Vol. 8.* Washington, DC: U.S. Government Printing Office.

Mosher, D. L. (1986). The Meese Commission: "I told you so." *Sexual Coercion and Assault, 1,* 151–159.

Mosher, D. L., & Sirkin, M. (1984). Measuring a macho personality constellation. *Journal of Research in Personality, 18,* 150–163.

Mulvihill, D., Tumin, M., & Curtis, L. (1969). Crimes of violence. Staff report submitted to the National Commission on the Causes and Prevention of Violence (Vols. 11–13). Washington, DC: U.S. Government Printing Office.

Mynatt, C. R., & Allgeier, E. R. (1985, June). Sexual coercion: Victim reported effects of acquaintance and social contact. Paper presented at the annual meeting of the Midcontinent Region of the Society for the Scientific Study of Sex, Chicago.

Mynatt, C. R., & Allgeier, E. R. (1987). Attributions of responsibility by victims of sexual coercion. Manuscript submitted for publication.

Nelson, J. F. (1979). Implications for the ecological study of crime: A research note. In W. H. Parsonage (Ed.), *Perspectives on victimology* (pp. 21–28). Beverly Hills, CA: Sage.

Panton, J. H. (1978). Personality differences appearing between rapists of adults, rapists of children and nonviolent sexual molesters of female children. *Research Communications in Psychology, Psychiatry, and Behavior, 3*, 385–393.

Parcell, S. R., & Kanin, E. J. (1976, September). *Male sex aggression: A survey of victimized college women.* Paper presented at the Second International Symposium on Victimology, Boston.

Parrot, A. (1983). *Acquaintance rape and sexual assault prevention training manual.* Ithaca, NY: Cornell University, Department of Human Service Studies.

Polk, K., Adler, C., Bazemore, G., Blake, G., Cordray, S., Coventry, G., Galvin, J., & Temple, M. (1981). *Becoming adult: An analysis of maturational development from age 16 to 30 of a cohort of young men.* Final report of the Marion County Youth Survey. Eugene: University of Oregon.

Rada, R. T. (1978). Classification of the rapist. In R. T. Rada (Ed.), *Clinical aspects of the rapist* (pp. 171–132). New York: Grune & Stratton.

Rader, C. M. (1977). MMPI profile types of exposers, rapists, and assaulters in a court services population. *Journal of Consulting and Clinical Psychology, 45*, 61–69.

Rapaport, K., & Burkhart, B. R. (1984). Personality and attitudinal correlates of sexually coercive college males. *Journal of Abnormal Personality, 93*, 216–221.

Resick, P. A., Calhoun, K. S., Atkeson, B. M., & Ellis, E. M. (1981). Social adjustment in victims of sexual assault. *Journal of Consulting and Clinical Psychology, 49*, 705–712.

Ruch, L. O., & Chandler, S. M. (1982). The crisis impact of sexual assault on three victim groups: Adult rape victims, child rape victims, and incest victims. *Journal of Social Science Research, 5*, 83–100.

Ruff, C. F., Templer, D. I., & Ayers, J. L. (1976). The intelligence of rapists. *Archives of Sexual Behavior, 5*, 327–329.

Russell, D. E. H. (1984). *Sexual exploitation.* Beverly Hills, CA: Sage.

Sack, W. H., & Mason, R. (1980). Child abuse and conviction of sexual crimes: A preliminary finding. *Law and Human Behavior, 4*, 211–215.

Sales, E., Baum, M., & Shore, B. (1984). Victim readjustment following assault. *Journal of Social Issues, 40*, 117–136.

Sanday, P. R. (1979). *Female power and male dominance: On the origins of sexual inequality.* Cambridge, England: Cambridge University Press.

Schlafly, P. (1981). Testimony before the Committee on Labor and Human Resources, Washington, DC.

Schram, D. D. (1978). *Forcible rape: Final project report.* Washington, DC: National Institute of Law Enforcement and Criminal Justice, Law Enforcement Assistance Administration, U.S. Department of Justice.

Scully, D., & Marolla, J. (1984). Convicted rapists' vocabulary of motive: Excuses and justifications. *Social Problems, 31*, 530–544.

Scully, D., & Marolla, J. (1985). "Riding the bull at Gilley's": Convicted rapists describe the rewards of rape. *Social Problems, 32*, 251–263.

Selkin, J. (1975). Rape: When to fight back. *Psychology Today, 8*, 70–76.

Selkin, J. (1978). Protecting personal space: Victim and resister reactions to assaultive rape. *Journal of Community Psychology, 6*, 263–268.

Skelton, C. A. (1984). *Correlates of sexual victimization among college women.* Unpublished doctoral dissertation, Auburn University, Alabama.

Smithyman, S. D. (1979). Characteristics of "undetected" rapists. In W. H. Parsonage (Ed.), *Perspectives on victimology* (pp. 99–120). Beverly Hills, CA: Sage.

Spence, J., & Helmreich, R. (1978). *Masculinity and femininity.* Austin: University of Texas Press.

Stock, W. E. (1982, November). *The effect of violent pornography on women.* Paper presented at the annual meeting of the Society for the Scientific Study of Sex, San Francisco.

Three boys, aged 6–8, accused of raping 7-year-old girl. (1981, June 1). *Sexuality Today*, p. 3.

Tieger, T. (1981). Self-rated likelihood of raping and the social perception of rape. *Journal of Research in Personality, 15*, 147–158.

Tsai, M., Feldman-Summers, S., & Edgar, M. (1979). Childhood molestation: Variables related to differential impacts on psychosexual functioning in adult women. *Journal of Abnormal Psychology, 88*, 407–417.

U.S. Department of Justice. (1980a). *Criminal victimization in the United States, 1973–1978 trends.* Bureau of Justice statistics. National Crime Survey Report NCS-N-13 (NCJ-66716). Washington, DC: U.S. Government Printing Office.

U.S. Department of Justice. (1980b). *Sourcebook of criminal justice statistics (1979).* Washington, DC: U.S. Government Printing Office.

U.S. Department of Justice. (1985). *Uniform crime reports.* Federal Bureau of Investigation. Washington, DC: U.S. Government Printing Office.

Vera, H., Barnard, G. W., & Holzed, C. (1979). The intelligence of rapists: New data. *Archives of Sexual Behavior, 8*, 375–378.

Weis, K., & Borges, S. S. (1973). Victimology and rape: The case of the legitimate victim. *Issues in Criminology, 8*, 71–115.

Wolfe, J., & Baker, V. (1980). Characteristics of imprisoned rapists and circumstances of the rape. In C. G. Warner (Ed.), *Rape and sexual assault* (pp. 265–278). Germantown, MD: Aspen Systems Co.

Zellman, G. L., & Goodchilds, J. D. (1983). Becoming sexual in adolescence. In E. R. Allgeier & N. B. McCormick (Eds.), *Changing boundaries: Gender roles and sexual behavior* (pp. 49–63). Palo Alto, CA: Mayfield Publishing Co.

TEACHING STUDENTS WHAT THEY THINK THEY ALREADY KNOW ABOUT PREJUDICE AND DESEGREGATION

Elliot Aronson grew up in a working-class area of Revere, Massachusetts. While majoring in economics at Brandeis, he wandered into an introductory psychology course being taught by Abraham Maslow. Inspired by Maslow's passionate humanism, he switched into psychology and decided to go on to graduate school. He received an MA at Wesleyan University in 1956 (where he worked with David McClelland on achievement motivation) and a PhD in social psychology at Stanford in 1959 (where he worked with Leon Festinger).

He entered Stanford in 1956, the same year that Leon Festinger completed a manuscript called "A Theory of Cognitive Dissonance." Reading a rough draft of that manuscript was the beginning of his love for social psychology. In dissonance theory's heuristic elegance he found some intriguing questions raised about social influence and human motivation and cognition—and he found the answers to some of those questions through laboratory experimentation.

In 1971, he was happily experimenting on social influence when the local schools desegregated, producing riots, violence, and turmoil. He was called in as a consultant. His classroom observations led him to suspect that the highly competitive atmosphere dominating most American classrooms was exacerbating an already difficult situation. He designed a series of field experiments (described in this chapter), which changed the focus of his future research from solely basic to mostly applied.

Aronson is currently a professor of psychology at the University of California at Santa Cruz. During his career he has taught at Harvard, the University of Minnesota, and the University of Texas. He has written over 100 research articles and 13 books including *The Social Animal* and the *Handbook of Social Psychology* (with Gardner Lindzey). Aronson has received numerous prizes for research, teaching, writing, and contributions to the public interest. These include the American Association for the Advancement of Science award for creative research in social psychology, 1970; the Donald Campbell Prize for distinguished research in social psychology from the American Psychological Association's (APA) Division of Personality and Social Psychology, 1980; the APA Distinguished Teaching Award, 1980; the Gordon Allport Prize for contributions to intergroup relations (awarded by the Society for the Psychological Study of Social Issues), 1981; the APA National Media Award for his book, *The Social Animal*, 1973; citation as Professor of the Year from the Council for the Advancement and Support of Education, 1981. He has received distinguished teaching awards from the University of Texas and from the University of California at Santa Cruz. In 1986, he was elected president of APA's Division of Personality and Social Psychology.

ELLIOT ARONSON

TEACHING STUDENTS WHAT THEY THINK THEY ALREADY KNOW ABOUT PREJUDICE AND DESEGREGATION

Social Psychology and Prejudice

One of the tricky things about teaching social psychology is that all of us are social psychologists—the students no less than the instructor. This makes social psychology both exciting and challenging. It is exciting because it deals with problems and issues that are current and relevant in the student's lives. Because students are social animals, they are constantly interacting with other people, forming hypotheses, and drawing conclusions about phenomena that are at the essence of social psychology: Why people like or dislike one another, how people come to influence one another, form prejudices against others, and so forth. Each student is a social psychologist—each student is not a physicist, a chemist, or even a cognitive psychologist in quite the same way.

For example, students might watch a powerful TV docudrama such as "The Day After" and speculate about its effectiveness in changing attitudes about the nuclear arms race. In social psychology there are dozens of experiments dealing with communication effectiveness as a function of the source of the communication, the degree of fear arousal, the vividness of the message, and the degree of discrepancy between the message and the initial attitude of the audience. Similarly, social psychologists study antecedents of interpersonal attraction; we can expose students to these findings at a period in their lives when most of them are deeply concerned with being liked, finding a kindred spirit, or even building an enduring relationship. Most students have experienced or witnessed some form of prejudice (e.g., racism or sexism) and wonder about what causes it and how one might reduce it. That is the excitement; because social psychology is dealing with topics and issues that make a difference in a student's life, as a teacher I find it exciting to provide ways for them to confront issues that they already know are important.

Teaching social psychology is also challenging. Because students are amateur social psychologists, they have already thought about these issues and are well aware of some of the folk wisdom (e.g., absence makes the heart grow fonder or birds of a feather flock together). They may feel that they already know most of the answers or that social psychology is nothing but common sense. There are a lot of data in social psychology that do coincide with common sense, which tends to confirm in students the feeling that social psychologists are foolish academics who set up elaborate procedures in order to prove the obvious. For example, when I tell students that the credibility of the source of a communication is a major factor in influencing opinion, I am not surprised to be greeted by a room full of yawns. And if I spend much time discussing those data, I deserve what I get.

This situation is even more complex. There are very good data on a process aptly labeled the *hindsight bias* (Fischhoff, 1982; Fischhoff & Beyth, 1975). After an event (e.g., an election or a football game), people show a strong tendency to remember their prediction of the outcome as being much closer to the actual outcome than it was. Based on these data, I would guess that once students hear or read the results of an experiment, most will erroneously convince themselves that they could have easily predicted the outcome in advance. Thus the challenge of teaching social psychology comes from setting oneself the task of showing students that the knowledge generated by social psychology is usually more than simple "bubba" knowledge— that is, something more than one's grandmother always knew without the benefit of a PhD.

This does not mean that we should avoid teaching those data that coincide with common sense. This would be both silly and dishonest. The solution lies in the fact that every commonsensical finding contains exceptions to the rule that are intriguing and interesting—and not predictable from a knowledge of common sense—but *are* predictable from a knowledge of social psychology theory. For example, I can tell students that, by and large, people like those who are kind to them or who say nice things about them—just as Dale Carnegie said (ho hum). But then I can show them the research demonstrating that people tend to like others who are nice to them, but will like the person even more if that other person was initially nasty and subsequently treated them nicely (Aronson & Linder, 1965). Or, that under certain specifiable conditions unsavory or dishonest people can be more persuasive than nice, decent, moral people (Walster, Aronson, & Abrahams, 1966). Or, that although providing a person with the promise of a huge reward for performing a specific action does increase the probability that he or she will perform that action (common sense), providing them with a small reward increases the probability that, once performed, the action will be enjoyed and therefore will be performed over and over again—not common sense, but predicted by social psychology theory (Festinger & Carlsmith, 1959).

One of my favorite activities as a teacher of introductory social psychology is to describe vividly Milgram's (1974) study, which is an ingenious and diabolical demonstration of the powerful tendencies toward obedience. In this experiment, a person whom the subject believes is a researcher instructs the subject to administer a series of shocks of increasing voltage to a person wired up in the next room. I ask the students to pretend that they are the subjects and to raise their hands if they think they would go all the way in administering the shocks. My courses usually consist of about 250 students; typically two or three raise their hands. I then inform them that in the actual situation over 60% of the students obeyed to the very end. I drive home the point: Most people, even trained psychiatrists, vastly underestimated the percentage of people who would succumb to obedience pressure and go all the way under these circumstances.

For me, the single most interesting topic to teach—the topic where both the challenge and the excitement are highest—is the topic of prejudice and prejudice reduction. One of the reasons that it is both exciting and challenging is that students are pretty sure what prejudice is and that prejudiced people are numerous, yet almost no one believes that he or she is prejudiced. But, in fact, all people have some prejudices and cherish some stereotypes—even if it is only a prejudice a person holds against sexists, racists, or other assorted "rednecks"—whoops, see what I mean?

Most stereotypes are relatively harmless—after all, part of the human tendency is to go beyond the information given. For example, if I ask my students to visualize a dedicated computer programmer most will come up with a mental image of a person that they would characterize as "some kind of nerd." If I ask them to visualize a distinguished surgeon, almost no one will come up with the picture of a warm, attractive woman.

But this is merely a preface to the heart of the topic—which is to demonstrate that even "good" people (like my students and me) can engage in stereotyping that is potentially harmful and even dangerous. The first great task of the instructor is to find a way of demonstrating this to students. The exact manner in which this is done depends on the time, place, and circumstances. For example, in the late 1960s it was relatively easy to demonstrate to students in the northeast that Lyndon Johnson's Texas accent made him sound dumber to them than he would have if he had spoken with an accent and inflections more like John F. Kennedy's. Admittedly, this example is a bit dated; most undergraduates were toddlers when Johnson's accent last rang throughout the land. But with a little effort and ingenuity, most instructors will be able find numerous examples of stereotyping that pertain to a substantial number of the students in their region or university. It is well worth the effort, because only by doing this, can we succeed in our mission of making the issue real, alive, personal, and vivid for the students—and take it out of the textbook and place it into their lives.

Prejudice Reduction: Desegregation

As interesting as this aspect of prejudice is, it is even more interesting to deal with the topic of prejudice reduction, because most students have been subjects in one of the grandest and most ambitious experiments in prejudice reduction ever. I refer, of course, to the desegregation of public schools in the United States. The striking thing about desegregation is that, although most students favor it and believe it works, when pressed most will admit that in their personal experience it was anything but an unqualified success! If we can establish that experience in the minds of the students, we can begin a truly exciting teaching experience in which social psychology theory and research can demonstrate convincingly why it did not work for them and how it can be made to work. This can be done in a manner that is not obvious bubba psychology, with an explanation that makes perfectly good sense to them only after it has been explained. I regard the research on desegregation to be one of social psychology's finest hours: as a body of research, as a contribution to society, and as a teaching strategy. And in the hands of teachers who have just a bit of the ham in them, it plays just like a detective story.

I will briefly sketch in the background of this detective story. In 1954, when the Supreme Court outlawed school segregation, hopes ran high that the United States might be on its way to a better society. At that time, many believed that if youngsters from various ethnic and racial backgrounds could share the same classroom, stereotypes would fade because of shared experiences and the development of cross-ethnic friendships. It was thought that ultimately these youngsters would grow into adults who were largely free of the racial and ethnic prejudice that has always plagued society.

The case that brought about the Court's landmark decision was

Brown v. Board of Education of Topeka, Kansas (1954); the decision reversed the 1896 ruling (*Plessy v. Ferguson*), which held that it was permissible to segregate racially, as long as equal facilities were provided for both races. In the *Brown* case, the Court held that psychologically there could be no such thing as the constitutional premise of "separate but equal" because forced separation, in and of itself, implied to the minority group in question that its members were inferior to those of the majority. To quote from the *Brown* decision:

> Does segregation of children in public schools solely on the basis of race, even though the physical facilities and other "tangible" factors may be equal, deprive the children of the minority group of equal educational opportunities? We believe that it does . . . to separate Negro school children from others of similar age and qualifications solely because of their race generates a feeling of inferiority as to their status in the community that may affect their hearts and minds in a way unlikely ever to be undone. . . . We conclude that in the field of public education the doctrine "separate but equal" has no place. Separate educational facilities are inherently unequal.

The *Brown* decision was not only a humane interpretation of the Constitution, but it was also the beginning of a profound and exciting social experiment. The testimony of social psychologists in the *Brown* case as well as in previous, similar cases in state supreme courts suggested strongly that desegregation would not only reduce prejudice but also increase the self-esteem of minority groups and improve their academic performance (Stephan, 1978).

The Effects of Desegregation

What was the result of this social experiment? The most careful scholarly reviews of the early research show few, if any, benefits (see St. John, 1975; Stephan, 1978). For example, according to Stephan's review, there was not a single study that showed a significant increase in the self-esteem of minority children as a result of desegregation; in fact, in fully 25% of the studies, desegregation was followed by a significant decrease in the self-esteem of minority children. Moreover, Stephan reported that desegregation reduced the prejudice of Whites toward Blacks in only 13% of the school systems studied. The prejudice of Blacks toward Whites increased in about as many cases as it decreased. Similarly, studies of the effects of desegregation on the academic performance of minority children presented a mixed and highly variable picture; the dominant finding was that where grades were affected at all, the trend was negative—toward a decrease in academic performance.

This rather bleak picture was vividly captured in Lukas's *Common Ground* (1985), which is a poignant analysis of the desegregation of Boston's schools. In this brilliant piece of reportage, Lukas viewed the desegregation process through the eyes and lives of three families: a working-class Irish family who felt that their schools and neighborhood were threatened by the "invasion" of Black children; a Black family whose children were being bused into a hostile area; and an upper-middle-class, liberal family that worked hard for desegregation only to see their dreams go awry.

Classroom Competition and Desegregation

Once you have given students the history of desegregation, you can challenge them to come up with a common sense hypothesis of the effects of desegregation based on their own experience. The student hypotheses can then be compared to the actual effects of desegregation. My own experience was similar to the one Lukas (1985) described—except that mine occurred in Austin, Texas, rather than in Boston. Moreover, because I was a social psychologist doing experiments in interpersonal relations and self-esteem when desegregation produced turmoil in the Austin classrooms, the school authorities asked me to come in, not simply to observe and report it (as Lukas did), but to see if there was anything that could be done to make the situation better for the kids.

My colleagues and I began with the elementary school. The first thing we did was systematically observe the process. We tried to do this with fresh eyes—as if we were visitors from another planet—and the following scenario is most typical of what we observed.

> The teacher stands in front of the class, asks a question, and waits for the children to indicate that they know the answer. Most frequently, 6 to 10 youngsters strain in their seats and wave their hands to attract the teacher's attention. They seem eager to be called on. Several other students sit quietly with their eyes averted, as if trying to make themselves invisible. When the teacher calls on one of the students, there are looks of disappointment on the faces of those students who were eagerly raising their hands but were not called on. If the student who is called on comes up with the right answer, the teacher smiles, nods approvingly, and goes on to the next question. This is a great reward for the child who happens to be called on.
>
> At the same time that the fortunate student is coming up

with the right answer and being smiled on by the teacher, an audible groan can be heard coming from the children who were striving to be called on but were ignored. It is obvious they are disappointed because they missed an opportunity to show the teacher how smart and quick they are.

Through this kind of process, students learn that there is one and only one correct answer to any question the teacher asks—that is, the answer the teacher has in mind. The students also learn that the payoff comes from pleasing the teacher by actively displaying how quick, smart, neat, clean, and well-behaved they are. If they do this successfully, they will gain the respect and love of this powerful person. The teacher will then be kind to them and will tell their parents what wonderful children they are. There is no payoff for the children in consulting with their peers. Indeed, they feel that their peers are their enemies—to be beaten. Moreover, collaboration is frowned on by most teachers; if it occurs during class time it is seen as disruptive, and if it takes place during an exam, it is called *cheating*.

In this elementary-school classroom competition, the stakes were very high—because the youngsters were competing for the respect and approval of one of the two or three most important people in their world. If you are a student who knows the correct answer and the teacher calls on one of your peers, it is likely you will sit there hoping and praying he or she will come up with the wrong answer so you will then have a chance to show the teacher how smart you are. Those who fail when called on, or those who do not even raise their hands and compete, have a tendency to resent those who succeed.

Frequently, the "losers" become envious of the successful students, perhaps they tease them or ridicule them by referring to them as "teacher's pets." They might even use physical aggression against them in the school yard. The successful students, for their part, often hold the unsuccessful students in contempt; they consider them to be dumb and uninteresting. The upshot of this process is that friendliness and understanding are not promoted among the children in the same classroom—quite the reverse. The process tends to create enmity even among children of the same racial group. When ethnic or racial unfamiliarity is added, or when tension brought about by forced busing soured the stew of an already unhappy process, the situation can become extremely difficult and unpleasant.

A particularly dramatic example of dysfunctional competition was demonstrated by Sherif, Harvey, White, Hood, and Sherif (1961). I am referring to the classic "Robber's Cave" study, in which the investigators encouraged intergroup competition between two teams of boys at a summer camp. This competition created fertile ground for anger and hostility even in previously benign, noncompetitive circumstances—like watching a movie. Positive relations between the groups were ultimately achieved only after both groups were required to work cooperatively to solve a common problem.

The Jigsaw Method

My colleagues and I (Aronson, Blaney, Sikes, Stephan, & Snapp, 1975; Aronson, Blaney, Stephan, Sikes, & Snapp, 1978) have contended that whatever differences in ability that might have existed between minority children and White children prior to desegregation were emphasized and exaggerated by the competitive structure of the learning environment. Furthermore, because segregated school facilities were rarely equal, minority children frequently entered the newly desegregated school at a distinct disadvantage, which was made more salient by the competitive atmosphere.

It was this reasoning that first led us to develop the hypothesis that interdependent learning environments would establish the conditions necessary for the increase in self-esteem and performance and the decrease in prejudice that many naively expected to occur simply as a function of desegregation alone. Toward this end we invented and developed a highly structured method of interdependent learning and systematically tested its effects in a number of elementary and secondary school classrooms. The aim of this research program was not merely to compare the effects of cooperation and competition in a classroom setting. Rather, our intent was to devise a cooperative classroom structure that could be utilized easily by teachers on a long-term, sustained basis and to evaluate the effects of this intervention via a well-controlled series of field experiments. In short, this project was an action research program aimed at developing and evaluating a classroom atmosphere that could be sustained by the classroom teachers long after we researchers had packed up our questionnaires and returned to the laboratory.

The method, called the *jigsaw method,* is described in detail elsewhere (Aronson, 1984; Aronson et al., 1978; Aronson & Goode, 1980; Aronson & Yates, 1983). Briefly described, students are placed in six-person learning groups. The day's lesson is divided into six paragraphs such that each student has one segment of the written material. Each student owns a unique and vital part of the information that, like the pieces of a jigsaw puzzle, must be put together before any of the students can learn the whole picture. The individual must learn his or her own section and teach it to the other members of the group. The most important aspect of this method (and one that makes it unique among cooperative techniques) is that each student has a special, vital gift for the other group members—a gift that is unattainable elsewhere.

An example will clarify: In our initial experiment, we entered a fifth-grade classroom in a newly desegregated school. In this classroom, the children were studying biographies of famous Americans. The upcoming lesson happened to be a biography of Joseph Pulitzer, the famous publisher. First, we constructed a biography of Pulitzer that consisted of six paragraphs. Paragraph one was about his ancestors and how they came to this country; paragraph two was about Pulitzer as a little boy and how he grew up; paragraph three described him as a young man, his education, and his early employment; paragraph four was about his middle-age and how he founded his newspaper; and so forth. Each major aspect of Joseph Pulitzer's life was contained in a separate paragraph.

We mimeographed our biography of Pulitzer, cut each copy of the biography into six one-paragraph sections, and gave every child in each of the six-person learning groups one paragraph about Pulitzer's life. Thus each learning group had within it the entire biography of Pulitzer, but each individual child had no more than one-sixth of the story. Like a jigsaw puzzle, each child had one piece of the puzzle, and each child was dependent upon the other children in the group for the completion of the big picture. In order to learn the biography, each child had to master a paragraph, teach it to the others, and listen carefully while each of his or her groupmates recited.

The Expert Group

Each student took his or her paragraph and went off alone to master it. The child then consulted with fellow experts from the other learning groups. That is, if Bill had been dealt Pulitzer as a young man, he would then consult with Nancy, Carlos, and Samantha who were in different jigsaw groups and had also been dealt Pulitzer as a young man. In the expert groups, the children utilized one another as consultants to rehearse and clarify for themselves the important aspects of that phase of Pulitzer's life.

This part of the process is of great importance in that it provides time, space, and practice for the less articulate and less skillful students to learn the material, and it affords them an opportunity to make use of the more adept students as models for organizing and presenting their report. Without the mediation of this expert group, the jigsaw experience might have backfired. That is, as Brown (1986) pointed out, if we are not careful, the jigsaw classroom can be a little like baseball: If the boy or girl playing right field keeps dropping fly balls, it hurts the team and the teammates might begin to resent him or her. Thus if you are dependent on the performance of, for example, a Mexican American boy who is less than perfectly articulate in English, you might resent him—unless he has a clear idea of how to present the material. The expert groups provided just such an opportunity and were crucial to the success of the enterprise. Even so, things rarely went as smoothly in practice as they did on the drawing board.

The Jigsaw Group

After spending from 10 to 15 minutes with their fellow experts, the students came back into session with their original six-person groups. The teacher then informed them that they had a specified amount of time (usually from 20 to 30 minutes) to communicate their knowledge to one another. They were also informed that at the end of the time (or soon thereafter) they would be tested on their knowledge. When left to their own resources, the children eventually learned to teach and to listen to one another. The children gradually learned that none of them could do well without the aid of each person in the group—and that each member had a unique and essential contribution to make.

But cooperative behavior does not happen all at once. Typically, several days pass before children can use this technique effectively. Old habits die hard. The students in our experimental group had grown accustomed to competing during all of their years in school. For the first few days, most of the youngsters tried to compete—even though competitiveness was dysfunctional.

I will illustrate with an actual example that was typical of the way the children stumbled toward learning the cooperative process. In one of our groups there was a Mexican American boy, whom I will call Carlos. Carlos was not very articulate in English, which was his second language. He had learned over the years how to keep quiet in class because frequently, when he had spoken up in the past, he was ridiculed. In the jigsaw group, initially, he had a little trouble communicating the contents of his paragraph to the other children; he was very uncomfortable about it. This is not surprising because, in the jigsaw system that we introduced, Carlos was forced to speak, whereas before he could always de-individuate himself and keep a low profile in the classroom.

But the situation was even more complex than that—it might even be said that, long before jigsaw had been introduced, the teacher and Carlos had entered into a conspiracy. Carlos was perfectly willing to be quiet. In the past, the teacher had called on him occasionally; when he tried to answer, he would stumble, stammer, and fall into an embarrassed silence. Several of his peers would make fun of him. The teacher had learned not to call on him anymore. The decision probably came from the purest of intentions—the teacher simply did not want to humiliate him. But, by ignoring him, the teacher had written him off. The implication was that he was not worth bothering with—at least the other students in the classroom got that message. They believed there was one good reason why the teacher was not calling on Carlos—he was stupid. Indeed, even Carlos began to draw this conclusion. This is part of the dynamic of how desegregation, when coupled with a competitive process, can produce unequal-status contact and can result in even greater enmity between ethnic groups and a loss of self-esteem for members of disadvantaged ethnic minorities.

In the six-person jigsaw group, Carlos, who had to report on Pulitzer as a young man, had a hard time. Although he had learned the material quite well in the expert group, when it was his turn to recite in his jigsaw group, he grew very nervous. He stammered, hesitated, and fidgeted. The other youngsters in the circle were not very helpful; they had grown accustomed to a competitive process and they responded out of this old habit. They knew what to do when a fellow student stumbled—especially a student whom they believed to be stupid. They ridiculed him, put him down, and teased him. During our experiment, it was Mary who was observed to say, "Aw, you don't know it, you're dumb, you're stupid. You don't know what you're doing."

In our initial experiment, the groups were being loosely monitored by a research assistant who was floating from group to group. When this incident occurred, our assistant made one brief intervention: "OK, you can do that if you want to. It might be fun for you, but it's not going to help you learn about Joseph Pulitzer's young manhood—and the exam will take place in an hour." Notice how the reinforcement contingencies had now shifted. No longer did Mary gain much from putting Carlos down—in fact, she now stood to lose a great deal. After a few days and several similar experiences, it became increasingly clear to the students in Carlos' group that the only way they could learn about Pulitzer as a young man was by paying attention to what Carlos had to say.

Moreover, they began to develop into pretty good interviewers. Instead of ignoring or ridiculing Carlos when he was having a little trouble communicating what he knew, they began asking friendly, probing questions—the kind of questions that made it easier for Carlos to communicate what he knew. Carlos began to respond to this treatment by becoming more relaxed; with increased relaxation came an improvement in his ability to communicate. After a couple of weeks, the other students concluded that Carlos was a lot smarter than they had thought he was. They began to see things in him they had never seen before. They began to like him. Carlos began to enjoy school more and began to see the White students in his group not as tormentors but as helpful and responsible people. Moreover, as he began to feel increasingly comfortable in class and started to gain more confidence in himself, his academic performance began to improve. It is important to emphasize that the motivation of the students is not altruistic; rather, it is primarily self-interest, which in this case, happens also to produce outcomes that are beneficial to others.

Each group remained intact for approximately six weeks. The groups were then dissolved and re-formed. This was done in order to increase the diversity of experience that each youngster could have, that is, so that each youngster could have an opportunity to interact with a great many of his or her fellow students of various ethnic groups.

Benefits of the Jigsaw Method

Students in the jigsaw groups showed significant increases in their fondness for their groupmates both within and across ethnic boundaries. Moreover, children in jigsaw groups showed a significantly greater increase in self-esteem than did children in the control classrooms. This was true for White children as well as for ethnic minority children. Most children in the jigsaw classrooms also showed relatively greater liking for school than those in traditional classrooms.

The major results were replicated and refined in several experiments in school districts throughout the country. For example, Geffner (1978) introduced jigsaw in Watsonville, California. As a further control (for the possibility of a Hawthorne effect), Geffner compared the behavior of children in classrooms using the jigsaw technique with that of children in highly innovative (but not interdependent) classroom environments as well as with traditional classrooms. Geffner found consistent and significant gains only in the cooperative classrooms. Specifically, children in these classes showed increases in self-esteem as well as increases in fondness for school. Negative ethnic stereotypes were also diminished. That is, children increased their positive general attitudes toward their own ethnic group as well as toward members of other ethnic groups to a far greater extent than did children in traditional and innovative classrooms.

Conventional wisdom has long held that if one designed a classroom structure that increased the joy of education or led students to appreciate themselves and each other better, this joy would occur at the expense of fundamental learning. Thus when the public is periodically made aware of the fact that children are not learning as much in school as they might, there is usually an outcry to "eliminate the frills" and "get back to basics." Research on the jigsaw classroom and other cooperative techniques has proved the general wisdom to be bankrupt.

My colleagues and I made our first systematic attempt to assess the effects of jigsaw learning on academic performance in Austin

(Lucker, Rosenfield, Sikes, & Aronson, 1977). The subjects were 303 fifth- and sixth-grade students from five elementary schools. Six classrooms were taught in the jigsaw manner, and five classrooms were taught in the traditional manner by highly competent teachers. For two weeks children were taught a unit on colonial America taken from a fifth-grade textbook. All children were then given the same standardized test. The results showed that White students performed just as well in jigsaw as they did in traditional classes (means = 66.6 and 67.3 respectively). Minority children performed significantly better in jigsaw classes than in traditional classes (means = 56.6 and 49.7 respectively). Only two weeks of jigsaw activity succeeded in narrowing the performance gap between White and minority students from more than 17% to about 10%. Interestingly, the jigsaw method had the same results for high ability students: Students in the highest quartile in reading ability benefitted just as much as students in the lowest quartile.

Since then, a number of experiments have been done on academic performance comparing the jigsaw method, as well as other cooperative methods, with the usual competitive classroom. In a recent analysis of the literature, Slavin (1983) found striking support for cooperative classroom structures. Of the 46 studies Slavin designated as methodologically sound, 63% found significantly higher academic performance in cooperative classrooms, whereas only 4% favored competitive classrooms. The remaining studies were insignificant.

Conclusion

The results reported in this chapter offer substantial evidence supporting the value of the jigsaw method in raising self-esteem and academic performance, in reducing intergroup enmity, and in increasing the attractiveness of school. My colleagues and I have also shown why this structure is particularly beneficial to underachieving linguistic minorities such as Mexican Americans. Moreover, in 1984, to commemorate the 30th anniversary of the *Brown* decision, the U.S. Civil Rights Commission issued a report on the effects of desegregation. In this report, Austin was named as one of two cities where school desegregation worked in an exemplary manner. Although there were undoubtedly many factors that helped make desegregation effective in Austin, when one considers the turmoil that occurred in that city during the early weeks of desegregation, one can only conclude that the jigsaw classroom did play a major role in the successful outcome of that great social experiment.

I hasten to add that the jigsaw technique is merely one of several cooperative strategies developed more or less independently by several social psychologists. These include those developed by Slavin and his colleagues at The Johns Hopkins University, Cook and his colleagues at the University of Colorado, Johnson and his colleagues at the University of Minnesota, and Sharan and his colleagues in Israel (see Slavin et al., 1985). Although each of these techniques has its own unique flavor and its own special advantages and disadvantages, they all essentially involve a far higher degree of student interdependence than does the traditional classroom. And all produce results similar to those discussed here.

It is important for the teacher to note that all of these techniques were developed independently and virtually simultaneously, for it demonstrates the vigor of the zeitgeist in social psychology—that is, these ideas are part and parcel of the legacy of social psychologists. None of us researchers did anything spectacularly original; we merely applied and extended the results of classical experiments by Sherif et al. (1961) and Deutsch (1949) that were in the literature waiting to be developed and applied. The point for the teacher to make is that social psychology is a science with a body of accumulated knowledge—some of which is commonsensical, some of which is not. Those who apply this knowledge to problems in the real world are basing their work on solid experimental evidence. If society chooses to ignore this body of knowledge in implementing policy, the probability of success is limited.

In 1954, I was a college senior majoring in psychology and terribly excited about the Supreme Court decision on school desegregation. I was sure it would produce desirable results. I hasten to point out that although many laypersons (like myself, in 1954) believed that equal status contact would somehow be enough to bring about a major decrease in prejudice, very few sentient social psychologists were that optimistic. As my old friend Stuart Cook (one of the social psychologists who filed the well-known amicus brief in 1954) subsequently pointed out, certain preconditions would have to be met. These preconditions were stated most articulately by Allport in his classic book, *The Nature of Prejudice* (1954), published the same year as the Supreme Court decision:

Prejudice . . . may be reduced by equal status contact between majority and minority groups *in the pursuit of common goals*. The effect is greatly enhanced if this contact is sanctioned by institutional supports (i.e., by law, custom or local atmosphere), *and provided it is of a sort that leads to the perception of common interests and common humanity between members of the two groups.* (p. 281, italics mine)

It required many years of stumbling and fumbling since 1954 before my colleagues and I arrived at a strategy that enabled us to set up the kinds of conditions in the classrooms that Allport felt were essential. The point is that knowledgeable social psychologists like Allport and Cook (based, in part, on earlier laboratory experiments by Deutsch) knew that desegregation, in and of itself, would not produce the reduction in prejudice and increase in self-esteem that many naively expected. Furthermore, they had a good idea of what had to be done to achieve the ideals behind the idea of desegregation. Educated laypersons, like myself (when I was a college senior), and my current students tend to use common sense instead of sound theory—and therefore, are often wrong. In this case, we were wrong because we somehow believed that contact alone would do the trick. This is not a trivial observation; when people expect too much, their disappointment can lead to pessimism and despair rather than to an organized and informed search for the right combination of variables to produce the anticipated effect. Part of the challenge of becoming an experimenting society involves developing and testing theories that are sensible and based on good, solid empirical evidence.

I have tried to present a story about social psychologists and their attempt to come to grips with one of society's most enduring problems. The story has a beginning, a middle, but not quite an end. The end will come when the institutionalization of cooperative learning techniques in schools throughout the country becomes a matter of public policy. For a social psychologist, it is frustrating to have arrived at a method with demonstrated value and witness its nonapplication in the vast majority of school districts in this country. If this society wants to become an experimenting society in the best sense of the term, it must learn to implement programs which have been proven to be beneficial. But there is hope. One of the great benefits of being able to teach social psychology lies in the hope that somewhere among my undergraduate students (and yours) are people who will be impatient with the status quo in education. These are the people who will write an ending to my little story.

References

Allport, G. W. (1954). *The nature of prejudice.* Reading, MA: Addison-Wesley.

Aronson, E. (1984). Modifying the environment of the desegregated classroom. In A. J. Stewart (Ed.), *Motivation and society* (pp. 319–336). San Francisco: Jossey-Bass.

Aronson, E., Blaney, N., Sikes, J., Stephan, C., & Snapp, M. (1975, February). Busing and racial tension. *Psychology Today,* pp. 43–50.

Aronson, E., Blaney, N., Stephan, C., Sikes, J., & Snapp, M. (1978). *The jigsaw classroom.* Beverly Hills, CA: Sage.

Aronson, E., & Goode, E. (1980). Training teachers to implement jigsaw learning: A manual for teachers. In S. Sharan, P. Hare, C. Webb, & R. Hertz-Lazarowitz (Eds.), *Cooperation in education* (pp. 47–81). Provo, UT: Brigham Young University Press.

Aronson, E., & Linder, D. (1965). Gain and loss of esteem as determinants of interpersonal attractiveness. *Journal of Experimental and Social Psychology, 1*, 156–171.

Aronson, E., & Yates, S. (1983). Cooperation in the classroom: The impact of the jigsaw method on inter-ethnic relations, classroom performance and self esteem. In H. Blumberg & P. Hare (Eds.), *Small groups* (pp. 119–130). London: Wiley.

Brown v. Board of Education of Topeka, Kansas, 347 U.S. 483 (1954).

Brown, R. (1986). *Social psychology: The second edition.* New York: Free Press.

Deutsch, M. (1949). An experimental study of the effects of cooperation and competition upon group process. *Human Relations, 2*, 199–231.

Festinger, L., & Carlsmith, J. M. (1959). Cognitive consequences of forced compliance. *Journal of Abnormal and Social Psychology, 58*, 203–210.

Fischhoff, B. (1982). Debiasing. In D. Kahneman, P. Slovic, & A. Tversky (Eds.), *Judgment under uncertainty: Heuristics and biases.* New York: Cambridge University Press.

Fischhoff, B., & Beyth, R. (1975). "I knew it would happen": Remembered probabilities of once-future things. *Organizational Behavior and Human Performance, 13*, 1–16.

Geffner, R. A. (1978). The effects of interdependent learning on self-esteem, inter-ethnic relations, and intra-ethnic attitudes of elementary school children: A field experiment. Unpublished doctoral thesis, University of California, Santa Cruz.

Lucker, G. W., Rosenfield, D., Sikes, J., & Aronson, E. (1977). Performance in the interdependent classroom: A field study. *American Educational Research Journal, 13*, 115–123.

Lukas, J. A. (1985). *Common ground.* New York: Knopf.

Milgram, S. (1974). *Obedience to authority.* New York: Harper & Row.

Plessy v. Ferguson, 163 U.S. 537 (1896).

Sherif, M., Harvey, O. J., White, J., Hood, W., & Sherif, C. (1961). *Intergroup conflict and cooperation: The robber's cave experiment.* Norman, OK: University of Oklahoma Institute of Intergroup Relations.

Slavin, R., Sharan, S., Kagan, S., Hertz-Lazarowitz, R., Webb, C., & Schmuck, R. (Eds.). (1985). *Learning to cooperate, cooperating to learn.* New York: Plenum Press.

Slavin, R. (1983). When does cooperative learning increase student achievement? *Psychological Bulletin, 94*, 429–445.

St. John, N. (1975). *School desegregation: Outcomes for children.* New York: Wiley.

Stephan, W. G. (1978). School desegregation: An evaluation of predictions made in *Brown v. Board of Education. Psychological Bulletin, 85*, 217–238.

Walster, E., Aronson, E., & Abrahams, D. (1966). On increasing the persuasiveness of a low prestige communicator. *Journal of Experimental Psychology, 2*, 325–342.

TIMOTHY B. JAY

COMPUTERS AND PSYCHOLOGY

Timothy B. Jay was born in Dayton, Ohio. His fairly routine childhood included playing sports, being a rock and roll musician and an Eagle scout, and working for minimum wages in a variety of jobs. At the age of 16 he discovered how fascinating people-watching was in local shopping malls. In high school, he read Lenny Bruce, Eric Berne, and Freud and made up his mind to attend Miami University and become a psychologist. In working toward a BA in psychology, he concentrated on linguistics, language, and communication. He then traveled directly to Kent State University to work in Joe Danks' Psycholinguistic Institute in research on language comprehension. His master's degree in 1974 and a PhD in 1976 covered the little-studied area of verbal obscenity, and he was noted some 10 years later in the *Wall Street Journal* as the "preeminent scholar of profanity" in the country. It was at Kent, when Danks was off to Princeton, that Jay became interested in human factors by taking Jim Dooling's course on the subject.

After graduating from Kent, Jay secured a tenure track spot at North Adams State College in Massachusetts. In 1979–1980 he worked with computer guru Al Bork, through the National Science Foundation's Chautauqua course on teaching science with microcomputers. He has published, edited, consulted, presented, and trained in-service extensively on the topic of computer-assisted instruction.

He continues to write about computers, obscene speech, and popular culture and psychology. He is currently researching how to use computers to teach birth control education and is writing a book on dirty word usage.

TIMOTHY B. JAY

COMPUTERS AND PSYCHOLOGY

Introducing Computers to Psychology Students

I am compelled to make two preliminary remarks before discussing the role of computers in psychology. First, most of the revolution in microcomputers in psychology has occurred within the last decade or two. Computers, software, and research on them are evolving so rapidly that much of what I have written here may be obsolete in a few years. Second, psychology instructors should teach introductory students with unfaltering enthusiasm about subjects that are interesting, true to our discipline, and important to the lecturer. Computers are interesting to students because we make them seem so. Computers and technology are topics that many freshmen do not associate with psychology. Once the topic is presented, most students become attentive and enthusiastic about future uses and employment trends for psychologists with computer training. A discussion of computers and psychology will show students the extent to which psychologists are involved in the electronic revolution, and how psychologists' research will influence our future environments and quality of life.

People do not decide to use computers merely because of a flashy piece of software or expensive hardware. People decide to use computers because they see the applicability of them. To lecture on computers or any other technology-oriented topic, psychology instructors must be knowledgeable and up to date about the uses of computers for psychology, and they must maintain some confidence as they lecture. You will be a better lecturer on computers when you also have some hands-on experience with the machines and software; otherwise you will feel intimidated by your students who know more than you do about computers. In short, not all introductory psychology instructors should choose to lecture on computers. Your students will be the first to know when you are out of touch. So, do not venture lightly into this domain unless you are willing to do some outside reading and periodic updating of your notes.

How do psychologists use computers? What is the psychological impact of computers on people? What should introductory psychology students be told? Computers are used in a wide variety of settings, on a wide variety of tasks, and for a number of purposes. According to Taylor (1980) a computer can be a tool, a tutor, or a tutee. Because of its programmed intelligence, it can be an actor or can be acted upon. A computer is not passive, but rather an interactive device with multiple dimensions. As with any tool, some of us have received specific training using computers for statistical analysis or for computer-assisted instruction. Others have received training in counseling or therapy first, and later adopted the computer when they saw its potential role in jobs they were doing already. Thus, there is no one course of entry into the field. Taylor (1980) is a good general source that outlines the major roles that computers can play. Another more recent analysis of the effects of computers in the behavioral sciences is presented by Elwork and Gutkin (1985), whose bibliography is valuable for those of you just becoming interested in computers and psychology.

Many college students are surprised by the scope of microcomputer use by psychologists and have more to learn. Because employment in computer-related fields is on the rise, students are interested in the topic. Knowledge of this diversity opens a broader horizon for potential postgraduate work. Students arrive in an introductory course thinking that psychology is about rats and dreams. They leave with a more accurate and open view of who psychologists are and what we can do. Computers take psychologists off of the couch and into the future. Discussions about human–machine distinctions, the ethical use of patient profiles, and the humanity of computerized therapy have proven to be enthusiastic, regardless of the level of students' knowledge about computers.

All students should learn that no single discipline has a corner on the computer market, that psychologists are uniquely qualified to measure and evaluate the impact of computers on people, and that psychologists' views are critical to assess where and how computers will be used in education, on the job, and at home. The topic of computers and psychology should not meet the same fate as "new math," when children brought out their homework and parents promptly left the room. Computers will resonate in discussions at many levels, not only at school or on the job. We should be quick to use our hypothetico–deductive methods to tell the public what is happening and what might happen with this new technology (see Abelson, 1986; Foster, 1986).

In this chapter I present the major uses of computers by psychologists, how computers relate to traditional courses and topics in undergraduate programs, and where computers might appear in the future. Demonstrations, exercises, and class materials are also suggested. My goal is to present the breadth of computer use in contemporary applied and academic settings rather than to pursue any one issue in detail or provide a literature review.

First, I provide some preliminary information regarding the use of computers for nonspecific purposes. The experienced computer user may find these points routine, but many of the accepted practices, jargon, and analogies employed by computer users need to be explained to the less experienced lecturer.

The Importance of Computer Literacy

Computer literacy is not a stable, well-defined concept; it is a function of context. Computer literacy has the three major semantic dimensions: skill, knowledge, and effect (see Jay, 1981a, for a working definition). When you finish reading this chapter, you will be knowledgeable, but not fully literate, because being computer literate means not only knowing but the ability to do as well. A more purposeful question might be, "What does computer literacy mean for psychologists?" Here we can focus on what psychologists do with computers. The bottom line is that to be computer literate you should be able to make computers do something.

Why should psychologists be concerned with computer literacy, and why should we talk about computer literacy in introductory courses? Psychologists have always been interested in education and instruction. The definition of literacy requires a sensitivity to the underlying knowledge and overt skills that are involved in demonstrating it. Instructional psychologists are experts at examining and defining such abilities. Furthermore, this definition will have an impact on children and the activities they engage in at school.

What is a computer? On the surface this looks like a naive question; however, I pose it to define what types of machines or hardware are commonly used. Currently much of the work done on computers in psychology is performed on configurations of microcomputers (e.g., Apple, TRS-80, or IBM PC) or on configurations of large main-frame machines (e.g., Digital or Cyber), which would be accessed on a time-sharing basis. Microcomputers are autonomous or "stand-alone" devices that allow freedom and flexible use. Mainframes are larger and more expensive and are used by a number of people simultaneously. One must also consider home computers and video games, because the video game format is becoming a major medium of electronic education. Interpret the question, "What is a computer?" as you would "What is an automobile?" and you will see the need to be flexible when defining the concept.

How do you make a computer do something? The best advice for converting computer illiterates to computer literates is to learn by doing. Those of us trained in computer programming (e.g., FOR-TRAN, Pascal, or LISP) or number crunching (e.g., SPSS, SAS, or BMD) will testify that no matter how much time we spent listening to lectures and reading manuals, the real achievement came from using a program, finding the mistakes, correcting the mistakes, and obtaining success. There is no other way. We learn by doing it. Get a machine, get a manual, and get a problem to be solved that is intrinsically interesting and important. Then work on that problem until you are satisfied.

Although some manipulations can be learned while working in isolation, it is best to work in teams. A team consists of a good student programmer, an expert in teaching, and an expert in the subject matter of interest. Add one artist or graphic designer if visual presentation is important. This team could produce interactive materials for one course of instruction. One of the great failures of instructional software is that it was designed almost solely by computer programmers without supervision and evaluation by methodologists in instruction or psychology.

Defining computer literacy, examining how computer materials are produced, and evaluating those materials are important dimensions of the computer industry. Psychologists have some of the answers and must play a role from the initial stages of these processes. We would be wise to make a plea to all of our students regardless of their backgrounds that it will be necessary for those making future decisions about technology to have a sound psychological understanding of people targeted to be affected by computers and other programmable devices.

How Is a Human Like a Machine?

Computer users think about computers and people in somewhat similar terms, to the extent that computer software and human thought processes are considered similar. Gardner's (1985) recent examination of the field of cognitive science provides an excellent historical analysis of the integration of cognitive psychology, philosophy, and computer simulation. At least two powerful analogies emerge in cognitive science, the idea that both humans and machines process information and the idea that some human capabilities can be simulated in computer programs. A more recent analysis of computer analogies to the mind–brain issue was presented by Pribram (1986). These analogies are basic to understanding how computers are and will be used by psychologists. In addition, analogies illustrate how psychologists conceive of humans and machines and provide a convenient linguistic vehicle for such notions.

The information-processing analogy. One powerful message derived from the study of computers is the idea that information is first input into a system, then it can be stored for some period of time, and later it can be retrieved. Computer scientists use these basic stages to show how data are entered, stored, and found in the computer, whereas cognitive psychologists use them to illustrate how human memory operates. This analogy to electronic data processing, neural functioning, or memory processes, once termed cybernetics, is one of the most powerful ideas in contemporary psychology.

When introducing computers to students, equate the movement of data via computer to human information processing. Once established, the analogy is useful to discuss forgetting, study skills, memory search, and some higher order perceptual processes. Forgetting is like putting data in memory but not knowing where to retrieve it. Forgetting from overload is similar to being able to do only a limited number of things at one time on the computer (i.e., serial processing). Forgetting as a result of input failure means not paying attention or not putting the fact in memory in the first place—like reading by skimming, or daydreaming during a lecture. If the information-processing analogy has not been incorporated in your method of presentation, make an effort to translate your notes about memory and language into these useful, computer-oriented terms.

You could point out, through an instructional–cognitive analysis, that studying a psychology text is like putting a lot of new information into a computer memory. Students have to pay attention to the text, encode the concepts, and store them in memory. A professor's test determines if the information got into the memory bank and got there in the right form. Information may be missing or faulty. Teachers give feedback to students about the nature of the faulty information, and students can debug the memory to correct the faults. Many of these on-line activities, such as encoding, storing, and debugging, take place in active memory, as in a computer's random access memory (RAM), which is limited in the number of things it can hold and can be lost during events such as an electrical power failure. These time and space limitations of computers are similar to the limitations on the short-term or working memory of humans.

These basic information-processing stages are best introduced early in a lecture on human learning and thought processes. They can also be useful to differentiate between children's and adults' memory, experts' and novices' memory, normal and abnormal processing, and instructional and educational psychology, which could be discussed later with other topics in the course. I will not go into more detail about how to translate your notes into the information-processing mode, but I suggest reading *Human Information Processing* (Lindsay & Norman, 1972), which was designed for introductory courses and provides a good vehicle for translating your notes and many light-hearted examples and analogies.

The artificial intelligence analogy. Can a machine have intelligence? An idea with wide applicability in an introductory course is the notion that machines can operate like humans or simulate human functions. This idea challenges students to define intelligence, thinking, creativity, logic, decision making, prediction, and control of human behavior, in relation to what a computer can be programmed to do.

Gardner (1985) has defined artificial intelligence (AI) as a computer program that produces output that would be considered intelligent if done by a person. The computer simulates processes that are normally associated with the human brain. The emergence of the computer and the type of thinking behind AI helped cognitive psychologists break from behaviorists with a new language of information, flow, stages of processing, logic, and the internal representation of knowledge. Research may focus on simulating a particular human ability such as interpreting or perceiving objects in a scene or on simulating a conversation between a doctor and a patient. Artificial intelligence challenges the idea that the notions of mind and purposeful thought are uniquely human.

A controversial issue in AI research is the ability to simulate on a computer the therapeutic interaction that doctors have with patients. As I discuss later, psychologists continue to create more realistic interactions and effective dialogue for various types of abnormal populations. Psychology students seem receptive to programs that play chess at various levels of expertise, but they are less comfortable with programs that produce art, poetry, or advice. People feel challenged by a machine that acts creatively or produces material once considered uniquely human.

The benefit of such a challenge is to present psychology as science, with the goal to construct a more precise explanation for how human minds operate on environments. As psychologists gain more accurate knowledge about human processes and behavior, the distinction between humans and machines becomes more blurred. Computer simulations allow us to determine how well our understanding and theoretical explanations of people can be logically documented and tested in a human–machine interaction. With our new creations, the old formulations are destroyed and new ground is uncovered. Such is the nature of any creative endeavor, whether science or art. Revolutions in psychological theory, especially in an area as volatile as computers, are inevitable: The old must constantly make way for the new.

The Computer as a Psychologist's Tool

A brush in the hands of an artist is used differently than when in the hands of a housepainter. Computer tools are employed for a variety of different reasons and in a variety of different ways, as we infer when we say, "She uses computers on her job." As a computing tool or machine, psychologists employ computers in two major ways.

First, it may be a device to control, record, or manipulate other laboratory devices. Here it is preprogrammed to operate in certain ways under certain conditions. Numerous articles in the journal *Behavior Research Methods, Instruments, & Computers* (BRMIC) are valuable to investigate how computers can be employed on-line in academically based psychology laboratories in eye movement, speech technology, simulation, and computer-assisted instruction (Castellan, 1981, 1982). There are also several recent works on the topic of computers and psychology that contain basic information and laboratory examples (Cozby, 1984; Deni, 1986; Peden & Steinhauer, 1986). Second, computers are used for the hands-on task of "number crunching." Here the computer is programmed to perform routine mathematical or statistical calculations for research. Another more specific function is to score and evaluate psychological tests or inventories.

Both of these uses not only save labor but also produce consistent results. Accuracy in scoring a Rorschach test, for example, is a function of the specificity of known criteria for a person to complete that task and the ability to translate those criteria into computer programming statements. In other words, the computer can do the same task that a psychologist can, when we can specify to the computer what the person does. Consider the procedures necessary for factor analysis. These calculations used to take hundreds of hours when attempted by hand. Even with minimal error rates these numbers were not beyond suspicion. However, computers have made factor analyses as routine as simple mathematical functions performed with hand calculators.

A recent survey of undergraduate psychology curricula indicates that the most prominent use of computers in undergraduate psychology programs appears in courses on experimental and statistical methodology (Scheirer & Rogers, 1985). At the present time computers are perceived as and used as tools. This situation will change with more time and money.

Computer-Related Topics in Introductory Psychology

In this section I describe common topics in introductory psychology texts for which instructors could include a discussion of computers. I use *Introduction to Psychology* (Atkinson, Atkinson, & Hilgard, 1983) as an example of a typical introductory text; it is one of the most widely used books, and many others have copied its form and content. Thus when I refer to the topic of language or memory, you can think in terms of the presentation in a standard text.

The order of appearance of these topics is based primarily on the amount of computer-related material relative to the topic. I begin with human factors because there is a lot of material about computers and people from this domain. The rest of the topics are equally interesting to me and my students, but there is less research to present on them. You may find it better to adapt this material to your existing lecture scheme than to accept my order of presentation verbatim. That is, a discussion of human factors and people with disabilities could be coordinated with a discussion of human factors, counseling, or rehabilitation. You should decide where these topics would fit best and would require minimal revision of your current plans. You may also want to consult analyses and reviews of the role that computers play in contemporary psychology courses, including laboratory demonstrations and applications (Balsam, Fifer, Sacks, & Silver, 1984; Butler, 1986; Butler & Kring, 1984; Castellan, 1986a, 1986b).

Human Factors and Ergonomic Design

One of the most attractive areas of experimental psychology is the applied, interdisciplinary concern of human factors. Over the years, my lecture and slide presentation on human factors has been so popular that students not enrolled in my course come in to see the show. I also teach an upper division course on human factors and repeatedly have had both psychology majors and nonmajors enroll in the course because they were so intrigued by the subject. Whatever changes you make to your course plans, be sure to develop a good lecture on the topic of human factors and design.

One of the goals of human factors research is to create an environment that is compatible with human behavior and characteristics.

Many examples from the military, space, business, and manufacturing can be derived from the professional literature or your own experience (Cordes, 1985). Human factors psychology and computers are particularly compatible fields: As human factors educators have recognized, computer literacy is important in understanding the human as a processor of information and as a physical engine (Geyer, Pond, & Smith, 1986).

Human factors psychology offers the opportunity for information-processing psychologists to provide their unique and valuable input, besides making a very good salary. There are many openings for human factors psychologists at all levels of employment and the salary range is so attractive that students will remain attentive to your lecture on that basis alone. I am happy to say that many of my former students who have entered the human factors field not only make more money than I do but also live in a much warmer section of the country.

Human–machine systems. Human factors psychologists work to create an environment that is both effective and efficient for human performance. At the same time, they try to promote health, satisfaction, and human values both at home and at work. One important human factors topic is human–machine systems (HMS), that is, the interface between humans and computers. It is difficult to imagine any computer operating without some, even minimal, human intervention; therefore, there are a large number of different interfaces.

Variables involved in HMS are diverse and numerous, including physical arrangements of components and psychological, physiological, or biomechanical considerations. Human factors psychologists are involved with all phases of design and improvement in the interface between humans and machines. The physical variables of HMS include the shape of the machine, keyboard design, use of colors, biomechanical constraints imposed by the senses, body, and brain. Seemingly obscure factors such as keyboard slope, key colors, character font, and screen background contrast can have significant impact on the performance of workers. These notions may fit in the discussion of human perception or physiology. Psychological variables include attention span, memory capacity, perception, and language processing. The amount of information relayed, presentation rate, feedback complexity, or delay in a human–machine system must be assessed. These ideas are covered in discussions on human cognition or language in introductory texts.

Physiological variables come into play in HMS because of factors such as the shape of the human hand, body postures, fatigue, caloric intake, scheduling of rest periods, eye strain, muscle tension, use of limb or trunk supports, or workstation lighting conditions. These factors can affect production and the satisfaction of workers. The physical, psychological, and physiological characteristics of job demands must be weighed and accounted for in developing work environments that maximize performance, health, and happiness.

Current topics of interest in HMS involve the physiological and psychological effects of sitting at a computer terminal. Issues involve eye strain, complications with pregnancy, job satisfaction, productivity monitoring, pacing of work scheduling or rest periods, and designing the proper workstation. Focusing on these issues as variables subject to empirical examination allows the instructor to reinforce the notion that psychological knowledge is advanced by hypothesis testing and helps remove these issues from the emotional, worker versus management slant provided by the popular press.

One growing demand in HMS is for personnel psychologists who can match people who are good with and like machines to the jobs that require such a personality. Because computer technology came on the scene so rapidly, currently many workers are highly dissatisfied with computers. Workers feel abused and spied upon by the technology; management is trying to create a more productive atmosphere.

The computer is used as a task simulator for pilots, doctors, and military personnel. Several issues of the journal *Human Factors* contain intriguing research that provides valuable lecture and discussion material on this topic. Nickerson's (1986) recent text is a valuable compendium of human factors information and projects areas of concern for human factors practitioners for the future. McCormick and Sanders (1982) provide a good foundation for lectures. The *Human Factors* newsletters and conference proceedings are rich sources of lecture materials, as are the publications of APA's Division 21, Applied Experimental and Engineering Psychology.

Another major area in human factors engineering is designing environments and devices to meet the needs of people who have disabilities. The computer is playing a major role in both school and home environments for those with physical impairments. Visual, auditory, reading, communication, and memory abilities can all be enhanced or enabled with computers. Computers are also used in improving locomotion, limb replacement, and prosthetics. These issues are especially relevant to a discussion of special education rehabilitation and counseling people who have disabilities. Lecture material can be obtained on enhanced visual presentations, vocalization enablement or synthesis, and reading machines in the *Journal of Learning Disabilities,* which has a section on computers and computer aids in each issue. Jerrold Petrofsky's work (see Chizeck, 1985) at Wright State University on computer-controlled walking in paralyzed individuals has received national recognition and provides a dramatic example of how computers can change the life of those with spinal cord injuries.

Controversial issues in human factors include using computers to make pilot decisions, monitor military weaponry, control robots, and communicate to humans. Why are these areas controversial? They replace the burden of decision making for people who are under stress or have high information load. When the machine makes the decision or part of it, who is responsible for the fate of the plan? Imagine an aircraft accident involving a computer-aided decision. Who is responsible for the accident—the airline, computer manufacturer, software designer, or pilot? Such is the nature of technology; with each labor-saving move, risk is escalated and the burden of responsibility shifts. In order to improve life and work, some risks must be taken. The question is when to use machines and when to use humans in this interface.

Consider these psychological issues in the current human factors literature. What mission-control decisions for a flight crew should be made by humans and which should be automated? How will computers change our cars (see Rowand, 1986)? In a hostile environment, when should human intervention be supplanted by a robot? Raise these issues in the classroom for a stimulating discussion.

Cognitive Science

Cognitive science incorporates a combination of ideas from artificial intelligence and information-processing research to linguistics, physiology, and computer science. Research compares the manner of human cognition with its machine representation. The major underlying processes considered are perception, pattern recognition, memory search, problem solving, decision making, hypothesis testing, intelligence, creativity, visual processing, and communication. Cognitive processes have long been explored as human abilities. The assumptions and theories about them are being simulated and evaluated now with computer models. The topic is commonly presented in introductory texts in chapters on human cognition, problem solving, language, or perception. Gardner's (1985) recent book on cognitive science is a valuable source of lecture material. I will point out a few examples of research and simulation from the field of cognitive science. I have chosen some of the more dramatic and entertaining projects; however, they are still representative of the field, even if they are fun to talk about.

My students have been fascinated by Scragg's (1975) program, LUIGI, developed to explore how we answer questions about processes: how, what, and why? LUIGI has a database, Kitchenworld, containing objects found in a kitchen and a set of procedures for manipulating those objects. LUIGI simulates simple actions for cooking and preparing foods and answers questions about the processes, such as "How do you toast bread?" or "What utensils do you need to prepare cookies?" You can ask students to answer the process questions first, then compare their answers to LUIGI's. Students readily appreciate the problem space that LUIGI represents, because they all have some knowledge about cooking. The literalness of computer programs and the precision they require become evident when you read the protocol in class.

Neuropsychology

A topic that has always titillated cognitive psychologists is that of the relation between neural activity and thinking. Some cognitive psychologists are schooled in physiology, but most are not. Those who are schooled in physiology tend to be interested in the brain activity correlates of information-processing stages. Perhaps the field of cognitive science will eventually merge with neuropsychology, but currently both fields remain at different levels of abstraction in explaining intelligent processes. Computers can be useful in bridging the two fields.

Computers have been employed in psychophysiology to monitor electroencephalogram (EEG) signals associated with tracking processes, discrimination, short-term memory, and cognitive resource management. This technology can also differentiate between novices and experts at these tasks, as simulated in a video game format (Donchin, 1983). In addition to differentiating between novice and expert users, these physiological processes can be monitored over short time periods to plot fatigue effects or, over longer periods, recovery from brain trauma.

Computers allow the monitoring of event-related brain potentials (ERPs) from the EEG or brainwave recordings, which provide an indicator of human information processing. Donchin (1983) used video games to plot ERP changes in relation to fluctuations in computer game strategies. The games simulate different levels of mental workload depending on the level of problem challenge presented by the machine. They have been used in research for the U.S. Air Force to simulate how cognitive and physiological components of a skill such as battle mission planning are affected by stress. Donchin varied the objects or target positions, their detectability or discriminability, short-term memory load, and resource (equipment and fuel) management to discover what the brain does under simulated stress.

When I talk about Donchin's research in class, I am reminded of a recent movie, *Firefox*, in which Clint Eastwood pilots a plane that employs a rocket firing system, using brainwaves as the launching mechanism. Because many students have seen the movie, instructors can link military and psychological research with the kinds of machines that might exist in the future. Moreover, brain wave research is not just science fiction; the military has been working on this tech-nology for some time.

Cognitive Development

What role does the computer play in human mental and social devel-opment? How can the information-processing analogy be applied to cognitive development? Are computers changing family interaction? These are some of the issues raised by the topic of computers and human growth, found in every introductory course.

When I offer seminars to educators about computer-assisted instruction (CAI), I make a comparison between the Piagetian no-tions of assimilation (fitting information into the existing cognitive schemes) and accommodation (changing cognitive schemes because of new or discrepant information) and what we do in the classroom as instructors. To me Piaget's ideas not only speak to child cognition but also to the acquisition of information in any information-process-ing system, human or machine. With the assumption of input, stor-age, retrieval, assimilation, and accommodation, I can go on to talk about education, programming computers, and children. These anal-ogies are presented early in my course to be used later when I discuss educational psychology and CAI.

A child comes into the world with some knowledge but has much knowledge to acquire about life through problem solving, searching, playing, and manipulating the environment. Obviously a great deal of raw information storage is going on. Sometimes children build in-accurate schemes of the world, and these ideas have to be debugged or replaced. A child also may not find information previously ob-tained about the world either because of improper retrieval strategies or a failure to store the material properly in the first place. Based on years of playing with the world, children eventually become experts of a sort in a variety of problem-solving domains, for example, play-ing cards, developing motor or creative skills, or building a detailed memory bank about a certain subject (mollusks, for example). I offer this extended analogy between Piaget and information processing in order to set the stage for further lectures.

Fortunately, there is a direct link from Piaget to children's use of computers. In his frequently cited book, *Mindstorms* (1980), Papert explains how children experience mathematical concepts by using computers. He has referred to his book as an exercise in an applied genetic epistemology. You cannot get any more Piagetian than that! Papert and his colleagues at MIT have also developed a computer language called LOGO and a robot-like device known as the "turtle" to give children the means of expressing previously abstract mathe-matical knowledge about geometry in physical, graphic, and objective forms. Moving the turtle about with LOGO commands, the child demonstrates his or her level of understanding about both the world of geometry and computer programming.

There are a great number of assumptions and untested hypotheses that keep people skeptical about this research, but the enthusiasm and uniqueness of this approach to cognitive development deserves attention. I should add that the LOGO language is one of the best languages to introduce to computer novices of any age. The LOGO commands are simple and build on the existing database by adding information stored previously. The effects of programming on the turtle provide almost immediate feedback to the programmer. The system is also highly visual and animated, which gives it an added advantage over other languages that are highly abstract.

Another area to consider in computer-assisted instruction is the effect of computerized learning on family and social processes for children. Lepper (1985) and Malone (1983) have formulated some of the major conclusions and posed future questions about children and computers. Their work has focused to a great degree on motivational factors within educational systems and in computer software design that is not only attractive to children but also effective in teaching them something. Malone, for example, has identified the variables of fantasy, challenge, and curiosity that underlie the intrinsic motivation to learn from video games. He also has presented crucial questions: How does playing these games transfer to real world tasks? How does video learning fit into traditional curricula?

Creasey and Myers (1986) have studied the impact of video games on children. What happens when video games enter the home? According to this study, involvement with the games is high initially, but usage soon drops off. Leisure activities with television, arcade games, and movie watching decrease during the initial period but differences soon disappear. Ownership of these games did not jeopardize homework time or grades in math or English. Children's peer interactions and popularity did not change either. Parents, take note: Buying a video game for your child will not greatly alter his or her activities.

Education

When is a computer as effective as a teacher? What motivates students to interact with machines rather than teachers? When should computers be used in schools? What could computers not replace? Are there sex differences in computer learning? These are some of the questions researchers ask when studying the instructional impact of computers. This area is a strong working ground for psychologists because they can provide the empirical data with which to answer these questions (Jay, 1983).

One of the most effective methods of teaching psychology majors about instructional computing is to have them create and test a learning module of their own design. Convince them that they have expertise about some area of knowledge and then work through the stages of CAI development. Not surprisingly, they will teach about subjects such as 35 mm photography, exercise and diet, the rules of ice hockey, and favorite drinks among college students. This approach provides the personal incentive to stay with the task and renders some valuable new ideas for CAI. I believe this approach applies not only to teaching new psychology students but also to experienced psychology faculty.

My colleagues and I are currently asking the question, "Can computers deliver birth control education?" We capitalize on the nonpersonal aspect of the device, important in related therapeutic interventions, to produce an educational dialogue about a sensitive topic for teenagers. We know that teenagers are attracted to computer technology. They are deficient in birth control and contraceptive knowledge. And they would be embarrassed less by a machine than by a high school guidance counselor. Enter the efficient, cheap, nonjudgmental computer. Our data suggest that compared with paper and pencil formats, the computer is just as effective at teaching birth control information (Jay & Bingley, 1986).

A more extensive attempt to deliver education about sex, as well as about alcohol use, suicide prevention, drug effects, and health-related issues is the development of BARN (body awareness resource network). Developed at the University of Wisconsin by Gustafson and his colleagues (Bosworth, Gustafson, Hawkins, Chewning, & Day, 1983), BARN provides an extensive array of microcomputer software targeted to pre-teens and teenagers on the topics just mentioned. You can obtain an up-to-date progress report by writing the authors and you can preview some of the BARN system for microcomputers through the *Encyclopedia Britannica* in Chicago.

Another domain of study focuses on the roles that computers can play in improving the quality of education. According to an analysis by Lepper (1985), the major dimensions that computers can affect are intrinsic motivation, learning styles, curriculum, and educational philosophy. To date there is much debate and controversy but little real longitudinal data with which to decide how computers can best be used in education. A recent review of instructional psychology addresses the nature of computers in relation to important educational variables under study (Pintrich, Cross, Kozma, & McKeachie, 1986). These researchers found that computers can be ineffective when presenting educational materials in a game-like format. They also found, however, that computers reduced the time students spent on tasks in some instances. The important conclusion, however, of this and almost all of the present research on computers is that it is difficult to separate the effects of the type of media used and methods of presentation.

Another question concerning the use of computers in education is to what extent does computer-assisted instruction (CAI) transfer to skills and problem solving in the real world? Kulik, Kulik, and Bangert-Downs (1985) surveyed 32 comparative studies and showed that generally CAI has had a positive effect on achievement scores of elementary school children. These positive impacts, however, weaken in secondary schools and weaken again in college populations. These authors also point out the methodological difficulties in making accurate assessments of computers in educational settings at the present time.

Can the computer assist populations of students who have disabilities or special learning needs? This question appears both in human factors literature and instructional technology. A recent review by Manion (1986) reports positive effects of CAI on attention and performance characteristics of autistic students. Other groups with behavior disorders that are affected positively by CAI include hyperactive students, who spend more time on tasks with computers, and institutionalized juvenile children who have social, emotional, and learning problems. Another example has been cited by Hasselbring and Crossland (1981), who studied the effects of CAI with spelling problems in students with learning disabilities. Pay particular attention to the *Journal of Educational Psychology, Educational Technology,* and *Journal of Learning Disabilities* for specific issues. Be warned that much of the literature is positively biased. There are numerous methodological problems with educational literature, usually stemming from lack of proper (or in some cases, any) control groups and confounding methods of instruction.

Social issues in CAI cannot be separated from educational ones. Today psychologists are concerned with differences in advantaged versus disadvantaged students in terms of access, parental and family interaction with computer homework, sex differences in access and usage, and the effect of computers on peer interaction and socialization. A source of surveys and research on the use of microcomputers in schools is the Center for Social Organization of Schools at The Johns Hopkins University (Becker, 1986). The Center will mail these reports to you upon your request. These national summaries are quite valuable to assess what is actually happening in our schools and with our children and dollars.

The computer is not a panacea. It has been injected into an existing system of education with its own power structure and resistance to change for reasons other than instruction (Jay, 1982). In some cases the computer has created a new or better way of doing an old job. Sometimes, it creates an entirely new job. Unfortunately, sometimes, computers have recapitulated previous problems with sex differences, racial differences, and social or communication difficulties. Kohl (1983) has recently discussed the issue of social equity and computers, and the Becker surveys from Johns Hopkins elaborate the appearance of previous problems reappearing with the use of new technology.

Personality and Social Psychology

How is communication changed within an organization when computers are introduced? How do students communicate with computers? What do people do to computers when frustrated? What is a computer crime? Under what conditions are communications via computer networks valuable? These are some of the major questions being asked about the social impact of computers on groups of people.

When computer game arcades became the contemporary electronic version of the poolroom, parents became concerned that these games would pollute the minds and bodies of the young. To date there is no substantial data to support this contention, and psychologists and teachers would probably benefit from avoiding the issue in the popular press without research to support this highly subjective matter (see Brooks, 1983).

Another social issue was uncovered by Emmett (1981), who found that when IBM introduced an electronic mail network for internal communications and messages, it evolved into a vehicle for complaints. Personal attacks on management, erosion of constructive criticism, the appearance of joke telling, and complaints about working conditions appeared, reflecting underlying tensions among employees. The network allowed employees to "let off steam and get out old hurts," according to one worker. Important here is the indication that new media involving computers will be used in unconventional and unpredictable ways. Psychologists will be needed to assist in the design and restructuring of these systems.

The social psychological impact of computerized communication has been more recently reviewed by Kiesler, Siegel, and McGuire (1984). Both technological and social aspects of computer-mediated communication networks are poorly understood and need to be researched to determine how they affect communication. Some of the major issues are concerned with etiquette, aggressiveness, decision making, attribution, and anonymity or depersonalization. These are issues previously studied by psychologists, who will now have to turn their attention to these same issues in new contexts.

Applications of Computers to Clinical Psychology

Simulating Language

The premise that systems with identifiable rules, operators, and goals can be simulated by computers affects all disciplines. This premise challenges fields such as art, music, poetry, and psychotherapy that have seemingly vague parameters. Opponents of computer simulation in these areas think that simulations would alter the magic qualities of their efforts. Thus we call the machinations of a magician "magic" until the magician shows us how the trick was performed. All simulations seek to understand complex human processes, not to destroy creativity or artistic endeavors.

One of the earliest simulations to appear in psychological literature was Weizenbaum's (1966) attempt to study natural language communication between humans and machines. The program, known as ELIZA, was an experiment to see if a conversation between a user and a computer program could be carried out. The dialogue that appears in many introductory psychology texts was compared to that which might occur when a therapist reacted to a patient's remarks. From this premise followed the notion that the machine was being designed to replace or at least demystify psychotherapy. Actually, Weizenbaum was more interested in identifying "keywords" used during input, making appropriate responses, and cutting system response time than in putting therapists out of a job.

Another simulation that is perhaps more interesting to students is Colby's (1973) PARRY, designed to simulate the underlying factors involved in paranoid thought processes. This simulation is used to instruct clinical psychology students about paranoia and what major variables of the syndrome appear in doctor–patient interactions. PARRY has been field tested in two natural ways. In one case psychiatrists were told to communicate with a patient via teletype; sometimes the patient was an actual paranoid patient from a locked ward, other times it was PARRY. In another case, psychiatrists read dialogues, generated either from real interviews with real patients or from talking to PARRY. In both cases PARRY was convincing to professionals. These dialogues make good lecture material. Ask your students to rate the two sources for paranoia before telling them about PARRY.

The ability of computers to simulate language has broad implications for psychotherapy. A computer does not make faces, get upset, lose patience, scowl, or worry. Although most of us "normal" people prefer to talk to other normal people about ourselves (Dupee & Jay, 1983), those among us with psychological disorders have a different opinion. The nonpersonal computer may be effective and even preferred for dealing with some problems that are difficult to discuss with another person, regardless of how empathetic the doctor or therapist may be. For these reasons computers have been effective in dealing with a variety of psychological disorders, such as alcohol abuse, adherence to antidepressant drug therapy, and sexual dysfunction.

Recently a colleague and I asked college students about the types of sources of help they would seek for various problems (Dupee & Jay, 1983). When we did not see "computers" among their responses, we later listed sets of problems and sets of sources of help that included computers. Again computers were virtually ignored in responses. Were computers of no value in providing health services? Of course not! We were just asking the wrong population. When you ask people who have real psychological disorders, you get a different answer. Anyone who has witnessed how inhumane, depersonalized, and institutionalized many modern social services appear knows why a computer would be a refreshing alternative to some health care providers.

There are a number of sources that could be recommended on the topic of computers in clinical practices. Credit should be given to Greist and his colleagues at the University of Wisconsin, who have been at the forefront of this technology for over 20 years. His reviews are highly readable and thorough (see Greist & Klein, 1981). A recent book of readings on many aspects of psychotherapy from word processing to rehabilitation contains an extensive bibliography of related research as well (Schwartz, 1984). Another collection of readings on the topic of technology in mental health systems contains several integrated chapters of note (Sidowski, Johnson, & Williams, 1980). Of special interest are the chapters on computer psychotherapists (pp. 109–117), behavioral treatment (pp. 119–137), and the work of Greist and Klein (pp. 161–181). These texts alone provide a wealth of information and examples for lecture material by some of the leading figures in computers and mental health. Finally, I found a review by Zarr (1984) valuable because it focused on patient guidelines for computer psychotherapy instead of the more typical issues of hardware and software.

Assessment Instruments

The issue of using computers to assess disorders or administer psychological tests is of great relevance to many health care providers (Matarazzo, 1986; McCullough, Farrell, & Longabaugh, 1986). The appearance of computer versions of popular psychological tests is fairly recent. As with many other types of software (e.g., in education or industry), these programs are offered by many different vendors and remain to be fully field tested and validated. Clinical psychologists who use software for MMPI or Rorschach testing, for example, are challenged with questions about invasion of privacy, cost containment, legal liability, third party payments, and the accuracy of interpretation. It appears that the use of software in testing will grow in the future and our discipline must be well informed about the consequences of using these programs. Aside from these legal, moral, and financial considerations, we should look at what computerized mental health care is doing for patients and providers.

Patients appear to be positive about the use of computers in assessment. Moore, Summer, and Bloor (1984) tested women from an antenatal clinic on their fifth postnatal day to determine their psychological state and to find out if computer assessment was acceptable to these women. A separate paper and pencil attitude survey about the computer revealed almost unanimous acceptability and ease of use. More recently, Lukin, Dowd, Plake, and Kraft (1985) compared computerized versus traditional paper and pencil methods for assessment of anxiety, depression, and reactance. Their analysis revealed no significant differences between scores on these measures across administration format.

Diagnosis

The role of computers in helping doctors diagnose clinical problems has been under investigation for more than 20 years (see Feurzeig, Munter, Swets, & Breen, 1964). Feurzeig's early attempt to develop a computer aid for medical diagnoses is a good example to use to introduce the concept of making clinical decisions based on conversations between doctors and patients. The protocol from this early report is a useful one to read in class. Note that the ability to make accurate diagnoses of any sort depends on the quality of conversation, sequential logic of questioning, and knowledge base involved (see Arons, 1984, for a discussion of computer dialogues). The history and current state of the art of clinical judgment was assessed by Kleinmuntz (1984). He examined the nature of human judgment, formalization of medical and statistical reasoning, decision rules, and making predictions in the clinical task environment—all of which require a sound understanding of cognition and human information processing. With an understanding of these abilities and a background in making diagnoses or clinical judgments, you will be better prepared to launch into any specific type of clinical problem solving with computers.

Treatment Success

Depression. One of the difficulties with patients in treatment for depression is that they do not always adhere to their schedules for taking antidepressant drugs. Compliance to regular therapy is low. Between 25% and 50% of the patients fail to take a significant portion of their medication. BARRY, an on-line computer program, was developed to supervise adherence to drug treatments for depression (Sorrell, Greist, Klein, Johnson, & Harris, 1982). BARRY uses a dialogue to monitor both level of depression and medication adherence along with problems such as drug side effects. BARRY has been fairly successful and also offsets the extra supervision, which is expensive and inconvenient, although also therapeutically effective. BARRY's dialogues are valuable for class discussion of depressive disorders and of computer adjuncts.

Another program designed to deal with depression is MORTON (Selmi, Klein, Greist, Johnson, & Harris, 1982), which uses a first-person dialogue to administer the Beck Depression Inventory and to administer cognitive behavior therapy. MORTON conducts an interview and assigns homework for the patient. The goal of the program is to alleviate dysphoric affect in the depressed person. Again, a dialogue from the article is useful in class.

Alcohol abuse. It must be difficult for people with socially unacceptable habits like alcohol abuse to discuss these behaviors with others, including help givers. Some researchers have examined whether the computer makes it easier for patients to deal with problems such as alcohol abuse. For example, Lucas, Mullin, Luna, and McInroy (1977) addressed the issue of computer versus psychiatrists' effect on interviewees with alcohol-related illnesses. Each patient was interviewed three times, once by computer and twice by different psychiatrists. They found that patients reported greater amounts of alcohol consumption to the computer versus the psychiatrist, which implies that patients were more honest with the machine. In two other studies assessing patients' attitudes about computer interrogation, results indicated that patients had very positive views of computer aids. Men and young patients were especially positive about the programs (Lucas, 1977; Lucas, Card, Knill-Jones, Watkinson, & Crean, 1976).

Skinner and Allen (1983) tested the notion that computers could elicit more accurate reports about consumption. They compared alcohol, drug, and tobacco users' reports from face-to-face, self-report, and computer interview formats but found no significant differences in either level of problems or consumption reported. When rated by the subjects, the computer format was less friendly but more relaxing, interesting, and faster than the other two methods. Computer interrogation was most acceptable to clients with good visual–motor skills and least acceptable to those with good educational background or with defensive personalities. Their results should be compared with Lucas et al. (1976) to give a more complete picture of interrogation effects.

Phobias. One of the leaders in the attempt to automate procedures used in systematic desensitization is Lang (Lang, 1980; Lang, Melamed, & Hart, 1970). For each phobia patient, fear is associated with specific fearful stimuli, which in the course of treatment must be made less fearful. The systematization amounts to determining the fear stimuli, the patient's level of arousal, presenting the stimuli, and monitoring the reduction in autonomic activity (heart rate) over a period of time. This application is obviously a good candidate for computerization.

Ten years after their initial attempt to automate the procedure, Lang (1980) has developed a digital computer version that is flexible and responsive enough to provide a solution. SAM (Self-Assessment Mannequin) is a computer-generated graphic display used to monitor arousal and emotional imagery. Biofeedback is monitored by the computer as are changes in physiological activity that are sent to the subject to employ in a desensitization program. Lang has also made some future projections about computerized desensitization. His work is the kind to watch and to present to a class in relation to other types of therapy. A recent sample of other applications in behavior therapies was reported by Klepac (1984).

Carr and Ghosh (1983) wanted to determine if computers could assist in assessing and treating phobic patients. Treatment of phobias must include an initial, detailed behavioral assessment (2 to 3 hours). Paper questionnaires are of little use; they are long and impersonal and may be returned not fully completed. These authors developed a computer interview to categorize phobia type, assess the intensity of specific fears and avoidance behavior, and to define the precise behavioral targets for use in a desensitization program. More than half of their subjects, outpatients referred to a clinic by a general practitioner, preferred the computer to a clinician. The automated assessment by computer provided the advantages of being economical, precise, and objective, and of saving the clinician time. To see more clearly how an automated desensitization program operates, a look at Lang's work is helpful.

Rehabilitation

Can computer games help patients recover from brain damage? What can computer skills do for juvenile delinquents or inmates in jails? Do computers help autistic patients communicate better to others? These are some of the questions being asked under the rubric of rehabilitation. Computers have been employed in this domain for several years.

Stone (1983) reported on a program to assist juvenile offenders by providing them with computer programming skills. In some cases the computer can be used in corrections education as a means of providing computer literacy and to boost deficient reading or writing skills. In this particular report, computer programming was offered as a vocational skill to increase ex-offenders' job opportunities. Computer programming and computer software produced by inmates is also a source of employment within some jail settings.

Video games have been employed to assist and monitor the rehabilitation of patients with brain injuries (see Lynch, 1983). Fine motor functions and eye–hand coordination can be assessed as patients play video games. Recently Lynch (1986) has reviewed the sources of software for cognitive rehabilitation in the areas of simple and complex reaction time, visual scanning and tracking, memory, visual spatial skills, and higher cognitive functions. These packages allow the clinician the options to select the appropriate software for a given patient population and setting. Weir (1983) has also used video games for recreation and rehabilitation when dealing with victims of cerebral palsy and autism.

Applications of Computers to Students

Academic Advising

Curriculum counseling occurs on every campus, in every major, for almost every professor, and almost every student majoring in psychology. As long as the requirements for graduation remain stable, the task has clear goals and rules. Although I enjoy talking with my advisees, I prefer to discuss career plans and preparation rather than to simply restate the requirements for graduation that appear in the course catalog. The process of acquiring this information is well defined, repetitive, time consuming, and easily understood; therefore it is a good candidate for computerization. I created ADVISOR to help both me and my students appreciate the requirements of graduating as a psychology major at North Adams State.

ADVISOR unfolds in a question and answer format. First, the program asks the student whether he or she has completed general education courses required of all students. Where a selection among courses is possible, for example, among literature courses, the student indicates which course he or she took. General education courses are queried first because they are of primary importance, followed by psychology courses. These course options appear in an order that is most effective to reach graduation, given course sequencing and prerequisite restrictions. Again, where options occur, the student responds to a menu presentation. A final hard copy of each student's dialogue is made. This copy, when accurately done, indicates all the courses taken and reminds the student of those that remain. The student retains this record and uses it to supplement the official transcripts that he or she would otherwise have to purchase from the registrar. The exercise can also be required by advisers to ensure that students have initiated preparation for registration.

My students can read the school's catalog, talk to ADVISOR, or talk to other students about curricular requirements. The burden of completing these courses is theirs and taking the internally controlled or self-monitoring approach reminds them of what lies ahead. I also hear less of the "I didn't know I had to take that course" following ADVISOR contact. My advising sessions are hence more personally directed to the students and are more socially pleasant.

It is important to note that users have a number of options, of which the computer version is one. ADVISOR saves time and effort, has infinite patience, and will not be late for an appointment. ADVISOR was created in a fairly well defined domain of rules and procedures for graduation. We know that only a few students actually read their college catalogs and that they forget what they have read. Because of its interactive nature, ADVISOR forces students to think about course selection. Some of my students would probably prefer to talk to ADVISOR than to me!

I suppose that the next logical extension of academic counseling with computers would be career counseling. Cairo (1983) has reviewed some of these counseling systems, which are designed to provide career information instantaneously on a wide variety of occupations. Perhaps the most extensive program is SIGI (System for Interactive Guidance and Information), developed by the Educational Testing Service (see Chapman, Katz, Norris, & Pears, 1977, for review and field testing). SIGI has had a strong positive effect on a number of dimensions of career decision making; you should cite it when you talk about vocational counseling. A more recent review of career counseling was conducted by Pinder and Fitzgerald (1984), who found that computerized guidance systems improved career decision making for college students. Carrying the issue one step further, Hassett and Dukes (1986) explored the use of realistic computer-based training programs for employees of large corporations and students in professional schools.

Classroom Demonstrations and Media Presentations

There are a lot of ways to introduce to students the psychological implications of computers and their impact on our lives. Classroom demonstrations are especially effective because they take the burden off the lecturer, they are accepted enthusiastically by students, and they present material graphically. Students respond to and comprehend best new information that has some relation to what they already know about the world. Try to find examples of the use of computers in everyday life, especially some familiar to students. When these examples have psychological implications, bring them into the classroom for discussion. These demonstrations make the consideration of computers from a psychological viewpoint more real for students, and the topic will resonate with their lives in the real world. If you have a difficult time finding examples on your own, ask a few students interested in popular culture and computers for some suggestions. Faculty in communications, media, and computer science can also provide additional examples.

Those who use supplementary media such as tapes, movies, and other recorded materials should consider the role of computers in modern film. These can be presented outside of class time for discussion and critical review or can be related to other material in class. Films with strong computer themes include *Wargames, 2001, Metropolis,* and *The Andromeda Strain. The Andromeda Strain* is particularly good at showing the realistic use of advanced technology to solve a possible problem in an inductive, scientific manner. Students are enthusiastic about watching films and should benefit from relating these themes to research in their texts. They should also appreciate how many problems revolutionary technology can solve and initiate. They should see many psychological issues involved in these popular, commonplace events. Furthermore, the use of other media indicates that the instructor is widely read and up to date with current trends, which is crucial with a topic like computers. We have presented some of these films at North Adams and allowed our introductory students to write a review of them based on what they are reading in class. These written reviews then can be turned in for extra credit or used in small group discussions.

Another approach is to produce a computer-use slide show. I have slides depicting computer labs, secretaries' workstations, and students working privately. With these slides you can point out various human factors and social and instructional implications. The topic of computers and on-the-job health and safety issues can also be effectively depicted with slides. Posture, lighting conditions, seating, adjustability, eye strain, and distractions are easy to capture on film. Idiosyncratic versus group work settings demonstrate personality and instructional styles involved in computerized environments.

Classroom demonstrations of psychological software are also effective. You can purchase inexpensive packages for statistics, testing, interviewing, and scoring for well-known psychological materials. You can also create your own or use software created in other psychology methods or lab courses to show how computers are employed on your campus. The client-centered computer therapist, ELIZA, is a good demonstration of both the therapeutic technique and computer programming. These programs can be demonstrated interactively in small classes or set up for small groups to preview outside of class time for large lecture groups. These lab demonstrations can be prepared and monitored by upper level students. A benefit of using student-run labs is that introductory students are more likely to talk to the lab assistants and ask questions about the programs. In addition, it provides an opportunity to find out what upper level psychology majors with computer backgrounds can do.

The psychological effects of computers is also addressed in good science fiction literature. Negative effects were illustrated in Clarke's *The City and the Stars* (1956) and in Zamatien's *We* (1972). A more optimistic view can be found in Leonard's *Education and Ecstasy* (1968). These could be read outside the class for discussion, or specific passages could be detailed in your lecture. When you decide to talk about technological innovation such as with computers, you will find yourself pursuing two lines of thought and literature: one, readings from history about how technology and inventions have affected society, and two, futuristic predictions about society and technology. Being well read in both areas will enhance your understanding of today's research and developments. Those not well grounded in science fiction will be surprised to find many references to computers, robots, and intelligent programs in this literature. Of course, none of us know what the future will actually be like. But some of these science fiction scenarios may come true, and who better to make them so than psychologists!

Additional activities include field trips both on and off campus to study computer installations where psychologists or human factors people are employed. Computers are a topic in some modern musical recordings and video presentations. Students will perceive a different world when you point out both the existence of computers in popular culture and your awareness of these media.

Computerphobia

The reason I have been successful as an in-service trainer, consultant, and workshop leader is not because I am an expert at knowing about the guts of a machine, but because I know about the psychological guts of teachers and educators. A student of technology knows that innovation acceptance is not a hardware problem but a people problem. Getting people to use machines happens because a psychologist or someone with similar magic can understand a potential user first and then try to fit the device to that person. Psychologists are essential to finding this fit, and because computers are going to be more plentiful in the future, you should start thinking about what you are going to do about it now.

Besides considering how psychologists have chosen to use computers, another question arises when we ask what happens when we introduce new technology to novices or unwilling users? The impact of technology on workers is not unique to computers, of course; it has been around since the boss has tried to improve productivity. Computerphobia is just a more recent variant of an older technophobia. It is a topic worthy of scrutiny due to the growing use of computers at work and at school. Asking a worker to make changes in habits, competence, performance, and self-perception has far-reaching implications for our science. It is the human factors psychologist who is uniquely qualified to assess how people feel when the job environment changes and what changes in productivity are likely to occur.

In the late 1970s, when microcomputers came on the scene with full force, the proponents of this technology were very positive and enthusiastic. The proponents turned out to be manufacturers, vendors, and salespeople who were out to make profits and knew little about what would really happen to users' lives. I first saw computerphobia in the eyes of educators in elementary and high school settings when I was teaching seminars, workshops, and providing in-service training and consulting. Teachers were told by administrators with the backing of the local school board that during the next year they would make students computer literate. Computerphobics had fears about the machines, negative attitudes, and unrealistic thoughts about how they might damage them (see Jay, 1981b, 1985). Still my colleagues at schools of engineering and the like failed to see the population being affected. Even after computer illiterates were educated, the psychological problems did not end. Computerphiles are sometimes admired by fellow teachers, other times they are regarded with jealousy and misunderstanding. Social consequences for teacher and student alike remain to be fully understood.

How do we combat computerphobia? The introduction of any new technology into the home or workplace takes time and change. What makes people change? We will accept a new device if it will enhance our life-styles. Enhancement includes making life easier and safer, saving time, and making fewer errors. We have to perceive the device as being able to provide these enhancements through our experience with them, not just through the faith and word of the dealer. We need to have time to play with the device on our own and determine that we can operate it to our satisfaction. We need to accept the personality changes that will occur when we become competent. We will find that not only will our self-perception or self-efficacy be changed, but so will the way we are treated by others.

People and businesses must realize that computerization of a task makes performance on that task more objective. Thus the type and number of successes and failures can be recorded. Management hopes to improve productivity with these data but the workers do not know if this new accountability achieved by the computer records make that machine a work-saving device or a tattletail.

References

Abelson, P. H. (1986). Instrumentation and computers. *American Scientist, 74*(2), 182–192.

Arons, A. B. (1984). Computer-based instructional dialogs in science courses. *Science, 224,* 1051–1056.

Atkinson, R. L., Atkinson, R. C., & Hilgard, E. R. (1983). *Introduction to psychology.* New York: Harcourt Brace Jovanovich.

Balsam, P., Fifer, W., Sacks, S., & Silver, R. (1984). Microcomputers in psychology laboratory courses. *Behavior Research Methods, Instruments, & Computers, 16*(2), 150–152.

Becker, H. J. (1986). *Instructional uses of school computers.* Reports from the 1985 national survey. Baltimore, MD: The Johns Hopkins University, Center for Social Organization of Schools.

Bosworth, K., Gustafson, D. H., Hawkins, R. P., Chewning, B., & Day, T. (1983, October). Adolescents, health education, and computers: The body awareness resource network (BARN). *Health Education/Computers,* pp. 58–60.

Brooks, D. B. (1983). Video games and social behavior. In S. S. Baughman & P. D. Clagett (Eds.), *Video Games and Human Development: A Research Agenda for the '80s* (pp. 14–16). Cambridge, MA: Harvard Graduate School of Education.

Butler, D. L. (1986). Interests in and barriers to using computers in instruction. *Teaching of Psychology, 13*(1), 20–23.

Butler, D. L., & Kring, A. M. (1984). Survey on present and potential instructional use of computers in psychology. *Behavior Research Methods, Instruments, & Computers, 16*(2), 180–182.

Cairo, P. C. (1983). Evaluating the effects of computer-assisted counseling systems: A selective review. *The Counseling Psychologist, 11*(4), 55–59.

Carr, A. C., & Ghosh, A. (1983). Response of phobic patients to direct computer assessment. *British Journal of Psychiatry, 142,* 60–65.

Castellan, N. J., Jr. (1981). On-line computers in psychology: The last 10 years, the next 10 years—The challenge and the promise. *Behavior Research Methods & Instrumentation, 13*(2), 91–96.

Castellan, N. J., Jr. (1982). Computers in psychology: A survey of instructional applications. *Behavior Research Methods & Instrumentation, 14*(2), 198–202.

Castellan, N. J., Jr. (1986a). Issues in the effective use of computers in introductory and advanced courses in psychology. *Behavior Research Methods, Instruments, & Computers, 18*(2), 251–256.

Castellan, N. J., Jr. (1986b). *Microcomputer software for the undergraduate curriculum.* Chicago: Midwestern Psychological Association.

Chapman, W., Katz, M., Norris, L., & Pears, L. (1977). *SIGI: Field test and evaluation of a computer-based system of interactive guidance and information.* Princeton, NJ: Educational Testing Service.

Chizek, H. J. (1985). Helping paraplegics walk: Looking beyond the media blitz. *Technology Review, 88*(5), 55–63.

Clarke, A. (1956). *The city and the stars.* New York: Harcourt, Brace.

Colby, K. M. (1973). Simulations of belief systems. In R. C. Schank & K. M. Colby (Eds.), *Computer models of thought and language* (pp. 251–286). San Francisco: Freeman.

Cordes, C. (1985, July). Military waste: The human factor. *APA Monitor,* pp. 1, 17–18.

Cozby, P. C. (1984). *Using computers in the behavioral sciences.* Palo Alto, CA: Mayfield.

Creasey, G. L., & Myers, B. J. (1986). Video games and children: Effects on leisure activities, schoolwork, and peer involvement. *Merrill-Palmer Quarterly, 32*(3), 251–262.

Deni, R. (1986). *Programming microcomputers for psychology experiments.* Belmont, CA: Wadsworth.

Donchin, E. (1983). Video games in medical rehabilitation and learning. In S. S. Baughman & P. D. Clagett (Eds.), *Video Games and Human Development: A Research Agenda for the '80s* (pp. 30–32). Cambridge, MA: Harvard Graduate School of Education.

Dupee, L. D., & Jay, T. B. (1983). *Students' perceptions of computers as sources of help.* Paper presented at the Greater Boston Undergraduate Research Paper Convention, Suffolk University, Boston, MA.

Elwork, A., & Gutkin, T. B. (1985). The behavioral sciences in the computer age. *Computers in Human Behavior, 1,* 3–38.

Emmett, R. (1981, November). VNET or Gripenet? *Datamation,* 48–58.

Feurzeig, W., Munter, P., Swets, J., & Breen, M. (1964). Computer-aided teaching in medical diagnosis. *Journal of Medical Education, 39,* 746–754.

Foster, K. R. (1986). The VDT debate. *American Scientist, 74*(2), 163–168.

Gardner, H. (1985). *The mind's new science: A history of the cognitive revolution.* New York: Basic Books.

Geyer, L. H., Pond, D. J., & Smith, D. D. B. (1986). A summary of the proposal for the accreditation of graduate programs in human factors. *Human Factors Society Bulletin, 29*(1), 1–3.

Greist, J. H., & Klein, M. H. (1981). Computers in psychiatry. In S. Arieti and H. K. H. Brodie (Eds.), *American handbook of psychiatry* (pp. 750–777). New York: Basic Books.

Hasselbring, T. S., & Crossland, C. L. (1981). Using microcomputers for diagnosing spelling problems in learning-handicapped children. *Educational Technology, 21*(4), 37–39.

Hassett, J., & Dukes, S. (1986, September). The new employee trainer: A floppy disk. *Psychology Today,* pp. 30–36.

Jay, T. B. (1981a). Are you a computer illiterate? *The Computing Teacher, 8*(4), 58–60.

Jay, T. B. (1981b). What to do about computerphobia. *Educational Technology, 21*(1), 47–48.

Jay, T. B. (1982). The future of educational technology. *Educational Technology, 22*(6), 21–23.

Jay, T. B. (1983). The cognitive approach to computer courseware design and evaluation. *Educational Technology, 23*(1), 22–26.

Jay, T. B. (1985). Defining and measuring computerphobia. In R. E. Eberts and C. G. Eberts (Eds.), *Trends in Ergonomics/Human Factors II* (pp. 321–326). Amsterdam: North-Holland.

Jay, T. B., & Bingley, J. (1986, June). *Can microcomputers deliver birth control education.* Presented at Third Mid-Central Ergonomics/Human Factors Conference, Miami University.

Kiesler, S., Siegel, J., & McGuire, T. W. (1984). Social psychological aspects of computer-mediated communication. *American Psychologist, 39*(10), 1123–1134.

Kleinmuntz, B. (1984). The scientific study of clinical judgement in psychology and medicine. *Clinical Psychology Review, 4,* 111–126.

Klepac, R. K. (1984). Micro-computers in behavior therapy: A sampler of applications. *The Behavior Therapist, 7,* 79–83.

Kohl, H. (1983). Video games and formal education. In S. S. Baughman & P. D. Clagett (Eds.), *Video Games and Human Development: A Research Agenda for the '80s* (pp. 47–49). Cambridge, MA: Harvard Graduate School of Education.

Kulik, J. A., Kulik, C. C., & Bangert-Downs, R. L. (1985). Effectiveness of computer-based education in elementary schools. *Computers in Human Behavior, 1,* 59–74.

Lang, P. J., Melamed, B. G., & Hart, J. (1970). A psychophysical analysis of fear modification using an automated desensitization procedure. *Journal of Abnormal Psychology, 78*(2), 220–234.

Lang, P. J. (1980). Behavioral treatment and bio-behavioral assessment: Computer applications. In J. B. Sidowski, J. Johnson, & T. H. Williams (Eds.), *Technology in mental health care delivery systems* (pp. 119–137). Norwood, NJ: Ablex.

Leonard, G. (1968). *Education and ecstasy.* New York: Delacorte Press.

Lepper, M. R. (1985). Microcomputers in education: Motivatonal and social issues. *American Psychologist, 40*(1), 1–18.

Lindsay, P. H., & Norman, D. A. (1972). *Human information processing.* New York: Academic Press.

Lucas, R. W. (1977). A study of patients' attitudes to computer interrogation. *International Journal of Man-Machine Studies, 9,* 69–86.

Lucas, R. W., Card, W. I., Knill-Jones, R. P., Watkinson, G., & Crean, G. P. (1976, September). Computer interrogation of patients. *British Medical Journal,* pp. 623–625.

Lucas, R. W., Mullin, P. J., Luna, C. B. X., & McInroy, D. C. (1977). Psychiatrists and a computer as interrogators of patients with alcohol-related illnesses: A comparison. *British Journal of Psychiatry, 131,* 160–167.

Lukin, M. E., Dowd, E. T., Plake, B. S., & Kraft, R. G. (1985). Comparing computerized versus traditional psychological assessment. *Computers in Human Behavior, 1,* 49–58.

Lynch, W. J. (1983). Video games in medical rehabilitation and learning. In S. S. Baughman & P. D. Clagett (Eds.), *Video Games and Human Development: A Research Agenda for the '80s* (pp. 25–28). Cambridge, MA: Harvard Graduate School of Education.

Lynch, W. J. (1986). An update on software in cognitive rehabilitation. *Cognitive Rehabilitation, 4*(3), 14–18.

Malone, T. W. (1983). Video games and formal education. In S. S. Baughman & P. D. Clagett (Eds.), *Video Games and Human Development: A Research Agenda for the '80s* (pp. 49–52). Cambridge, MA: Harvard Graduate School of Education.

Manion, M. H. (1986). Computers and behavior-disordered students: A rationale and review of the literature. *Educational Technology, 26*(7), 20–24.

Matarazzo, J. D. (1986). Computerized clinical psychological test interpretations: Unvalidated plus all mean and no sigma. *American Psychologist, 41*(1), 14–24.

McCormick, E. J., & Sanders, M. S. (1982). *Human factors in engineering and design.* New York: McGraw-Hill.

McCullough, L., Farrell, A. D., & Longabaugh, R. (1986). The development of a microcomputer-based mental health information system: A potential tool for bridging the scientist–practitioner gap. *American Psychologist, 41*(2), 207–214.

Moore, N. C., Summer, K. R., & Bloor, R. N. (1984). Do patients like psychometric testing by computer? *Journal of Clinical Psychology, 40*(3), 875–877.

Nickerson, R. S. (1986). *Using computers: Human factors in information systems.* Cambridge, MA: MIT Press.

Papert, S. (1980). *Mindstorms.* New York: Basic Books.

Peden, B. F., & Steinhauer, G. D. (1986). FACES in the lab and faces in the crowd: Integrating microcomputers into the psychology course. *Teaching of Psychology, 13*(2), 85–87.

Pinder, F. A., & Fitzgerald, P. W. (1984). The effectiveness of a computerized guidance system in promoting career decision making. *Journal of Vocational Behavior, 24*, 123–131.

Pintrich, P. R., Cross, D. R., Kozma, R. B., & McKeachie, W. J. (1986). Instructional psychology. *Annual Review of Psychology, 37*, 611–651.

Pribram, K. H. (1986). The cognitive revolution and mind/brain issues. *American Psychologist, 41*(5), 507–520.

Rowand, R. (1986). Computers are changing our cars. *Lamp, 68*(2), 27–28.

Scheirer, C. J., & Rogers, A. M. (1985). *The undergraduate curriculum: 1984.* Washington, DC: American Psychological Association.

Schwartz, M. D. (Ed.). (1984). *Using computers in clinical practice: Psychotherapy and mental health applications.* New York: Haworth.

Scragg, G. W. (1975). Answering questions about processes. In D. A. Norman and D. E. Rumelhart (Eds.), *Explorations in cognition* (pp. 349–375). San Francisco: Freeman.

Selmi, P. M., Klein, M. H., Greist, J. H., Johnson, J. H., & Harris, W. G. (1982). An investigation of computer-assisted cognitive–behavior therapy in the treatment of depression. *Behavior Research Methods & Instrumentation, 14*(2), 181–185.

Sidowski, J. B., Johnson, J. H., & Williams, T. A. (Eds.). (1980). *Technology in mental health care delivery systems.* Norwood, NJ: Ablex.

Skinner, H. A., & Allen, B. A. (1983). Does the computer make a difference? Computerized versus face-to-face versus self-report assessment of alcohol, drug, and tobacco use. *Journal of Consulting and Clinical Psychology*, *51*(2), 267–275.

Sorrell, S. P., Greist, J. H., Klein, M. H., Johnson, J. H., & Harris, W. G. (1982). Enhancement of adherence to tricyclic antidepressants by computerized supervision. *Behavior Research Methods & Instrumentation*, *14*(2), 176–180.

Stone, A. (1983). Video games and social behavior. In S. S. Baughman & P. D. Clagett (Eds.), *Video Games and Human Development: A Research Agenda for the '80s* (pp. 16–18). Cambridge, MA: Harvard Graduate School of Education.

Taylor, R. P. (Ed.). (1980). *The computer in the school: Tutor, tool, tutee.* New York: Teachers College Press.

Weir, S. (1983). Video games in medical rehabilitation and learning. In S. S. Baughman & P. D. Clagett (Eds.), *Video Games and Human Development: A Research Agenda for the '80s* (pp. 28–30). Cambridge, MA: Harvard Graduate School of Education.

Weizenbaum, J. (1966). ELIZA-A computer program for the study of natural language communication between man and machine. *Communications of the ACM*, *9*(1), 36–45.

Zamatien, E. (1972). *We.* New York: Viking Press.

Zarr, M. L. (1984). Computer-mediated psychotherapy: Toward patient-selection guidelines. *American Journal of Psychotherapy*, *38*(1), 47–62.

GARY E. SCHWARTZ

PERSONALITY AND HEALTH: AN INTEGRATIVE HEALTH SCIENCE APPROACH

Gary E. Schwartz is currently a professor of psychology and psychiatry at Yale University, Director of the Yale Psychophysiology Center, Director of Yale's predoctoral and postdoctoral research training program in health psychology supported by the National Institute of Mental Health (NIMH), and Co-Director of the Yale Behavioral Medicine Clinic. He has served on NIMH and National Institutes of Health study sections, has been as Associate Editor of *Psychophysiology, Biological Psychology,* and *Health Psychology,* has been President of the Biofeedback Society of America and the Health Psychology Division of the American Psychological Association (APA), and is a Fellow of APA, the Academy of Behavioral Medicine Research, and the Society of Behavioral Medicine. His many awards include the 1972 Young Psychologist Award and the 1978 Early Career Award for Distinguished Research, both from APA. He has edited 10 books and authored approximately 150 articles and chapters.

Schwartz grew up in North Babylon, New York. He was deeply interested in mathematics, science, science fiction, soccer, and music. He loved animals, was interested in self-hypnosis and medical hypnosis, and enjoyed re-reading the 20-volume set of the *Book of Knowledge.*

At Cornell University Schwartz majored in psychology, minored in chemistry, and was introduced to the study of psychophysiology and the potential for learned control of autonomic responses. Schwartz saw a path for integrating his theoretical, research, and clinical interests. He was elected to the Premedicine and Psychology Honor Societies and graduated Phi Beta Kappa.

In graduate school at the University of Wisconsin, he studied psychophysiology and biofeedback with Peter Lang, psychopathology with Loren Chapman, and human physiology and biophysics. He transferred to the Department of Social Relations at Harvard University in 1977, where he worked closely with David Shapiro, Bernard Tursky, Andrew Crider, and Herbert Benson on the voluntary control of blood pressure and heart rate in normal and hypertensive persons, the psychophysiology of imagery, and the effects of predictability and control on physiological responses to stress (with Erwin Staub).

While an assistant professor, Schwartz focused on the psychophysiology of self-regulation, patterns of facial muscle tension during imagery and in clinical depression, cerebral laterality for patterns of emotional and cognitive processes, and the effect of repressive coping styles on physiological and behavioral responses to stress.

At Yale University, he and his colleagues have extended these themes through new aroma science research on the role of fragrances in altering mood and physiology (i.e., chemical psychophysiology) in normal people and in patients with psychological and medical disorders and in studies of the effects of music before, during, and after surgery; cognitive and brain mechanisms involving the unconscious processing of positive and negative emotional stimuli in repression and depression; the role of levels of emotional awareness and autonomic versus central nervous system laterality in physical and psychiatric disorders; as well as research testing of the opiate-peptide hypothesis of disregulation theory in repression, emotion, and disease.

Schwartz and his wife Jeanne just celebrated their 22nd wedding anniversary. Jeanne is a lecturer in the Department of Psychiatry, Clinical Coordinator of the Yale Behavioral Medicine Clinic, and Director of the Connecticut Center for Behavioral Medicine and Biofeedback. They live in a log home, share a love for American and Canadian Indian art, opera, mysteries, Maine, and most of all, their three Welsh Corgis (Thurber, Willy, and Nellie), to whom this lecture is dedicated.

GARY E. SCHWARTZ

PERSONALITY AND HEALTH: AN INTEGRATIVE HEALTH SCIENCE APPROACH

Introduction

In the teaching of introductory psychology, few topics are of more interest and relevance to students and faculty alike than are personality and health. The concept of personality as a set of qualities expressed in thought, feeling, and overt behavior that defines each person's uniqueness, is a common, if not universal, concept. Similarly, the idea that persons have the potential for a state of biological, psychological, social, and, for many, spiritual health also seems to be a common belief. Students and faculty come to courses in introductory psychology with specific individual beliefs about personality and health. In fact, it is difficult to imagine human beings without qualities of personality and health and beliefs about them.

When I was invited by the American Psychological Association (APA) to give the G. Stanley Hall Lecture in the area of health psychology, I asked myself the following four related questions:

1. What topics within health psychology are of special interest and relevance to students in introductory courses?

The assistance of Louise Leader in the preparation of this manuscript is gratefully acknowledged. Research reported was supported in part by National Science Foundation Grant #BNS-8318984.

2. What topics lend themselves to creative teaching techniques?

3. What topics are of special interest and relevance to those in the field of health psychology and to health care in general?

4. What topics need to be developed and integrated within the teaching of introductory psychology and also within health psychology and health care in general?

In order to prepare the answers to these qustions, I contacted approximately 25 leading psychologists and physicians whose work directly or indirectly dealt with the relationship between personality and health and requested copies of their most recent writings. This chapter also reflects my personal experiences in 15 years of teaching students about personality and health and my judgment of which topics are interesting and relevant to students and faculty. The chapter is not intended to be comprehensive but rather selective, representing what has worked in lectures and seminars, and what, for theoretical and applied reasons, is interesting and potentially important.

Initially, I did not intend to publish my lecture in this format. Unfortunately, before the APA convention, I came down with the flu, and I could hardly speak without bouts of uncontrollable, painful coughing. I began to heal, but the cough and attendant inability to speak prevented my giving the lecture on personality and health.

After the APA convention, a health psychologist wrote to wish me well and commented that it was "bad form" for someone about to give a major lecture on health psychology to become ill. I interpret the bad form not as getting sick per se but in failing to engage in appropriate healing behavior and, therefore, prolonging the illness and missing the convention.

This chapter is organized around nine conclusions that health psychologists have made about the relation between personality and health. These conclusions are a sampling of conclusions concerning health psychology today. They also reflect various degrees of speculation (i.e., hypothesis generation). These conclusions or ideas are discussed in separate sections of this chapter. The conclusions are

1. Individual differences are always present in effects of the mind on the body;

2. Stress is not stress is not stress;

3. Type A is not Type A is not Type A;

4. Low anxiety is not low anxiety is not low anxiety;

5. The five "dis's" hypothesis: disattention, disconnection, disregulation, disorder, and disease;

6. You cannot attend to your body without regulating your body;

7. Health promoting personality factors: hardiness, mindfulness, and relaxed affiliativeness;

8. Healthy repression: repression as a prerequisite to health;

9. Personality is a system, and all systems have personality.

Individual Differences Are Always Present in Effects of Mind on the Body

A Classroom Demonstration

One way to impress upon students that effects of the mind on the body can be easily demonstrated and that individual differences are the rule rather than the exception is to demonstrate voluntary control of heart rate. The larger the group, the more dramatic the findings and the more meaningful the experience.

In the demonstration, students are requested to get a partner and are told that each student will be able to serve as the subject and the experimenter at different times. After each pair determines who will be the subject first, they are told that they will participate in a heart rate control demonstration. There will be three trials, each one minute long. The first trial will be a resting baseline trial, the second, a heart rate increase trial, and the third, a heart rate decrease trial. The experimenters are requested to take their subjects' pulses. All students are requested to close their eyes. When all student experimenters can find their subjects' pulse, they are told when to start and stop each trial.

At the word *start*, the experimenter begins counting the pulses, and the subject is to either (1) simply sit quietly—the baseline trial, (2) attempt to raise his or her heart rate by thought processes (no gross body movements are allowed)—the heart rate increase trial, or (3) attempt to lower his or her heart rate by thought processes—the heart rate decrease trial. After each trial, the experimenter records the pulse in beats per minute and then closes his or her eyes again. After three trials are completed, the students switch roles. The same experimental procedure is repeated for another three trials.

The students are then instructed to calculate heart rate increase scores (increase minus baseline), heart rate decrease scores (decrease minus baseline), and total heart rate control scores (increase minus decrease) for their respective subjects.

At this point, to calculate findings for the class as a whole, the lecturer puts the following on the blackboard: 0 and below, 1–5, 6–10, 11–15, 16–20, 21–25, 26–30, and 31 and above. Each set of scores is called out and subjects are asked to raise their hands when the range reflecting their scores is stated.

In a sample of 100 students, it is common to obtain individual scores falling in all the ranges. Many scores will fall in the 1–5, 6–10, and 11–15 ranges. A surprising number will fall in the 20s and 30s, while some subjects will generate negative (increase minus decrease) scores.

Next, the students are asked to describe their conscious actions used to control their heart rate. It is common after the increase trial to receive reports of strategies, such as thinking aggressive thoughts, sexual thoughts, thoughts involving exercising, thoughts focusing on the feeling of the heart beat, and counting faster to oneself. This usually produces a lively discussion about what factors could account for such a wide range of heart rate control. Is it due to genetic differences in neural innervation of the heart, history of heart disease in the family, history of athletic training, implicit use of breathing or muscle tension, arousibility of the person, awareness of the pulsations, ability to imagine scenes, experimental error, discomfort in being touched, or other aspects of performance anxiety? At this point the lecturer could discuss selected studies on individual differences in voluntary control from biofeedback, meditation, relaxation, imagery, or hypnosis literature.

This demonstration illustrates the four following major conclusions:

1. People have the capacity to use their minds to influence their bodies, and they may have done so in the past more often than they realize.

2. The degree of the voluntary control effect varies for many reasons, including biological, psychological, and social factors.

3. When given the choice, people select different strategies in controlling their physiology that reflect aspects of their unique personalities.

4. The degree of control may have positive effects (e.g., good imagery) or negative effects (e.g., poor homeostasis).

This demonstration can be performed in a 50-minute lecture. It is one that, when properly orchestrated, remains in the minds of students long after they have completed the course.

Stress Is Not Stress Is Not Stress: The Emotion Story

All people are exposed to stressors and experience varying degrees of stress in their lives. However, there are remarkable individual differences in people's self-reports and their physiological reactions to specific stressors.

Early research linking stress with disease and research linking personality with stress and disease are covered quite well in current introductory books on health psychology (e.g., Feuerstein, Labbe, & Kuczmierczyk, 1986). What is generally not covered is a perspective integrating literature on stress with the broader, evolving literature on emotion and its relation to personality and disease. That relation is the focus of this part of the chapter.

The literature on emotion is huge and growing. However, the core idea underlying the modern research on the varied aspects of emotion can be summarized in a way that encourages introductory psychology students to think about stress, personality, disease, and health in terms of differentiated systems.

Emotion is not a simple, unitary concept. It is unique, organized sets of systems of responses with evolutionary significance (Schwartz, 1986). Darwin (1872) believed that distinct emotions that exist in lower animals and people are genetically organized and are altered in their patterns of expression through experience (e.g., learning and cross-cultural research by Izard, 1971). Ekman, Friesan, and Ellsworth (1972) have demonstrated that at least six emotions are reliably recognized across cultures from expressions shown in the human face. These six emotions are happiness, sadness, anger, fear, surprise, and disgust.

Izard (1972) made a major advance with his development of the Differential Emotions Scale. He demonstrated that emotions as well as patterns of emotion could be reliably measured using straightforward rating scales. Izard proposed (and demonstrated empirically) that the emotions of anxiety and depression actually included various combinations of fundamental emotions. For example, Izard discovered that when people reported feeling depressed, they reported feeling not only sadness but also feeling various combinations of anger, fear, and disgust. Depression, for Izard, represented an emergent property (in systems terms) of a particular combination of fundamental emotions.

Different situations elicit different combinations of emotional experiences, and these patterns may be replicable across cultures. Using an abbreviated version of the Differential Emotions Scale, my colleague and I found that different patterns of emotional experience can be reliably assessed across situations (Schwartz & Weinberger, 1980) and within specific situations (Schwartz, 1986).

A Classroom Demonstration

Unique subjective patterns of emotional responses to different stressors can be demonstrated easily in the classroom. In this demonstration, students are instructed to take a sheet of paper and to list six different emotions across the top. My classes often use happiness, sadness, anger, fear, anxiety, and depression. The students are told that various situations will be described, and they are to imagine their feelings in each one. For a given situation, they are instructed to rate the levels of each of the six emotions on a 0–5 scale. For example, when given the situation, "Your dog has died," the students should rate how happy they would feel, how sad, how angry, how afraid, how

Table 1
Mean Ratings of the Degree of Emotions Reported by Yale Students in Response to Imaginary Depressing Situations

Item	Happiness	Sadness	Anger	Fear	Anxiety	Depression
Your dog dies	1.09	*4.08*	2.08	1.38	1.93	*3.34*
Your girlfriend/ boyfriend leaves you for another	1.13	*4.13*	*3.41*	2.11	*2.72*	*4.09*
You realize that your goals are impossible to reach	1.15	*3.64*	*3.00*	*2.48*	*3.08*	*3.67*

Note. Rating scale of 0–5; 0 = none of the specified emotion, 5 = very high level of the specified emotion. Italicized entries indicate high mean ratings. Adapted from Schwartz (1986) by permission.

anxious, and how depressed. A zero rating on happiness means very unhappy; a 5 rating means extremely happy.

In the course of the demonstration, students rapidly discover that different stressors evoke different patterns of emotions for the class as a whole, and that there are significant individual differences in specific patterned responses relative to the average pattern in a specific situation. Tables 1 through 6 show self-reported patterns of emotions for a random group of Yale students and a group of health care providers living in Italy for different sets of imagined situations. For the classroom demonstration, students are asked to raise their hands per emotion and per imagined situation when they gave high ratings (4 or 5). A quick count per emotion for the class is thus possible.

Consider the three imagined situations in Tables 1 and 2, and focus on the average response patterns. The primary emotions reported in response to "Your dog died" are sadness and depression. However, the response to "Your girlfriend or boyfriend leaves you for another" elicits anger and anxiety in addition to sadness and depression. Of particular interest to those researching stress is the item, "You realize that your goals are impossible to reach." This situation results in all five negative emotions being high. It is striking that these emotional patterns were observed in both Yale students and Italian health care providers.

Particularly relevant to college students are the two situations in Tables 3 and 4. Unlike those in Tables 1 and 2, which were selected because they were all items that were hypothesized to elicit feelings of depression but actually varied in the number of other negative

Table 2

Percent of Italian Health Care Providers Reporting High Levels of Six Emotions in Response to Imaginary Depressing Situations

Item	Happiness	Sadness	Anger	Fear	Anxiety	Depression
Your dog dies	0	52	13	0	17	26
Your girlfriend/ boyfriend leaves you for another	0	70	61	13	43	70
You realize that your goals are impossible to reach	0	61	61	30	70	74

Note. Each entry represents the percentage of subjects giving a 4 or 5 rating out of a scale of 0–5 for a given emotion to a given question. Italicized entries indicate high percentages. Adapted from Schwartz (1986) by permission.

Table 3

Mean Ratings of the Degree of Emotions Reported by Yale Students in Response to Imaginary Happy Situations

Item	Happiness	Sadness	Anger	Fear	Anxiety	Depression
You are accepted at Yale	4.18	1.14	1.04	1.96	3.04	1.09
You have just graduated from Yale	4.09	2.74	1.38	2.57	3.40	2.36

Note. Rating scale of 0–5; 0 = none of the specified emotion, 5 = very high level of the specified emotion. Italicized entries indicate high mean ratings. Adapted from Schwartz (1986) by permission.

emotions simultaneously evoked, the situations in Tables 3 and 4 were all items expected to elicit feelings of happiness. These situations also varied dramatically in the number of negative emotions evoked simultaneously. To the item, "You have just been admitted to the school of your choice," not only is a high level of happiness evoked, but also a high level of anxiety and a moderately high level of fear are evoked. This so-called happy item could as easily have been called an anxiety item or, from a systems perspective, a happy–anxiety pattern.

Contrast this pattern with that resulting from "You have just graduated from school." Again, not only are high levels of happiness and anxiety reported, but now levels of sadness, depression, and fear

Table 4
Percent of Italian Health Care Providers Reporting High Levels of
Six Emotions in Response to Imaginary Happy Situations

Item	Happiness	Sadness	Anger	Fear	Anxiety	Depression
You are accepted at school	*83*	0	4	13	*26*	4
You have just graduated from school	*61*	26	0	*39*	*70*	22

Note. Each entry represents the percentage of subjects giving a 4 or 5 rating out of a scale of 0–5 for a given emotion to a given question. Italicized entries indicate high percentages. Adapted from Schwartz (1986) by permission.

are also reported by both Yale students and Italian health care providers.

To the extent that different emotions evoke different patterns of physiological responses (Schwartz, 1986), it follows that patterns of physiological patterns should occur in situations evoking combinations of emotions. It is reasonable to hypothesize that the greater the number of conflicting negative emotions elicited in a given situation, the more stressful the situation will be and the more potential stress will be placed on the biological systems.

A preliminary, important step in testing this general hypothesis was taken by Sarason, Sarason, Potter, and Antoni (1985). They documented that stressors that were rated generally negative contributed more to the development of disease than did stressors rated generally positive. Extending this research, it would seem prudent to take an explicit patterning approach to the relation of stress to disease because positive situations can vary in the number of negative emotions simultaneously evoked, as illustrated in Tables 3 and 4.

The precise wording of the situations and, hence, people's perceptions of the situations can strongly influence the patterns of emotions elicited. As shown in Tables 5 and 6, the item, "You feel loved," is remarkable in that it evokes almost pure happiness without any negative emotion. (Is this why unconditional, positive regard and genuine, pure love may be disease preventing and health promoting?) However, if the wording is changed slightly to "You meet someone with whom you fall in love," the evoked emotions are mixed—happiness is accompanied by anxiety and some fear.

Once the average patterns per situation are computed, it becomes possible to interpret individual patterns as deviations from the general pattern. In Lacey's (1967) psychophysiological terminology,

Table 5
Mean Ratings of the Degree of Emotions Reported by Yale Students in Response to Imaginary Situations of Love

Item	Happiness	Sadness	Anger	Fear	Anxiety	Depression
You feel loved	*4.78*	1.28	1.13	1.19	1.57	1.19
You meet someone with whom you fall in love	*4.58*	1.20	1.04	2.00	*3.06*	1.33

Note. Rating scale of 0–5; 0 = none of the specified emotion, 5 = very high level of the specified emotion. Italicized entries indicate high mean ratings. Adapted from Schwartz (1986) by permission.

Table 6
Percent of Italian Health Care Providers Reporting High Levels of Six Emotions in Response to Imaginary Situations of Love

Item	Happiness	Sadness	Anger	Fear	Anxiety	Depression
You feel loved	*100*	0	0	22	*34*	0
You meet someone with whom you fall in love	*96*	0	0	*30*	*70*	0

Note. Each entry represents the percentage of subjects giving a 4 or 5 rating out of a scale of 0–5 for a given emotion to a given question. Italicized entries indicate high percentages. Adapted from Schwartz (1986) by permission.

there exists both *situational stereotype* of response (different responses to different situations) and *individual stereotype* (individual differences that can carry over across situations). By knowing the average emotional response patterns and the individual's particular response pattern to a given situation, the ability to predict the effects of specific stressors on illness and health should be improved.

Simply stated, stress is not stress is not stress. Depression is not depression is not depression. Happiness is not happiness is not happiness. This general principle, once well learned, helps psychologists interpret new findings linking Type A behavior with anger and the role of self-deception and the misguided self-reports of low anxiety in physical disease.

Type A Is Not Type A Is Not Type A: The Anger Story

Like the topic of stress, the topic of Type A behavior and its relation to cardiovascular disease is well known and covered in the current introductory books on health psychology. Modern researchers focus on dissecting the components of the Type A behavior pattern. This pattern lends itself well to classroom demonstrations.

A Classroom Demonstration

Students can interview the instructor using a copy of the rating form for a structured interview (Rosenman, 1977). The instructor can model Type A behavior at certain points in the interview and Type B behavior at others. Students can compare questions used in the Jenkins Activity Survey (Jenkins, Rosenman, & Friedman, 1967) with those in the Type A structured interview. It is important that students obtain a "feel" for the Type A concept by assessing the construct.

The major components of the Type A behavior pattern were viewed as being related to the following six interrelated but not identical characteristics: time-urgent, impatient, hard-driving, ambitious, competitive, and hostile. The description of the Type A pattern by Friedman and Rosenman (1974) is particularly telling:

> An action–emotion complex that can be observed in any person who is aggressively involved in a chronic incessant struggle to achieve more and more in less and less time, and if required to do so against the opposing efforts of other things or other persons. It is not psychosis or complex of worries or fears or phobias or obsession, but a socially acceptable—indeed often praised—form of conflict. Persons possessing this pattern also are quite prone to exhibit a free-flowing but extraordinarily well-rationalized hostility. As might be expected, there are degrees in the intensity of this behavior pattern. Moreover, because the pattern represents the reaction that takes place when particular personality traits of an afflicted individual are challenged or aroused by a specific environmental agent, the results of this reaction (that is, the behavior pattern itself) may not be felt or exhibited by him [or her] if he [or she] happens to be confronted by an environment that presents no challenge. For example, a usually hard-driving, competitive, aggressive editor of an urban newspaper, if hospitalized with a trivial illness, may not exhibit a single sign of [the] Type A behavior pattern. In short, for [the] Type A behavior

pattern to explode into being, the environmental challenge must always serve as the fuse for this explosion. (p. 84)[1]

The following points that Friedman and Rosenman (1974) made should be highlighted in light of the previous discussion: the concept of an action–emotion complex, a pattern of behavior and emotions, and an emphasis more on anger and hostility than on fear and anxiety (a pattern of emotions). Anger, then, should play a more prominent role in contributing to disease than anxiety in these individuals. The pattern reflects a potential for action that is released by particular environmental stresses related to challenge. Thus the Type A behavior pattern is an expressed pattern that lies dormant as a potential pattern until elicited. Finally, individuals do not always know that they are Type A. I will return to this in the next section, because it helps to explain why a self-report instrument such as the Jenkins Activity Survey, misses a subset of Type A people who perceive themselves to be Type B on the questionnaire but express the Type A behavior pattern when provoked in the structured interview.

It is becoming increasingly clear that certain components of the expressed Type A behavior pattern, such as time-urgency and competitiveness, are not in and of themselves health damaging or disease promoting. Rather, it is the tendency toward excessive anger and hostility that seems most related to the development of cardiovascular disease (e.g., Williams, Haney, Lee, Hong Kong, & Blumenthal, 1980). Moreover, Spielberger et al. (1985) have developed a State–Trait Anger Scale that parallels the State–Trait Anxiety Scale. In a series of studies they showed that trait anger is more related to high blood pressure than trait anxiety. Students may discover that studying the difference between anger items and anxiety items on the Spielberger instrument is instructive.

Fishing as Behavior Model

It is valuable to demonstrate to students the difference between the pattern of being time-urgent and alert versus the pattern of being time-urgent and angry. Especially important is demonstrating the difference between the pattern of being competitive and alert versus the pattern of being competitive and hostile. I have found that describing the following personal experience, and the empirical study triggered by it, helps students grasp this fundamental point.

In the late 1970s, I was in Oregon attending a meeting of scientists reviewing biobehavioral grant applications for potential funding.

[1] Reprinted from Friedman and Rosenman, (1974) by permission of Knopf. Copyright 1974 by M. Friedman.

Some of the grants submitted were on Type A behavior. Stephen Weiss was attending the meeting and suggested to me that we take a day off and go salmon fishing. This we did, but, while supposedly relaxing, we ended up talking about Type A behavior.

Weiss noticed certain aspects of my behavior that identified me as a Type B fisherman. I baited the hook and dropped the line over in a relaxed fashion, watched the gulls, and swayed with the swells. But what really struck him was my talking to the fish when they bit the hook: "That's nice" or "Take your time, I'm in no rush." We imagined measuring my blood pressure, heart rate, and levels of epinephrine and norepinephrine while I fished, and we decided that my cardiovascular and hormonal levels would probably be fairly low.

Weiss, we decided, was a Type A fisherman. He baited the hook rapidly, dropped the line over, and focused his attention on the rod. He did not talk to the fish. If he got a bite, his muscles tensed and his expression became alert and semi-anxious. A fighting fish got a fight in return. If the fish escaped from the hook, Weiss showed some frustration and anger. We also imagined his physiological readings and decided that his cardiovascular and hormonal levels would probably be mildly to moderately high.

We decided a man fishing in a boat across from us was a Type A+ fisherman. He was fishing with two poles, racing back and forth between them, and tangling his lines while cursing the fish that happened to be on the line beyond his reach. If the fish eluded him while others caught them, he would pull up the anchor in frustration, start the engine with a roar, and race to another part of the bay. We imagined that his blood pressure, heart rate, and levels of epinephrine and norepinephrine would be extremely high.

Each of us was fishing, supposedly involved in the same relaxing behavior. Yet, our styles were clearly quite different. It follows that fishing is not fishing is not fishing. Relaxation is not relaxation is not relaxation (Schwartz, Davidson, & Goleman, 1978), and therefore, exercise is not exercise is not exercise.

Funding to conduct research on "Type A and Type B salmon fishing" is unlikely, but it is possible to model the generic hypothesis in the laboratory to determine if style, when superimposed upon a relatively standardized behavioral activity, can influence physiological activities. Schwartz, Weinberger, and Singer (1981) conducted a study using the Harvard Step Test as a standard mild exercise test. Students with a background in acting were instructed for each trial to imagine walking up and down the step while expressing a given emotion, and then to actually walk up and down the step, expressing the given emotion nonverbally. The six conditions were happiness, sadness, anger, fear, a normal state, and a relaxed state. Each trial consisted of a baseline, an imagery period, an exercise period, and a recovery period. Heart rate and systolic and diastolic blood pressure were recorded during the baseline, at the end of the imagery trial, and three times during the recovery period (blood pressure was not recorded during the step test due to movement artifact).

During the imagery period, patterns of heart rate and systolic and diastolic blood pressure differed among all six emotion and control conditions. Most important were the data replicating the classic finding by Ax (1953): Fear was accompanied by a pattern of increased heart rate, increased systolic blood pressure, and no change or decreased diastolic pressure. Anger was accompanied by a pattern of increased heart rate, increased systolic blood pressure, and increased diastolic pressure. In other words, the greatest strain on the cardiovascular system occurred during anger (when the three components were increased).

Immediately following the exercise, the overall levels of cardiovascular response were much higher (20–30 mmHG increases in systolic blood pressure). Differences in patterns of responses between the emotions were discovered again. Interestingly, even though the subjects were voluntarily placing themselves in different emotional states while exercising and were simply relaxing after getting off the step, the recovery data indicated that systolic blood pressure recovered significantly more slowly following the expression of anger while exercising than following the expression of fear while exercising (even though the levels of response immediately upon sitting down were comparable). The effects of expressed anger on blood pressure seemed to linger more than that of expressed fear.

The description of my personal experience and the design of the step experiment and its results provide students with a graphic, readily understandable set of important implications concerning the expression of different emotions while engaging in various activities. The fact that some people's states of wellness and health improve with regular jogging while other people drop dead from heart attacks when jogging may be related to the style with which they exercise, which, in turn, relates to their attitudes and emotions (Schwartz et al., 1981). Remembering what Webster's dictionary said about personality (including physical and mental actions and attitudes), it is reasonable to pay closer attention to the specific patterns of emotional behavior expressed in response to specific situations. This should clarify more of the variance linking specific personality variables with specific diseases and health.

Low Anxiety Is Not Low Anxiety Is Not Low Anxiety: The Repression Story

A typical assumption that many students, faculty, and health care professionals make is that people generally have accurate perceptions

		Self-Deception and Impression Management	
		Low	High
Self-Report of Anxiety	High	High Anxious	Defensive High Anxious
	Low	Low Anxious	Repressors

Figure 1. A 2 × 2 table showing combinations of high and low self-reports of anxiety with high and low self-reports of self-deception and impression management. Adapted from Schwartz (1984) by permission.

of their experiences that they can report veridically. As a result, if someone produces a low score on a self-report test measuring variables such as stress, anxiety, depression, hostility, Type A behavior, and pain, the typical assumption is that the score is accurate. This assumption, unfortunately, is mistaken. Its consequences for theory, research, and clinical practice are far reaching and touch virtually all aspects of personality and health.

The literature on stress, anxiety, depression, hostility, Type A behavior, and pain is, for the most part, compromised by a fundamental error of reasoning and associated measurement. For instance, people scoring high on a self-report test of anxiety are typically compared with a low-anxiety control group. How is the control group selected? By choosing subjects with low scores on the self-report test.

However, a significant number of the subjects reporting low anxiety may be in error because they are either consciously lying or attempting to appear healthy, or they genuinely believe that they are low-anxious, although they are mistaken and are thus misperceptive, if not self-deceptive. Hence, the typical low-anxious control group may contain a subset of subjects who are actually high-anxious but unknowing or unable to admit it. Comparisons with the high-anxious experimental group will therefore be compromised, if not confounded.

Using the Marlowe-Crowne Social Desirability Scale (Crowne & Marlowe, 1964), my colleagues and I developed a procedure to separate subjects reporting low anxiety into accurate versus inaccurate subgroups (Weinberger, Schwartz, & Davidson, 1979). This scale contains two subscales, one assessing defensiveness or self-deception and the other assessing impression management or other-deception. As depicted in Figure 1, subjects that scored low or high on an anxiety text, for example, could simultaneously score either low or high on the Marlowe-Crowne (MC). If a given subject reported low anxiety and simultaneously scored low on the MC, the reports were probably genuine, and he or she would be classified as true low-anxious. However, if a given subject reported low anxiety and also scored high on the MC, his or her reports were probably questionable, if not mistaken, and therefore he or she would be classified as self-deceptive or a repressor. A similar distinction could be made for subjects reporting high anxiety. If their MC scores were low, the classification was true high-anxious. However, if their MC scores were high, the classification would be defensive high-anxious.

In the Weinberger et al. (1979) study, subjects completed 15 sentences that had neutral, sexual, or aggressive content, while heart rate, sweat gland activity, and frontalis muscle activity were continuously monitored. Response times (times to complete the sentences) were also recorded, and answer content was scored for types of denial and avoidance of threatening content.

The results were striking: Subjects who scored low on the self-report anxiety test and simultaneously low on the MC scale (true low-anxious) showed behavioral and physiological responses indicative of being genuinely low-anxious, as compared with subjects reporting high anxiety. However, self-deceptive subjects (those who scored low on the self-report anxiety test but simultaneously high on the MC) showed behavioral and physiological responses equal to, if not greater than, the high-anxious subjects! In other words, although the repressors reported being low-anxious (in fact, their self-reported anxiety scores were even lower than the true low-anxious subjects), their behavior and physiology indicated that they were very anxious.

It is important for students to understand that if the two subgroups of subjects (true low-anxious and repressive) were combined into one traditional "low anxiety" control group, few differences between low- and high-anxious subjects would be discovered. For research reasons alone, it is imperative to select the accurately reporting low-anxiety subjects to comprise the true low-symptom control group.

Repression of Type A Behavior

This same principle applies to research on Type A behavior. Weinberger et al. (1979) suggested that the structured interview (a common behavioral measure) is a better predictor of cardiovascular response and disease than the Jenkins Activity Survey (a self-report measure). That is, low scores on the Jenkins do not necessarily mean that the subject is Type B, because a number of Type B subjects may actually be Type A's without knowing it (a prediction made also by Friedman & Rosenman, 1974, quoted previously).

If a subset of people are generally anxious, depressed, angry, fatigued, or in pain, but they do not recognize or accept this information (feedback), they will fail to change their behavior in a health-promoting manner. Not only will their self-deception extend their exposure to potentially damaging stressors, but it will impair their ability to initiate self-regulating behaviors necessary to promote health. Systems theory provides a testable hypothesis concerning psychobiological mechanisms of self-deception as well as specific predictions concerning the promotion of disease and the impairment of health in repressive persons.

The 5 "Dis's" Hypothesis: Disattention, Disconnection, Disregulation, Disorder, and Disease

Systems Theory

Fundamental requirements for a system to exist and function are that the components must be connected and that information must be transmitted and processed accurately. The concept of self-regulation via feedback requires that the feedback must be connected to the system and that the feedback information must be transmitted and processed accurately. If, for whatever reason, the information is diminished, delayed, or distorted, the system's ability to self-regulate will be impaired. In the extreme case, if the information is not processed at all (i.e., disconnected), the system will be unable to self-regulate. It follows that some of its emergent (systemic) properties will be lost as a result of the impaired interconnections.

Students should understand that negative feedback involves subtraction (counteraction) that will return a system to some mean value (termed the *set point*). A simple mechanical system using negative feedback is the thermostat that causes a furnace to start, then to stop running. Positive feedback involves addition (action) that will advance a system to some extreme value. Negative feedback works to facilitate homeostasis (the term described by Cannon in *The Wisdom of the Body*, 1932, whereas positive feedback works to facilitate anti-homeostasis.

Most students (as well as health care providers) do not realize that both negative and positive feedback contribute to self-regulation. Both serve to interconnect components so that the system behaves in a self-regulating, predictable way. If the information is distorted or misperceived, or, in extreme cases, disconnected, the self-regulation will be impaired or cease altogether.

It is also not typically realized that when the feedback is connected, the system will begin self-regulating automatically, and it will work with a sense of purpose. For example, when a thermostat and a furnace are connected, a system interaction occurs immediately. The purpose occurs automatically, and the thermostat–furnace negative feedback system works for a stable temperature control around the set point. Thus in negative feedback, if the environmental conditions are relatively stable, the system will rise and fall around the set point in a rhythmic, orderly fashion.

Biological Systems

All healthy biological systems show rhythmic behavior that self-regulates the system automatically for the purpose of maintaining a stable internal milieu. However, in more complex systems, learning and experience can alter these fundamental processes. Learning can alter (a) the degree of connection of the component processes through variations in attentional processes and (b) the way in which information is interpreted, not only to enhance or distort it but even to reverse it (i.e., convert negative feedback into positive feedback and vice versa through cognitive and affective interpretations of the feedback). As a result, psychophysiological systems vary in the combinations or patterns of involuntary regulation (automatic, rhythmic, purposeful regulation) and voluntary regulation (interpretation and regulation of learned information) occurring in a given situation.

Integrating these various concepts and observations led me to the following conclusion: Connection (in the case of negative feedback) leads to self-regulation, which is expressed as order (i.e., rhythmic behavior) that occurs with a degree of ease (i.e., automaticity). One psychological mechanism for enhancing connectivity is attention and the voluntary control of awareness. Hence, there is a progression from attention to connection to self-regulation to order to ease.

To the extent that this is true, the opposite also must be true. If the connection is impaired or, in extreme cases, disconnected, self-regulation will not occur, the order will be impaired (i.e., increased disorder), and the system will no longer function with ease (i.e., disease). One psychological mechanism for reducing connectivity is disattention. To complete the parallel and logic, I coined the term disregulation (Schwartz, 1977). Hence, we now have the 5 "dis's": There is a progression from disattention to disconnection to disregulation to disorder to disease.

Returning to the previous discussion, it follows that repression (and self-deception) includes disattention to negative feedback cues that are essential for self-regulation and, hence, healing. The disattention promotes a state of relative disconnection (e.g., between the two hemispheres, termed a functional disconnection by Galin, 1974).

This state of neuropsychological disconnection induces a state of psychophysiological disregulation, which is expressed as increased disorder in biological, psychological, and social functioning. The disordered biopsychosocial functioning contributes to physical, mental, and social disease.

Supporting Research

Space precludes a detailed review of the past 10 years' research that provides encouraging support for each of the 5 "dis's." Does disattention lead to relative disconnection? In recent studies, researchers have found that repressive subjects showed greater evidence of cerebral laterality to positive versus negative emotions than true low-anxious subjects, as measured by such variables as lateralized facial behavior, lateralized eye movements, lateralized facial temperature, and measures of dichotic listening (reviewed in Schwartz, 1983, 1984).

Does relative disconnection lead to a state of relative disregulation? This is an inference, of course, just as stating that connection leads to self-regulation is an inference. However, does relative disconnection lead to relative disorder, as predicted by disregulation theory? Relative disorder can be measured. In a recent pair of studies, for example, Bowen and I (1984, 1985) found that repressive persons showed evidence of decreased cardiovascular homeostasis and decreased flexibility of self-regulatory functioning, which was correlated with evidence of relative neuropsychological disconnection as measured in facial laterality.

Finally, does the increased disorder contribute to increased disease? Researchers are beginning to provide evidence consistent with this critical link in the chain of logical "dis's." For example, in a 2-year prospective study following women who had malignant breast cancer surgically removed, Jensen (in press) found that the repressors (those who scored low on self-reports of anxiety but high on the MC—the non-complaining, so-called good patients) had very poor prognoses. In fact, he discovered that significantly more deaths occurred within the two years following surgery for the repressive patients. In addition, Jensen found that the prognosis was the worst for those women who also used "positive avoidant daydreams," which is a further disattentive strategy. Jensen interpreted his data as being consistent with disregulation theory.

Evidence that self-deception impairs health-seeking and health-promoting behavior was recently discovered in a laboratory study of individual differences in coping with pain using controlled electric shock stimulation (Jamner & Schwartz, 1986). Subjects who scored high on self-deception (repression) tolerated twice as much electric shock as subjects rated as low self-deceptive. The level of shock that low-self-deceptive subjects rated as painful was perceived by self-deceptive subjects as causing only discomfort.

Jamner and I (1986) proposed that repressive persons may generate in themselves natural opiate peptides as a primary biochemical mechanism for reducing their perception of pain. Whereas in some situations this mechanism can be adaptive (i.e., short-term situations involving potential physical danger), the chronic use of this strategy will lead to underestimating fatigue, pain, and other symptoms of stress and illness. As a result, these persons will continue to expose themselves to high levels of stressful stimuli as well as be discouraged from engaging in appropriate health-promoting behaviors. The Type A person, particularly the repressive one who scores Type A on the structured interview but Type B on the Jenkins self-report inventory, probably attempts to avoid feedback (biological, psychological, and social) while exercising (perhaps even while fishing).

The 5 "dis's" theory, although comprehensive and integrative, needs to be qualified. It should be viewed as a general framework or approach (i.e., a metatheory), rather than a specific theory per se. Also, the theory as described here is oversimplified. For example, it is possible to distinguish between *disregulation,* which is the absence of regulation, and *dysregulation,* which is faulty regulation (Schwartz, 1984). Should repression be described as a *dysease* (a faulty state of ease) rather than as a *disease* (the absence of ease, therefore unease)? Can repression ever be adaptive and health promoting? As will be pointed out in this chapter, not only can repressive coping styles be healthy under certain conditions, but also one may argue that the capacity for repression is a prerequisite for health and wellness.

You Cannot Attend to Your Body Without Regulating Your Body: The Imagery/Healing Story

If connection leads to self-regulation, and attention fosters psycho-neurophysiological connections, then attention to the body should lead to its self-regulation. If the connection of feedback loops (negative or positive) has automatic and purposeful qualities, then attention to the body should have automatic and purposeful effects on brain and body regulation whether or not the person is aware of it. Attention to one's body in a relaxed, friendly fashion should foster negative feedback connections (the normal, homeostatic process). However, attention to one's body in a tense, threatened fashion should foster positive feedback connections (and produce anti-homeostatic effects, such as hypochondriasis).

A Classroom Demonstration

It is very easy to demonstrate this in the classroom. Discussion about attention, connection, and self-regulation should begin after the demonstration so that students will have honest reactions. Instruct the students to put their pens and pencils down, find a comfortable positon, and close their eyes. Then say in a relaxed, peaceful, yet affirmative voice:

> What I would like you to do for the next couple of minutes, with your eyes closed, is simply attend to your breathing and experience your breathing going in and out, in and out, as it does naturally. Do not try to control your breathing. Simply experience it. You might imagine that you are on a wave floating up and down as your breathing goes in and out, in and out. Now sit quietly and experience your breathing until I tell you to stop.

After about one minute has passed, give the following instruction in a calm, peaceful fashion, "Now, whenever you are ready, you may open your eyes." Be quiet and wait for another minute; you will probably note that the students vary substantially in the time they take to open their eyes on their own. Some students will open their eyes immediately, whereas for others it often is necessary to say, "You should open your eyes now" after the minute has passed.

Then ask the class if they noticed anything happening to their breathing. The data from their reports typically turn out as follows:

1. Someone will report that his or her breathing slowed down. If you ask how many people experienced this, usually two thirds of the class will raise their hands. Some will say that their breathing did not change, and a few will report that it increased. Note this for later.

2. Someone will mention that his or her breathing became deeper and about two thirds of the class typically will agree. Also, some will report that the depth of their breathing did not change, while a few will report that it became more shallow.

3. Finally, someone will mention that his or her breathing became more regular. Usually, this is the last observation made. Often it is greeted with surprise and then recognition by most of the students. Typically, more than half of the students will agree that their breathing became more regular. The others will report no change in regularity or, for a few, less regularity.

The overall pattern is one of slower, deeper, and more regular breathing when subjects attend to their breathing without any requirement to control it and without any explicit instructions. Request that the students speculate on why the class's response, on the average, showed slower, deeper, and more regular breathing. Would the same thing happen to their breathing if they were instructed to pay attention to some other bodily response, such as pulse rate, or to feelings of heaviness? In laboratory research, I have found that the effects of attention on breathing are specific to voluntary attention to it. If subjects pay attention to their pulse, a different respiratory pattern occurs (often more shallow and irregular). Attention paid to sensations of heaviness results in breathing somewhat slower but not necessarily deeper (Schwartz, 1984).

Students often wonder what explains the large individual differences in the magnitude and direction of breathing effects, as well as the degrees of involvement in the task (for some students the "attend breathing" instructions induce a hypnotic-like state). Variables that should be mentioned are individual differences in voluntary control of attention, imagery ability, feelings of comfort about their bodies and comfort in following the instructions in a classroom situation, absorption and hypnotic susceptibility, general anxiety, and repressive defensiveness. Students should be encouraged to think about how they might design specific experiments to test these and other hypotheses and about the specific predictions that can be raised.

It is possible that a personality-oriented systems analysis can provide an explanation of why certain patients are able to enhance the restorative effects of their cancer surgery and chemotherapy by using healing-oriented images. In these patients, selective attention to the disordered part of their bodies in a relaxed, non-threatened manner should strengthen brain–body feedback and homeostatic function and facilitate self-regulation and healing.

It is also possible that, like Heisenberg's Uncertainty Principle in physics, it is impossible for a person to attend to his or her body without altering his or her physiology and behavior in predictable ways. Self-monitoring should therefore have active, biopsychosocial effects that, depending upon one's personality, will either promote health and wellness or impair health and encourage illness.

Health Promoting Personality Factors: Hardiness, Mindfulness, and Relaxed Affiliativeness

As discussed in the previous section, personality can play a role not only in preventing illness, but also in promoting health. Three recent concepts and associated research that bear directly on the issue of promoting health are hardiness (reviewed in Maddi & Kobasa, 1984), mindfulness (reviewed in Langer, 1987), and relaxed affiliativeness (reviewed in McClelland, 1986).

Hardiness

Kobasa (1979) proposed that hardiness describes a personality consisting of three interrelated orientations: commitment (versus alienation), control (versus powerlessness), and challenge (versus threat). Following Antonovsky (1979), Kobasa referred to these qualities as *resistance resources*. Hardiness parallels the concept of health as being the potential to be well.

Kobasa, Maddi, Puccetti, and Zola (1985) described hardiness as follows:

> 1. Persons high in commitment find it easy to involve themselves actively in whatever they are doing, being generally curious about and interested in activities, things, and people.
>
> 2. Persons high in control believe and act as if they can influence the events taking place around them through what they imagine, say, and do.
>
> 3. Persons high in challenge expect that life will change and that the changes will be a stimulus to personal development. (p. 525)

Consistent with the systems framework used in this chapter, people high in commitment can connect to external (and implicitly, internal) events in an open (i.e., relaxed attentiveness) and nonthreatened fashion. They are likely to exhibit a pattern of emotions dominated by happiness, excitement, and curiosity (interest). As a result, they become successfully part of more and more suprasystems, such as increased social relations and, hence, social support. They, therefore, effectively contribute to self-regulation of these larger systems of which they are part and experience a sense of control (rather than powerlessness). They are challenged more than they are competitive or combative (recall the earlier discussion of Type A behavior).

Using five scales selected from different personality instruments Kobasa et al. (1985) found that among male business executives identified as high in stressful events, "hardiness is the most important of the resistance sources studied" in predicting illness one year later. As the title of their book, *The Hardy Executive: Health Under Stress*, suggests (Maddi & Kobasa, 1984), people's perception of stress and their expectations about stress play an important role in determining whether it contributes to disease or promotes health.

Mindfulness

The concept of mindfulness (and its converse, mindlessness), which is a particularly playful and creative approach to a person's openness to experience, was recently proposed by Langer (1987). A mindless state of mind is one in which "minimal information is processed" or is "not readily available for conscious consideration," whereas a mindful state is one in which information is actively processed and where the individual is "fully engaged in creating categories and drawing distinctions." The concepts of mindfulness versus mindlessness generally parallel our discussion of attention, connection, and the processing of information versus disattention, relative disconnection, and processing of information minimally or mistakenly.

In a clever test of Langer's thesis, Alexander, Langer, Newman, Chandler, and Davies (1987) studied the effects of transcendental meditation (TM) on health and longevity in a group of elderly adults in a nursing home. Compared with a low-mindfulness (relaxation) control group who sat for the same 20-minute period as the TM group, 87.5 percent of the TM group were still alive three years later, compared with 62.5 percent of the control group. Moreover, supporting the idea that mindfulness is health promoting, current work by Janowsky, Piper, and Langer (cited in Langer, 1987) found, using a new scale of mindlessness/mindfulness (the M/MQ scale), that mindfulness was significantly related to a measure of immune function.

Langer was thinking in systems terms when she proposed that "if we had instruments sensitive enough to measure it, I believe we would find that an effect observed on any level simultaneously manifests itself on every level, be it molecular, or sociological." That this idea deserves consideration is supported by the remarkable recent research on the concept of relaxed affiliativeness.

Relaxed Affiliativeness

First proposed by McClelland (1986), relaxed affiliativeness is the combined motives of being relaxed and caring about others. Two of my favorite studies in the topic of personality and health, which I go into in great detail with my students, are the experiment in which Jemmott (1982) examined immune function in first-year dental students during that year and the study in which McClelland and Kirshnit (1984) examined immune function in college students who were watching a film about Mother Teresa.

In the experiment by Jemmott, the level of immune function in the 47 subjects was measured by mean concentration of salivary immunoglobulin A (S-IgA). The higher the S-IgA, the greater the capacity of the immune system to protect the oral tissues from disease. Measurements were done at times in the academic year when stress levels were predicted to be particularly low or especially high (see Figure 2). The dental students who care about people in a loving,

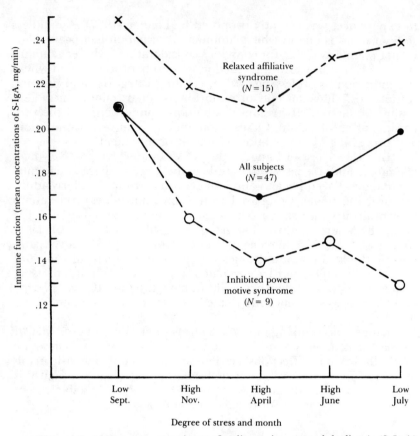

Degree of stress and month

Figure 2. Mean concentrations of salivary immunoglobulin A (S-IgA) during periods of low stress (September and July) and high stress (November, April, and June) for 47 first-year dental students that were placed into either a high relaxed affiliativeness group or high inhibited power group. During the academic term (November, April, and June), levels of immune function in saliva are reduced for the sample as a whole. Compared with the inhibited power group, the relaxed affiliative group started with higher immune values and recovered by June (exam time!). Adapted from Jemmott (1982) by permission.

relaxed fashion (high relaxed affiliativeness) began dental school with higher levels of immune function than did dental students who seem to desire power over people (and are in conflict about this motive). Moreover, by the last examination (June) and into the summer (July), the dental students high in relaxed affiliativeness returned to their initially higher immune function levels, whereas the dental students high in inhibited power continued to evidence further decreases in

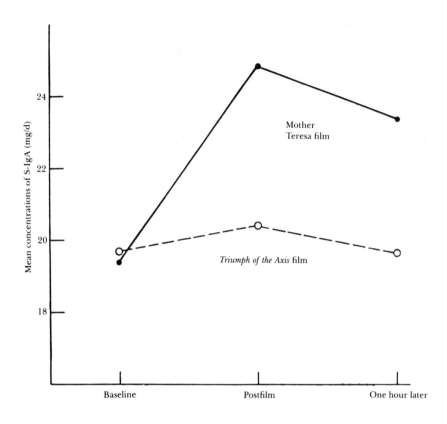

Figure 3. Mean concentrations of salivary immunoglobulin A (S-IgA) before (baseline), immediately after (postfilm), and one hour after watching one of two types of films. The Mother Teresa film is a very positive, inspiring film; the *Triumph of the Axis* film is neither positive nor inspiring. Reprinted from McClelland and Kirshnit (1984) by permission.

immune function, which is indicative of high stress.

The value of caring about people in a relaxed, loving fashion may have broad health significance (see Lynch, 1975, for an excellent discussion of these issues). Moreover, as the immune findings for the effects of watching the Mother Teresa film suggest (see Figure 3), the inspiration of love may have biochemical effects that increase the potential for wellness by increasing health (McClelland & Kirshnit, 1984).

McClelland (1986) has taken this research one step further by suggesting that "a view of love which takes both self-report (left brain) and fantasy (right brain) measures into account does a better job of predicting affiliative behavior than a view which relies solely on one or the other of the types of measures." This sounds curiously similar to our system that links self-deception and repression to a functionally disconnected brain and impaired health (that also includes the capacity to give and receive love effectively).

What happens, however, if a child grows up in a home where relaxed affiliativeness is minimally present among the family members, and the child's biological, psychological, and social self is threatened? Is the child's best adaptive strategy to become mindful, to treat the interactions among the family members as a safe challenge? Or, are there situations, particularly in early childhood, where the development of repression and self-deception is adaptive and potentially healthy?

Healthy Repression: Repression as a Prerequisite to Health

In a systems perspective, one should consider the possibility that not only are coping mechanisms such as repressions sometimes adaptive, and even healthy, but also that these coping mechanisms may actually be a prerequisite to health. The hypothesis that development of repression could, under certain circumstances, be healthy (repression could increase the system's potential to cope with certain stressors) was stimulated in part by clinical observations I made on patients whom I saw in the Yale Behavioral Medicine Clinic over a 5-year period (1981–1986). I treated a number of very intelligent, successful adults in their 30s and 40s whose biological, psychological, and social functioning was compromised in selective areas.

Their physical diseases included tension and migraine headaches, Crohn's disease, ulcers, allergies, hypertension, impotence, and vaginal herpes. All patients came to the clinic ostensibly for stress management, which quickly turned into psychotherapy (combining dynamic, behavioral, and humanistic perspectives). All of these patients had problems, to varying degrees, in experiencing certain negative as well as positive emotions; in thinking about certain issues in a non-defensive manner; and in developing effective, close, loving relationships with family and friends. Also, their childhood memories were remarkably impoverished and biased toward seeing their parents in a positive light.

This pattern of behavior fits the general style of repressive defensiveness. For each patient, his or her current problems tended to mirror certain experiences in childhood that could not be recalled initially or were rejected as being unimportant, if not irrelevant. However, as each therapeutic relationship developed, it became clear that, as a group, their family situations were quite destructive and that they had coped with this destructiveness in a remarkably adaptive fashion.

The striking quality about the people I saw in treatment was that they all elected to suppress their needs for love and affection; to push out of their minds feelings of loneliness, depression, anger, and fear; and to become overachieving children. They were obedient, responsible, and involved with school work (although they had few friends in school). They managed to do extremely well in school despite the serious problems at home and were able to leave home and go to college with relatively few memories of the past. They accrued some physical scars (e.g., severe migraines, Crohn's disease, and allergies) but were otherwise okay. Typically, their siblings tended to be more assertive, acting out against their parents or themselves (i.e., they were more likely to cope by resorting to drugs or alcohol, becoming sexually promiscuous, or doing poorly in school). The siblings were problems to their parents, to their teachers, and to themselves.

How did my patients happen to end up electing repression as the means of coping with these clearly high stress, unhealthy families? Was it because of their superior intelligence? Was it due to some psychophysiological differences that were genetically endowed (e.g., they were extra sensitive, high arousal children, which motivated them to push down and push away their feelings of pain, anxiety, and fury)? Did one of the relatives or friends of the parents model repressive defensiveness for the patient as a young child? The answers are not known and need to be assessed in future research concerned with the development of personality and its relationship to health.

The patients I saw in treatment were veritable masters at repression. My approach in therapy was to help them discover this "talent" and to help them label their repressiveness as a highly mastered tool which they should be proud of. Instead of feeling guilty for being mentally and physically sick, I encouraged them to reinterpret their prior coping as being remarkably adaptive, creative, and highly effective in helping them reach their present status. However, what was once necessary and highly adaptive is neither today. It is now safe for these patients to abandon this chronic strategy and to learn some new coping skills. This, of course, is easier said than done. However, the basic philosophy helps the patients to become hopeful and mindful and to see therapy as a positive challenge that they can approach with relaxed affiliation (in collaboration with their therapist, spouses, and children, when possible).

By definition, to *repress* means to push down and to push away. In order for a system to engage in selective tasks, it must have the ability to push down certain feedback and amplify other feedback. In psychological terms this is called *selective attention*. The student should be encouraged to think about the consequences for a system if it could not selectively push down information as needed. The consequences would be maladaptive, competing or conflicting information, if not information overload. If a system could not selectively inhibit feedback on a moment-to-moment basis, it could never function flexibly and adaptively in its ever-changing environment.

If one's present thoughts and previous memories could never be repressed, mental confusion or mental chaos (a state described clinically as schizophrenia) would result. People's capacity to push things out of awareness automatically is essential, if they are to be well and also if they are to be in good health and have the potential to heal. If I had to worry that various traumas from my past might emerge as unpredictable flashbacks while I was writing a lecture on personality and health, there would be obvious negative effects on my biological, psychological, and social functions.

If repression can be healthy and, moreover, if repressive processes are a prerequisite to healing and health, is it possible that the existence of disease plays an adaptive role in the promotion of health and wellness of the species and the ecology as a whole (see Schwartz, 1984)? The implications of this question are particularly far reaching and, therefore, potentially indicative of a shift in general paradigm.

Personality Is a System, and All Systems Have Personality: The Integrated Science Approach

There are many definitions and theories of personality. According to *Webster's Unabridged Dictionary,* 2nd edition, *personality* is not only the quality but, more importantly, the fact of being a particular person, having a personal identity and individuality. Personality also refers to habitual patterns and qualities of behavior as expressed by physical and mental activities and attitudes. These habitual patterns, considered collectively, reflect distinctive individual qualities of a person.

Habitual patterns of thoughts, feelings, and actions, considered collectively, define the person. These collective qualities also define a system. By Webster's definition, a *system* is a set or arrangement of things so related or connected as to form a unity or organic whole. A system is a regular and orderly way of doing something—an order, a method, or a regularity of behavior.

Personality is a collection of habitual patterns of covert and overt behaviors that define the individual as a whole, and a system is a connected set of regular, orderly ways of doing things—an organic whole. Thus personality reflects a system of behavior. The parallel

Table 7
Levels of Systems and Examples of Associated Academic Disciplines

Levels of Systems	Academic Disciplines	Interdisciplines
Groups of Groups	Political Science	Political Sociology
Groups of Organisms	Sociology	Social Psychology
Organisms	Psychology	Psychophysiology
Organs	Physiology	Neurophysiology
Cells	Cellular Biology	Biochemistry
Chemicals	Chemistry	Physical Chemistry
Atoms	Physics	Mathematical Physics
Abstract	Mathematics + Philosophy	

Note. Higher levels of systems and associated academic disciplines such as ecology and astronomy are not shown but follow the same general structure. Adapted from Schwartz (1982) by permission.

between personality and systems theory is strong. In systems terms, all entities behave. Behavior, in its most general sense, refers to the observed functioning of an entity. From the perspective of systems theory, all science is the study of behavior done in order to understand (by inference) underlying processes (behaviors) and their organization (their unique, habitual actions). Hence, a physicist studies the behavior of atoms, a biologist studies the behavior of cells and organs, and a psychologist studies the behavior of individuals. To the extent that the behavior of any entity being studied is habitual, patterned, and identifiable as an organized collection of activities, one can conclude that all entities have personality, or at least "entitality." When patterned psychological behavior is thought of as personality and patterned physiological behavior is thought of as "organality," it becomes clear immediately that personality and organality should be related to some degree within a given person.

Table 7 presents an organization of disciplines and interdisciplines that was derived from systems theory. In Table 7, wholes reflect the organization of their parts and lead to emergent properties or behaviors. (The term *emergent property* refers to observed unique properties that result from parts interacting mutually and collectively, just as unique personalities arise from the unique combination of components that comprise a person.) This table clearly shows the po-

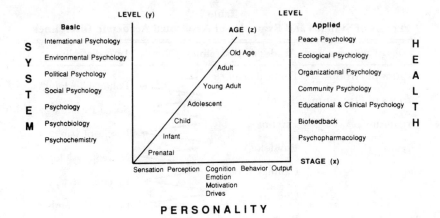

Figure 4. A tridimensional systems organization of (1) levels of basic systems (y axis left) and corresponding applied areas (y axis right), (2) stages of information processing (x axis), and (3) age. The diagram shows how psychology as a discipline can be organized from a systems perspective. Note that personality is not shown as a level on a single axis. This is because personality involves the intersection of the three dimensions across all the levels. Reprinted from Schwartz (in press) by permission.

tential for science as a whole to integrate by using a common meta-framework.

Personality is defined by habitual patterns and qualities of behavior of any individual as expressed by physical and mental activities and attitudes. Implicit in this concept of personality is its expression at multiple levels within one person. From a systems perspective then, an individual's personality will be expressed *biopsychosocially* (Engel, 1977), when one looks from the micro (bio) to the macro (social) or *social psychophysiologically* (Cacioppo & Petty, 1983), when one looks from the macro (social) to the micro (bio). Theoretically, a healthy person is one whose parts function collectively. They interact in an organized, synchronized manner. Conflicts within and between various levels in the person should lead to various degrees of dissociation and disorder.

The essence of both personality theory and systems theory is the concept of an organized whole that has a personality (in a generic sense) and is a system. This conclusion can be trivialized or it can be developed deeply. It may sound silly to talk, for example, about the personality of a rock. But beyond the silliness may lie an important conceptual truth. If a person behaved like a rock, the first thing one would conclude is that the person was stable, dependable, and strong. The person might also be described as quiet, heavy, non-responsive, and boring. Theoretically, from a systems point of view, it should be possible in principle to derive a collective set or pattern of dimensions describing classes of behavior that could be universally applied to all entities (all systems).

Figure 4 (from Schwartz, 1987, in press) illustrates organizing the discipline of psychology from a 3-dimensional systems perspective (levels, stages, and time). One may wonder, Where is the term *personality* in this organization? The answer is that the organization of these factors is the personality.

This can be translated into a simple classroom demonstration. Tell students to clench their fists in rage. This is both psychological and physiological. A clenched fist is achieved by tensing patterns of muscles, constricting blood vessels, and raising blood pressure accordingly. To act angry behaviorally is to act angry physiologically, at least to some degree. Psychological behavior is biological behavior at a correspondingly more complex, more highly organized level.

If personality is this closely linked with physiology (because organized psychological behavior is literally comprised of organized physiological behavior) then one would expect a strong link between personality and health. This provides the foundation for an integrated science approach to the study and applications of personality and health (Schwartz, in press).

References

Alexander, C., Langer, E. J., Newman, R., Chandler, H., & Davies, J. (1987). *Self-regulation procedures to enhance health and longevity: Transcendental meditation, mindfulness, and the elderly.* Manuscript submitted for publication.

Antonovsky, A. (1979). *Health, stress and coping.* San Francisco: Jossey-Bass.

Ax, A. (1953). The physiological differentiation between fear and anger in humans. *Psychosomatic Medicine, 15,* 433–442.

Bowen, W., & Schwartz, G. E. (1984). *Individual differences in cardiovascular flexibility and rigidity: Effects on cardiovascular differentiation to emotion.* Unpublished manuscript.

Bowen, W., & Schwartz, G. E. (1985). *Cardiovascular flexibility and rigidity: Relationship to repression, disregulation, and facial laterality in expressions of emotion.* Unpublished manuscript.

Cacioppo, J. T., & Petty, R. E. (Eds.). (1983). *Social psychophysiology: A sourcebook.* New York: Guilford Press.

Cannon, W. B. (1932). *The wisdom of the body.* New York: Norton.

Crowne, D. P., & Marlowe, D. (1964). *The approval motive: Studies in evaluative dependence.* New York: Wiley.

Darwin, C. (1872). *The expression of the emotions in man and animals.* London: Murray.

Ekman, P., Friesen, W. V., & Ellsworth, P. (1972). *Emotion in the human face.* Elmsford, NY: Pergamon Press.

Engel, G. L. (1977). The need for a new medical model: A challenge for biomedicine. *Science, 196,* 129–136.

Feuerstein, M., Labbe, E. E., & Kuczmierczyk, A. R. (1986). *Health psychology: A psychobiological perspective.* New York: Plenum Press.

Friedman, M., & Rosenman, R. H. (1974). *Type A behavior and your heart.* New York: Knopf.

Galin, D. (1974). Implications for psychiatry of left and right cerebral specialization: A neurophysiological context for unconscious processes. *Archives of General Psychiatry, 31,* 572–583.

Izard, C. E. (1971). *The face of emotion.* New York: Appleton-Century-Crofts.

Izard, C. E. (1972). *Patterns of emotions: A new analysis of anxiety and depression.* New York: Academic Press.

Jamner, L., & Schwartz, G. E. (1986). Self-deception predicts self-report and endurance of pain. *Psychosomatic Medicine, 48*(3/4), 211–223.

Jemmott, J. B., III. (1982). *Psychosocial stress, social motives, and disease susceptibility.* Unpublished doctoral dissertation, Department of Psychology and Social Relations, Harvard University, Cambridge, MA.

Jenkins, C. D., Rosenman, R. H., & Friedman, M. (1967). Development of an objective psychological test for the determination of the coronary-prone behavior pattern in employed men. *Journal of Chronic Diseases, 20,* 1271–1275.

Jensen, M. (in press). Psychobiological factors in the prognosis of breast cancer. *Journal of Personality Research.*

Kobasa, S. C. (1979). Stressful life events, personality and health: An inquiry into hardiness. *Journal of Personality and Social Psychology, 37,* 1–11.

Kobasa, S. C., Maddi, S. R., Puccetti, M., & Zola, M. A. (1985). Effectiveness of hardiness, exercise and social support as resources against illness. *Journal of Psychosomatic Research, 29,* 525–533.

Lacey, J. I. (1967). The evaluation of autonomic responses: Towards a general solution. *Annals of the New York Academy of Sciences, 67,* 123–164.

Langer, E. J. (1987). *Minding matters: The consequences of mindlessness/mindfulness.* Unpublished manuscript.

Lynch, J. J. (1975). *The broken heart.* New York: Basic Books.

Maddi, S. R., & Kobasa, S. C. (1984). *The hard executive: Health under stress.* Homewood, IL: Dorsey Press.

McClelland, D. C. (1986). Some reflections on the two psychologies of love. *Journal of Personality, 54*(2), 334–353.

McClelland, D. C., & Kirshnit, C. (1984). *Effects of motivational arousal through films on salivary immune function.* Unpublished paper, Department of Psychology and Social Relations, Harvard University, Cambridge, MA.

Rosenman, R. H. (1977). The interview method of assessment of the coronary-prone behavior pattern. In T. M. Rebroski (Ed.), *Proceedings of the Forum on Coronary-prone Behavior.* (DHEW Publication No. [NIH] 78-1451), pp. 100–103.

Sarason, I. G., Sarason, B. R., Potter, E. H., III, & Antoni, M. H. (1985). Life events, social support, and illness. *Psychosomatic Medicine, 47,* 156–163.

Schwartz, G. E. (1977). Psychosomatic disorders and biofeedback: A psychobiological model of disregulation. In J. D. Maser & M. E. P. Seligman (Eds.), *Psychopathology: Experimental models.* San Francisco: W. H. Freeman.

Schwartz, G. E. (1982). Psychophysiological patterning and emotion from a systems perspective. *Social Science Information, 21*(6), 781–817.

Schwartz, G. E. (1983). Disregulation theory and disease: Applications to the repression/cerebral disconnection/cardiovascular disorder hypothesis [Special issue]. *International Review of Applied Psychology, 32*, 95–118.

Schwartz, G. E. (1984). Psychobiology of health: A new synthesis. In B. L. Hammonds & C. J. Scheirer (Eds.), *Psychology and health: Master lecture series, Volume 3* (pp. 145–194). Washington, DC: American Psychological Association.

Schwartz, G. E. (1986). Emotion and psychophysiological organization: A systems perspective. In M. G. H. Coles, E. Donchin, & S. Porges (Eds.), *Psychophysiology* (pp. 354–377). New York: Guilford Press.

Schwartz, G. E. (in press). Personality and the unification of psychology and modern physics: A systems approach. In J. Aronoff, A. I. Rabin, & R. A. Zucker (Eds.), *The emergence of personality.* New York: Springer Publishing.

Schwartz, G. E., Davidson, R. J., & Goleman, D. J. (1978). Patterning of cognitive and somatic processes in the self-regulation of anxiety: Effects of meditation versus exercise. *Psychosomatic Medicine, 40*, 321–328.

Schwartz, G. E., & Weinberger, D. A. (1980). Patterns of emotional responses to affective situations: Relations among happiness, sadness, anger, fear, depression and anxiety. *Motivation and Emotion, 4*, 175–191.

Schwartz, G. E., Weinberger, D. A., & Singer, J. A. (1981). Cardiovascular differentiation of happiness, sadness, anger, and fear following imagery and exercise. *Psychosomatic Medicine, 43*, 343–346.

Spielberger, C. D., Johnson, E. H., Russell, S. F., Crane, R. J., Jacobs, G. A., & Worden, T. J. (1985). The experience and expression of anger: Construction and validation of an Anger Expression Scale. In M. A. Chesney & R. H. Rosenman (Eds.), *Anger and hostility in cardiovascular and behavioral disorders* (pp. 5–30). New York: Hemisphere/McGraw-Hill.

Weinberger, D. A., Schwartz, G. E., & Davidson, R. J. (1979). Low-anxious, high-anxious, and repressive coping styles: Psychometric patterns and behavioral and physiological responses to stress. *Journal of Abnormal Psychology, 88*, 369–380.

Williams, R. B., Haney, T. L., Lee, K. L., Hong Kong, Y., & Blumenthal, J. A. (1980). Type A behavior, hostility, and coronary atherosclerosis. *Psychosomatic Medicine, 42*, 539–549.

HENRY C. ELLIS

RECENT DEVELOPMENTS IN HUMAN MEMORY

Henry C. Ellis is a Distinguished Professor of Psychology at the University of New Mexico where he has been a member of the faculty since 1957. He served as Chair of the Department of Psychology from 1975 to 1984. He received his undergraduate degree from the College of William and Mary and his PhD in Experimental Psychology at Washington University in 1958. His research interests are in human memory, cognitive psychology, and emotion and cognition. He has published 6 books and approximately 70 articles and chapters. He has served as a visiting professor of psychology at the University of California at Berkeley, Washington University, and the University of Hawaii and was Distinguished Visiting Professor of Psychology at the U. S. Air Force Medical Center in San Antonio. He has received grant support from several agencies and has served as consulting editor for a number of journals. He is currently co-editor of *Cognition and Emotion*. He is a fellow of the Divisions of Experimental, Teaching, and General Psychology of the American Psychological Association (APA) and was the Annual Research Lecturer at the University of New Mexico in 1978.

Ellis was president of the APA Division of Experimental Psychology in 1985–86, president of the Southwestern Psychological Association in 1977–78, and president of the Rocky Mountain Psychological Association in 1968–69. He was Chair of the Council of Graduate

Departments of Psychology from 1977 to 1979 and a member of its executive board from 1976 to 1981. He was a member of APA's Education and Training Board, became Chair in 1983, and was a member of its Committee on Graduate Education. Currently, he is a member of the APA Board of Directors and a member of APA's Council of Representatives. He is also a consultant to a number of educational and legal agencies and is listed in *Who's Who in America.*

RECENT DEVELOPMENTS IN HUMAN MEMORY

In order to understand how people function in everyday life you need to know something about the way human memory operates. Memory refers to the processes involved in encoding information, storing it for later use, and accessing that record or representation of events and knowledge when you wish to use that information. It is difficult to imagine how you would function if you had no memory system for recording events: You would forever live in the immediate present and would truly wake up fresh each day with no memory of past events. Fortunately, except for certain severely ill and brain-damaged individuals, people are not condemned to live in the im-

Special thanks are due to Gil Einstein, Visiting Scholar at the University of New Mexico in 1986, for his helpful comments on an earlier draft of this manuscript. In addition, thanks go to my University of New Mexico colleagues who provided me with useful comments: Timothy Goldsmith, Robin Smith, John Gluck, Sidney Rosenblum, Janet Belew, Michael Dougher, and William Gordon. Thanks are due to Vivian Makosky, editor of this series and Associate Executive Director of APA, and Anne Rogers, formerly of the APA Educational Affairs Office, and two unknown reviewers who provided valuable remarks. I also wish to thank Jan Woodring, administrative officer in the APA Educational Affairs Office, for her friendship and her long-time distinguished support of issues involving the education and training of psychologists. Finally, thanks go to F. Chris Garcia, Vice President for Academic Affairs at the University of New Mexico, who has been instrumental in providing me research support over several years, which allowed me to conduct some of the work described in this paper.

mediate present but can rely extensively on the large store of knowledge and skills in their memories. And it is this ability to use this repertoire that allows for much of the flexible, problem-solving, and creative behaviors that are characteristic of humans.

Introducing the Topic of Memory

When I lecture on memory to introductory psychology students or to students in a beginning course in cognitive psychology, I find it useful to spend a little time placing the concept of memory in perspective and having the students think about the implications and significance of memory. One dramatic way of doing this is to get students to think about how difficult daily functioning would be if they had no memory. Another way is to illustrate the importance of memory in some familiar, commonplace activity such as conversing with friends, visiting the grocery store, or taking notes in class. My subsequent examples illustrate one way this might be accomplished. Those teaching the topic of memory will certainly develop their own strategies in introducing the topic.

Daily activities regularly involve memory. As you read a magazine article, listen to a lecture, or engage in conversation with others, you normally attempt to organize the information into some meaningful, sensible pattern. You think about the information, abstract the essential ideas, look for or impose some sense of structure, and try to relate the information to our existing knowledge. All of these activities involve memory processes.

In order to emphasize to students the pervasiveness of memory in everyday life, I like to illustrate this point using a familiar scene such as the following one: Reflect for a moment on a small period of time in your daily life. You have just finished a doubles tennis match with a group of friends, and you are seated around a table drinking coffee. Much of the immediate conversation focuses on the match and how each of you performed. Two members of the group have recently taken some brush-up lessons, and, as a consequence, their ground strokes have dramatically improved. Another had trouble with serving, and another felt that her performance at the net was mixed. Conversation then shifted to events of the past week, the resignation of the university president, speculation as to his replacement, and then to the impact of changing tax laws. A few new (and old) jokes were told by the group's raconteur, and then discussion shifted to plans for the week, including setting the date and time for the group's next tennis match. In all of this activity, I emphasize that one is remembering recent events and relating them to future events. Indeed, in telling a simple joke you rehearse the joke, organize the main points, and remember the punch line. In these brief few minutes, your memory has been very active, and yet, because the use of active memory is so commonplace, you may fail to recognize the pervasiveness and significance of your memory system. Indeed, for many people, it is only when memory fails that they become aware of the significance of it. People usually think about memory in terms of recollecting events from the past; however, they also use memory to plan for future events. This *prospective memory* is receiving increasing attention in light of the growing interest in everyday memory (Baddeley & Wilkins, 1984; Harris, 1984).

From the foregoing illustration it is clear that memory systems provide a sense of personal continuity in the world of work and play and helps people plan for the future. Thus it is no surprise that the memory system is seen as an integral part of cognitive psychology and as central to the understanding of other cognitive processes such as comprehension, problem solving, reasoning, and language. The contemporary study of memory occupies a core position in cognitive psychology, the study of which ranges from up-front perceptual processes to the complex activities of problem solving and reasoning.

I provide an overview of the human memory system in this chapter, describing how it is organized and how it functions, and I will review the major issues and trends in human memory and related cognitive processes. In examining human memory as an information processing system, I look at encoding, storage, and retrieval as three principal aspects of the system. Within this framework, I cover a range of topics, including attention and memory, elaborative encoding, imagery and memory, the nature of the memory code, the status of short-term memory, mnemonics and memory strategies, distinctiveness and elaboration, organization in memory, retrieval processes, memory and awareness, amnesia, developments in schema theory, memory for scripts, comprehension and memory, and memory for inferences. In addition, I briefly examine the role of several major classes of variables that influence memory, including the role of context, the role of emotional and mood factors in memory, and the role of individual differences, including personality variables. I emphasize the significance of the way material is processed as being important for memory and as distinct from where the processing occurs.

My objectives are fourfold: (1) to examine, briefly, memory as part of an information processing system; (2) to examine some important memory processes and some variables that influence memory; (3) to look at some of the applications of memory principles, particularly in the area of memory strategies and improving memory; and (4) to illustrate how the operations of memory can be readily demonstrated in classroom teaching.

Usually, the introductory psychology course permits an instructor to present only one or two lectures about memory. The material presented in this chapter could, if covered in detail, be presented in a number of lectures far exceeding the time normally available. The best way for the introductory psychology instructor to use this material for a single lecture is to carefully select one or two issues in each of the six major sections that follow: (1) what is memory; (2) stages of memory; (3) encoding; (4) retrieval; (5) comprehension, knowledge, and schemas; and (6) memory strategies and mnemonics. The instructor should, of course, pick topics that best meet their needs and the interests of their students.

What Is Memory?

Memory is a somewhat complex concept that is composed of several important processes. Memory is not an entity but rather an organization of processes that involves three stages: acquisition, storage, and retrieval. The first stage is *acquisition,* which is the process by which people perceive and encode information in memory. For example, as you read a book you pay attention to the material, usually the meaning, and thus encode the gist or essential features of it. And during acquisition, the information is recorded in the form of a memory trace. The second stage is *storage,* which is the maintenance of information over time; a storage process is needed in order to hold information for later use. Finally, *retrieval* refers to the means by which people access and use information in memory. Normally, retrieval involves an active search for stored information and is the process by which you get information out of storage and bring it to immediate awareness (Best, 1986; Stern, 1985). Information may be in storage but you may be unable to retrieve the information under some circumstances.

What Is Remembered?

What kinds of things are remembered? In describing the content of memory, Tulving (1983) has proposed that memory can be classified according to three types of content. One type of memory is *episodic,* that is, memory for specific episodes or events of life that are experienced by an individual. The fact that you can remember taking your car to the car wash yesterday or that you had toast and scrambled eggs for breakfast this morning are examples of episodic memory. A second type of memory is *semantic* memory, which represents general knowledge of the world. Knowledge about automobiles, such as who made the first car, knowledge of who was the first president, and even of the concept of president are examples of semantic memory. Notice that these are events that you have not personally experienced (episodes) but are part of your general knowledge of the world. The third type of memory is called *skill* or procedural memory (Anderson, 1985). Skill memories consist of a variety of cognitive skills such as reading and of motor skills such as driving a car or playing golf.

Semantic–Episodic Distinction

Not all psychologists have accepted the semantic–episodic distinction in memory and some contend that such a distinction is not needed. This view has been suggested as the result of several experiments that show that certain experimental manipulations can have the same effect on both semantic memory and episodic memory (Anderson & Ross, 1980; McKoon & Ratcliffe, 1979). The logic of this approach, in general, is to assume that if a variable produces the same effect under two presumably different memory systems, then the two systems may not really be distinct. The results of these studies suggest that the two memory systems share the same memory representation and that episodic memory is the activation of some portion of semantic memory. For a more detailed discussion of this issue, see Ellis and Hunt (1983) and Wessells (1982), and for a recent critical view of this distinction, consult McKoon, Ratcliffe, and Dell (1986). Also, a rejoinder that argues for the potential usefulness of the distinction is given by Tulving (1986), and a rebuttal is given by Ratcliffe and McKoon (1986).

If you choose to discuss the episodic–semantic distinction in your class, you should be prepared for an interesting discussion. One question that is very likely to arise is "I understand episodic memory because it is based on my personal experiences; however, where does semantic memory come from?" In other words, how do we acquire semantic memories? One answer to this question of how general knowledge develops has been to assume that general knowledge arises from abstracted episodic memories. Thus the basic units underlying what we call semantic memory derive from memories of specifically experienced events.

From this viewpoint, semantic memories are seen as generalized conceptual memories. This position has been most carefully developed by Schank and Abelson (1977), who contend that knowledge consists of scripts that are essentially memories of past events. Scripts are scenarios of events that are temporally organized, such as "going to a football game" or "going to a picnic." Going to a football game, for instance, represents one's knowledge of events that are likely to happen in sequence at a football game. This includes events such as (a) buying football tickets, (b) driving to the stadium, (c) parking the car, (d) entering the stadium, (e) getting seated, (f) watching the kickoff, (g) cheering for the team, (h) talking with friends, and (i) buying popcorn at halftime. Thus the script or idea of "going to a football game" is built up as the result of specific episodes, and, from this view, there is no distinction between semantic and episodic events.

The theoretical distinction between episodic and semantic memory and the necessity for this distinction will undoubtedly continue to be debated for some time. Psychologists differ with respect to the necessity of these two systems, and no complete resolution of this debate is yet present. One teaching suggestion on this issue is perhaps to note the distinction but to withhold discussion of the divergent views until completion of any single lecture on memory. After you have laid the framework for memory may be the best time to raise the distinction.

Finally studies of memory range from those done in laboratory settings to studies of memory in everyday settings (Bahrick, 1984; Bruce, 1985; Harris & Morris, 1984; Neisser, 1982). In a fascinating book, Neisser has assembled a vast range of papers on the processes of memory in natural contexts. Similarly Bahrick's pioneering work on very long-term memory for faces and for Spanish represents a remarkable accomplishment.

Stages of Memory

Approximately 20 years ago Atkinson and Shiffrin (1968) and Waugh and Norman (1965) proposed an information-processing model of memory. This model became so influential in a brief period of time that by 1970 it was known as the *modal* model of memory. It was also known as the *stage* model of memory because the researchers contend that the flow of information moves successively through the stages as it is being processed. In the various stage models, the human memory system is divided into three different stores or components: sensory memory, short-term memory, and long-term memory. Originally, these stages were seen as the formal structural components or the architecture of the memory system (Atkinson & Shiffrin, 1968) and were viewed as the permanent part of the memory system that set the boundaries within which memory processes operate.

Recent years have seen a modification of this earlier view of stage models. Today most cognitive psychologists are probably unwilling to endorse the idea of separate structural memory systems (Horton & Mills, 1984). These stages are now seen as various time frames in which humans are able to process information. This shift in thinking about the three memory stages does not imply that the information-processing approach is incorrect but rather that a strict structural view with discrete events at one and only one stage has been largely abandoned. Thus the stages refer to memories that last for milliseconds, for several seconds, minutes, days, weeks, months, or years.

Sensory Memory

The first stage of the human memory system is sensory memory. This system holds sensory representations, that is, fleeting impressions of events that impinge on the sense organs for a very brief period of time. These images or representations may be *iconic*, affecting the visual modality; *echoic*, affecting the auditory modality; or the images may affect any of the other senses. Everyone has experienced sensory memory. Consider the following demonstration: Close your eyes for about a minute; while closed, hold your hand approximately one foot in front of your face. Now blink once and be sure to keep your eyelids closed after you blink. The visual icon (image) of your hand will persist after your eyelids are closed but will begin to fade immediately.

At this point I should call your attention to what I regard as a very important aspect of teaching the subject of human memory. Whenever feasible, it is very desirable to illustrate concepts and principles of memory by simple classroom demonstrations of memory phenomena. This allows you to directly involve the students in their own memory processes and thus enrich their understanding with meaningful demonstrations. Students almost invariably find these interesting, and the demonstrations are likely to encourage lively and interesting discussions. A variety of memory phenomena and processes lend themselves to convenient classroom demonstrations, and I will periodically describe some of those I have found useful.

How long does visual sensory memory last? About one-third of a second. This estimate was arrived at by the classic studies of Sperling (1960) using the partial report technique, a procedure that has been frequently described. Of particular interest has been the fate of information in the sensory register. One thing that can happen is the decay of information in sensory memory (Averbach & Coriell, 1961). Another possible consequence is the integration of information, which is simply the combination of two images. Compelling evidence for integration has been demonstrated by Eriksen and Collins (1967) and Turvey (1973). In the Eriksen and Collins experiment, subjects were shown two separate patterns of dots, which, when superimposed, combined to form three letters. The subjects were never shown both pairs simultaneously, but were shown one pattern for 6 milliseconds followed by a second pattern for 6 milliseconds with a delay ranging from 0 to 500 milliseconds. The subjects were then able to identify the three letters at better than chance levels, demonstrating the integration of the two stimuli. A third fate that may befall the icon is erasure, which has been shown in experiments of backward masking (Didner & Sperling, 1980).

There are still unanswered questions in the domain of sensory memory. One concerns the locus of the visual icon. As Haber (1983) has noted, there are two possible locations, one in the retina and the other in the brain. McCloskey and Watkins (1978) have suggested that the icon must operate beyond the retina and is at least partly controlled by the central nervous system. Another issue concerns the necessity to postulate a separate iconic storage system. Merikle (1980), for example, has suggested that different aspects of a stimulus may be encoded at different rates by the nervous system. More generally, although there is basic agreement about the facts of sensory memory, there is some disagreement regarding the interpretation of some of the experiments in this area. For a critical discussion of these issues, the interested reader will want to examine the papers by Haber (1983), Coltheart (1980), Neisser (1976), and Turvey (1977).

Short-Term Memory

The short-term memory system is often regarded as a mental workbench (Baddeley, 1976; Klatzky, 1980) and is the center of activity in the information-processing system. Information can be brought into short-term memory from two sources: It can come from the sensory memory store, or it can be activated from long-term memory. In either case, information in short-term memory lasts in the order of seconds and shows a rapid loss after about 20 seconds (Peterson & Peterson, 1959). An important aspect of being able to keep large amounts of information in short-term memory is the process of *chunking*, which is the process by which people organize items they wish to remember into larger units (Miller, 1966). Chunking can involve both verbal and spatial memory, such as memory for chess positions (Chase & Ericsson, 1982). An especially powerful demonstration of chunking was shown in a subject who was extensively tested: After much practice he was able to hold 82 items in short-term memory as a result of enhanced skill in chunking (Ericsson & Chase, 1982). The basic findings of short-term memory have been described in many sources (e.g., Best, 1986; Ellis & Hunt, 1983; Reed, 1982; Stern, 1985) and will not be reviewed here. Rather, I will talk about the status of short-term memory and how our thinking about it has evolved in recent years.

Long-Term Memory

Long-term memory represents the vast store of knowledge we have about the world. The capacity of the long-term store is virtually infinite, and many memory theorists have regarded long-term memory as permanent. The permanence of long-term memory, however, has been questioned by some (e.g., Loftus & Loftus, 1980). Many psychologists regard long-term memory as permanent, based upon a range of experimental evidence that suggests that information residing in long-term memory can be accessed under specific conditions. Such a view recognizes that forgetting occurs because information is not always accessible.

Distinguishing Short-Term from Long-Term Memory

Much of the earlier research on short-term memory had the ultimate goal of establishing the characteristics of short-term memory and of demonstrating that these characteristics differ from long-term memory. This research was motivated by efforts to demonstrate theoretical differences between short-term and long-term stores. Three basic characteristics were proposed to distinguish short-term from long-term memory. These characteristics were *trace life* or duration of the memory code, the *capacity* of short-term memory, and the nature of the *memory code*. In addition to these three features, arguments were made about differential effects of variables on short- and long-term memory, and clinical case studies were also used to support the arguments for a dual memory system.

Let us examine just one of these characteristics, the nature of the memory code. Initially, psychologists believed that the presumed different memory structures affected the nature of the memory code (cf. Wickelgren, 1973). For example, acoustic errors were prominent when subjects retrieved material from short-term memory, whereas semantic confusion was prominent in retrieval from long-term memory. This type of finding led psychologists to theorize that the short-term memory code was acoustic in nature, whereas the long-term memory code was semantic in nature. And a difference in types of memory code thus argued for two different memory systems.

Subsequently, it was demonstrated that people do have semantic information in short-term memory as well as acoustic information in long-term memory (cf. Drewnowski & Murdock, 1980). As a result, most psychologists are unwilling to argue for theoretical differences in the two memory systems based on presumed differences in the nature of the memory code. Similarly, other researchers began to question any sharp division of memory into separate structures or stages, and by 1975 many psychologists had abandoned the notion of separate storage systems of memory. The principal reason to propose discrete stages of memory was the original assumption that each stage allowed for some unique processes to operate. But if memory processes can occur at several stages, then the necessity to postulate separate stages disappears. What this represents is a retreat from the earlier thinking of discrete, separate stages and a shift in emphasis to memory processes.

This shift in emphasis can be misleading. It does not mean that the information-processing approach to memory is wrong. The stage approach has been useful because it forced psychologists to focus on the processes that take place at each stage and on understanding these processes. In summary, although the theoretical distinction between short-term and long-term storage has blurred, there is still agreement that we have a short-term, or working, memory and a long-term, more permanent memory system. This simply means that a rigid division between the two separate memory systems, at a theoretical level, is probably an overstatement (Best, 1986); nevertheless, it is still useful at a descriptive, functional level to delineate between the activities of the short-term and long-term memory systems without necessarily implying the existence of two separate storage locations.

A principal task has been to understand the structure or organization of long-term memory. As noted earlier, the content of long-term memory includes episodic information, semantic memory or general knowledge, and the representation of procedural information. A most important development since the late 1960s has been the construction of models of semantic memory that attempt to describe the organization of general knowledge.

Models of Semantic Memory

Models of semantic memory are generally classified into three types: network models (e.g., Collins & Loftus, 1975), set theory models, and feature-comparison models (e.g., Smith, Shoben, & Rips, 1974). The network models have received the greatest attention, particularly the more recent propositional network models. Complete and full descriptions of these models are available in the literature so I shall only briefly refer to them.

The first major network model was developed by Collins and Quillian (1969). In this model, concepts were hierarchically organized into logically nested subordinate–superordinate relations. For example, information about birds can be stored as part of the class mammals, then as information specific to birds, then, as information relating, for example, to bluebirds, in the hierarchy mammal–bird–bluebird. In addition, the model made the assumption of cognitive economy in which information about a concept was stored in only one mode in the conceptual hierarchy. But it was not long before evidence against the basic assumptions developed, in particular the notions of hierarchical organization (e.g., Rips, Shoben, & Smith, 1973) and cognitive economy (Conrad, 1972). Subsequently, Collins and Loftus (1975) developed a spreading-activation model that responded to some of the concerns raised about the Collins–Quillian model. The basic unit, however, was still a conceptual node. Further developments of network models have generated the propositional network models in which the basic unit of memory is the proposition rather than a word or a single concept (Anderson, 1976; Anderson & Bower, 1973; Norman & Rumelhart, 1975). A proposition is the smallest unit of knowledge that can be asserted and have truth value, that is, that can allow us to decide if it is true or false. In this sense, propositions are "idea units" that describe relations among events, objects, or concepts. The latest revision of Anderson's (1983) ideas incorporates the notion of spreading activation as a major part of his thinking. All of these models emphasize that information held in long-term memory is organized in the form of vast associative networks.

In summary, many models have been proposed to describe the structure of semantic memory and to account for retrieval from semantic memory. For details the interested reader should refer to the extensive literature on this topic. In teaching this topic to introductory students, my recommendation is to describe briefly a general version of one of the network models to illustrate how knowledge is represented and how retrieval occurs.

Encoding

Although the classic information-processing models of memory (e.g., Atkinson & Shiffrin, 1968) emphasized the importance of memory processes such as selective attention, rehearsal, coding, and organization, they did so within a structural framework. These processes occurred within certain stages or were important in transferring information from one stage to another. However, the fundamental assumption of stage models was that memory is determined by the stage at which the information is processed. As psychologists became increasingly interested in studying memory processes, the focus shifted from the locus of processing to how the information is processed. And with this shift psychologists developed views of memory with which they sought to understand how various memory processes affected the representation of information in memory. For an overview of some of the conceptions of encoding see Ellis (1973).

Selective Attention

The process of encoding begins with selective attention. Years ago William James (1890) argued that attention is the key to better memory, and the point is still true today. People are bombarded by a vast array of stimuli in their daily activities, but they can attend to only a small fraction of these events. Because one cannot process all the information in the environment, only those features of information that are selected for careful attention are strongly implanted in memory.

How does selective attention operate? A variety of theoretical accounts of selective attention have been proposed over the past 30 years, and it is beyond the scope of this chapter to review them. What have emerged as influential are capacity models of attention (Kahneman, 1973) that show the process as one of allocating resources to selected inputs. In one important conceptualization, Johnston and Heinz (1978) proposed a flexible, multimodal model that allows the human to adopt any mode of attention demanded by a particular task.

What gets attended to? In general, people attend to those things that interest them and are important to them. Strong emotional or physically intense stimuli as well as unusual events get people's attention.

Automatic Versus Effortful Processing

An important distinction has been noted by Hasher and Zacks (1979) between automatic and effortful processing. Automatic processes are those that require no allocation of capacity, whereas effortful processes do. Examples of automatic processing include the encoding of frequency and spatial information. Effortful processing includes various cognitive activities, such as organization, elaboration, rehearsal, and imagery.

The predictions stemming from this distinction regarding memory for frequency and spatial information are quite straightforward. Because these are processed automatically, they should not be affected by an array of factors such as instructions and practice and incidental versus intentional instructions. In contrast, effortful processes do require the allocation of capacity, and they are affected by these variables. Preliminary studies have supported the usefulness of this distinction and how it relates to memory.

Levels of Processing

Craik and Lockhart (1972) proposed the idea of levels of processing and rejected the stage notion that the locus of processing determined what was placed in memory. Instead, they contended that stimulus information can be processed in a variety of ways. The essential idea is that the learning of anything can require several types of processing that vary along a continuum of depth. At the initial levels of processing, stimuli are analyzed for their gross physical features such as lines, angles, and contours. At intermediate levels the process of stimulus recognition occurs, and in the final levels the stimulus is processed semantically. The levels of processing idea also contended that if meaning is encoded, then the event will be remembered better than if the surface, perceptual features are encoded. Thus semantic or meaningful features facilitate better retention than do nonsemantic features.

One important implication of the levels of processing idea is that a multistage conception of memory was no longer necessary to account for differences among sensory, short-term, and long-term memory. The factors that appeared to affect each stage differently could now be explained in terms of processing differences at various levels. And good memory was the by-product of semantic analysis resulting from a greater depth of processing.

A number of studies in which instructions were manipulated using orienting tasks have supported this general idea. In a classic study, Hyde and Jenkins (1969) demonstrated the importance of orienting tasks in affecting the retention of word lists. Subjects were given word lists and two different sets of instructions. One group rated the words on a pleasantness scale, a semantic orienting task, whereas a second group merely determined whether each word contained the letter *e*, a nonsemantic orienting task. Following this procedure, the subjects were given a surprise recall task in which the group using the semantic orienting task showed considerably better recall. Regardless of the type of semantic task used, these orienting instructions have been shown, under a number of conditions, to produce better memory than do nonsemantic orienting tasks, provided that the target information was semantic (e.g., Einstein & Hunt, 1980; Hunt, Elliott, & Spence, 1979; Jacoby, Craik, & Begg, 1979; Parkin, 1984). Similar results were obtained with pictures of human faces (Bower & Karlin, 1974).

These demonstrations of the powerful effects of orienting tasks can be conveniently adapted for classroom use. My favorite is to conduct a classroom experiment in which half the class receives written semantic orienting instructions and the other half receives written nonsemantic orienting instructions prior to learning, say, a list of words. The surprise free recall task can be administered in class and the data quickly collected. The results are always impressive and usually generate an interesting, in-depth discussion as to why semantic processing leads to better memory. To prevent any knowledge contamination, of course, the demonstration should be given first, followed by a description of experimental findings.

The interesting theoretical question is: Why should semantic processing support better memory? The original version of levels of processing (Craik & Lockhart, 1972) suggested that semantic information lasts longer than nonsemantic information. This has been shown not to be the case (e.g., Stein, 1978) in that nonsemantic information can be retained for just as long as semantic information can. Thus alternative explanations for the effectiveness of semantic processing were sought. In addition, several theoretical problems were raised with the levels concept (e.g., Baddeley, 1978; Nelson, Walling, & McEvoy, 1979) so that it became necessary to modify the initial version.

Maintenance Rehearsal and Elaboration

An important distinction has been made between maintenance and elaborative rehearsal (Craik & Lockhart, 1972; Craik & Watkins, 1973), which provides the basis for one modification of the levels idea. Maintenance rehearsal refers to the continued repetition of information in short-term memory in order to keep the information available. This process presumably does not strengthen memory for the information but just keeps it briefly activated. However, some researchers have found that even maintenance rehearsal can improve recall (e.g., Maki & Schuler, 1980; Rundus, 1980). In contrast, elaborative rehearsal refers to deeper rehearsal of the information, in which the information is related to one's existing knowledge.

In an attempt to modify the depth hypothesis as originally formulated, Craik and Tulving (1975) proposed that semantic processing produces a more *elaborated* encoding than does nonsemantic processing. Elaboration, by virtue of relating the to-be-remembered information to other information already in memory, broadens one's knowledge about the information. As Hunt and I have noted, the heart of the elaboration idea is captured by the suggestion that something is better remembered if it is related to other known facts (Ellis & Hunt, 1983). But why should elaboration produce better memory? One answer to this question lies in the notion of distinctiveness.

Distinctiveness

Distinctiveness is the idea that if events are more unique, in the sense of being more distinctive, then they will be more memorable. The process of elaboration is seen as leading to more distinctive, and hence more memorable, traces: With more elaborate encoding, more will be remembered about an event. Elaboration increases the likelihood of sampling more unique or distinctive features, thus making the memory more discriminable from other memories. A series of experiments have confirmed the importance of distinctiveness (Hunt & Elliott, 1980; Hunt & Mitchell, 1982). Thus distinctiveness is an important hypothesis to account for the effects of semantic processing and elaboration. One of the virtues of distinctiveness is that it leads to more discriminable memory traces and to greater resistance to interference (Battig, 1979).

Cognitive Effort

One other element that can account for processing effects on memory is cognitive effort. A number of researchers have reported that the allocation of capacity, or effort, in various tasks is related to better memory (e.g., Ellis, Thomas, & Rodriguez, 1984; Jacoby, 1978; O'Brien & Myers, 1985; Swanson, 1984; Tyler, Hertel, McCallum, & Ellis, 1979). In one such experiment, Tyler et al. (1979) measured cognitive effort by the use of a secondary task paradigm with subjects who made decisions about words that could fit in sentences. Following the processing of the items, subjects were given a surprise retention test. Difficulty was assessed by reaction time to the secondary task problem during processing. The results showed that there was better retention for the more difficult items. This finding raises the question of whether the effort or capacity allocation causes better memory. The results, of course, show simply a correlation between effort and memory, not a causal relationship. Tyler et al. (1979) suggested one explanation in terms of elaboration and another in terms of distinctiveness. In either case, the effects of cognitive effort on memory are thought to be explained in terms of the processes just described, rather than in terms of a direct causal effect of effort.

Not all studies have shown that effort is positively correlated with memory. For example, Zacks, Hasher, Sanft, and Rose (1983) had their subjects do a variety of tasks that appeared to require varying amounts of cognitive effort. Using the anagram task described by Tyler et al. (1979), they failed to find that solving more difficult anagrams produced better memory. Other tasks were also used with similar negative findings. Although the cognitive effort effect has been reported in a number of studies, these negative findings indicate that the boundary conditions of the effect are yet to be fully understood (Ellis et al., 1984).

From the viewpoint of teaching, a discussion of the role of cognitive effort in memory can lead to an interesting class interaction. This discussion can be raised in the context of whether "studying hard" produces increased memory of the material being studied, and if so, then a further discussion of how this comes about can be of considerable interest. You might consult Einstein, McDaniel, Dunay, and Stevens (1984) and McDaniel, Einstein, Dunay, and Cobb (1986), who make the argument that whether or not cognitive effort makes a difference in memory depends upon the extent to which the task encourages encoding of information that is not routinely extracted from the to-be-learned material. For example, if the task requires the subject to do considerable organizing or structuring of the material, and if the structure of the text is not encoded obligatorily, then effort is important. Otherwise, if effort promotes processing of information that is insufficiently induced by the text itself, then effort is not an important factor. Their framework provides an important advance in understanding how effort operates.

Generation Effect in Memory

One interesting phenomenon in memory has been called the generation effect: When information that is to be remembered is actually produced or generated by a person, it is better remembered than when the material is simply given to a subject with instructions to read it (e.g., Slamecka & Graf, 1978). The generation effect has been demonstrated in situations in which the subject must generate (or read) opposites to a list of words, or where they must complete a sentence with a word. The generation effect occurs even if subjects try but fail to generate the items (Slamecka & Fevreiski, 1983).

A variety of explanations have been offered for this effect, but at present none of them seems completely satisfactory. Explanations include the possibility that generation involves an increased number of cognitive operations, more distinctive memory traces, enhanced organization, and greater cognitive effort. The generation effect is consistent with the long-standing notion that there is something important about one's own activity in learning and remembering. It will require further study, however, to delineate the precise processes that can account for this finding.

Organization

Another important encoding strategy involves the process of organization. Organization is the process by which people group discrete, individual items into larger units or chunks of information (see Ellis & Hunt, 1983). Items and events can be organized in a number of ways including into conceptual, perceptual, and functional categories. I view organization as a type of memory strategy that may be used in attempts to facilitate memory.

The classic studies of organization were list-learning studies using free recall. Organization differs from elaboration in that elaboration involves relating an item to information in long-term memory, whereas organization involves grouping or combining individual items within the set of to-be-learned materials. Thus elaboration involves enriching some new knowledge by relating it to what is already known, whereas organization involves grouping information according to categories or similarities. Almost any form of organization seems better than none. The positive effects of organization have been widely demonstrated, and the literature has been summarized nicely (e.g., Klatzky, 1980), so I provide only a few comments on it in this chapter.

Most researchers of organization in free recall have distinguished between experimenter-imposed organization and subjective organization. In the former category, the familiar studies of category clustering in free recall (e.g., Wood & Underwood, 1967) illustrate how humans use categories in organizing word lists. Similarly, Tulving (1962) illustrated the importance of subjective organization. And early researchers established that organizational effects could occur at both encoding and retrieval.

Although organization is a well-established process, interest in organization in list-learning studies has sharply declined in recent years. One important exception has been the conceptual distinction between relational processing and item-specific processing proposed by Einstein and Hunt (1980; Hunt & Einstein, 1981). Einstein and Hunt (1980) required subjects to learn either a categorized list or an unrelated list of words followed by both a free recall test and a recognition test. During learning, subjects were required to perform either a relational orienting task (taxonomic categorization) or an individual-item task (pleasantness rating). In the free recall test, the relational orienting tasks produced greater clustering then did individual-item tasks. In contrast, individual-item processing led to superior item recognition. Einstein and Hunt postulated that relational processing facilitates the formation of retrieval schemes for free recall, whereas item processing brings about better discrimination among the items. For example, relational knowledge that several words in the list were animals, along with individual-item information that something has stripes would help one to reconstruct the list item "zebra." A similar idea to account for processing effects in picture memory has been proposed by Ritchey and Beal (1980). A more general point of this research is that memory is facilitated by both organization and distinctiveness.

In recent years researchers of organizational processes have shifted to the study of text processing and schematic organization, which will be discussed in another section. For purposes of illustration, I prefer to highlight the use of organization with scripts or scenarios (e.g., Rabinowitz & Mandler, 1983) rather than to use list-learning demonstrations. I will describe the use of scripts later, but I should also acknowledge that having students freely recall categorized lists provides an easily understood demonstration of the effects of free recall. In connection to this, you can ask students how they recalled the lists and whether they generated the items from categories. This leads to a good discussion of organization and how it operates.

Imagery and Visual Codes

There has been a rebirth in the study of imagery in the past 20 years. For many years the subject of imagery was taboo, largely because it was regarded as mentalistic by many psychologists who were influenced by behaviorism. During the 1960s psychologists began to observe that imagery facilitated learning and memory, and they became interested in understanding the imagery process. In many ways the pioneering studies of Paivio (1969, 1971) played an important role in establishing the significance of imagery. In his initial studies, Paivio demonstrated the facilitative effects of imagery in paired-associate learning, and Bower (1972) was able to demonstrate that the facilitative effects of imagery could not be explained simply in terms of verbalization or related elaborative processes.

Paivio (1974) proposed that some information in memory may be stored in two forms: verbal codes and image codes. For example, a picture can be labeled and remembered by the use of a verbal code suggested by the label. In addition, the picture can be remembered by the use of an image code, which provides for better memory, because two codes are better than one. Moreover, Paivio argued that the image code also facilitates memory because the image contains greater detail, allowing for a more distinctive code.

Although Paivio has marshaled a considerable amount of evidence in support of dual code theory, a great deal of controversy has resulted, and many cognitive psychologists now question the necessity of having a separate image code. Pylyshyn (1973) was among the first to raise serious objections to dual code theory. The alternative proposed was propositional theory, in which all information is stored in the form of propositional codes. Although the experimental findings about imagery were not seriously questioned, the issue of how to interpret the imagery findings became the topic of debate (see Anderson, 1978; Kolers, 1983; Kosslyn, 1981; and Palmer, 1978). As Horton and Mills (1984) noted, the debate on the conceptual status of imagery has settled down for the moment. Nevertheless, these issues have not been fully resolved.

The important experimental work on imagery includes studies of mental rotation, mental travel, imagery and learning, mental comparisons, and interference with mental images. It is beyond the scope of this chapter to review this large amount of literature on imagery research, but I note a few aspects of it. The work on mental rotation has focused on the nature of mental operations (e.g., Shepard & Metzler, 1971). The starting point in their research was to examine some of the implications of the view that mental images are like pictures in the mind. Shepard and Metzler (1971) demonstrated, in a now classic study, that the time required to determine that two objects have the same shape is an increasing linear function of the angular separation of the shapes. Most subjects reported that they first made the match by "watching" themselves rotate the mental image and then deciding on a match. Similarly, psychologists studying mental travel (e.g., Kosslyn, Ball, & Reiser, 1978) provided further evidence for the direct storage of visual information. In Kosslyn's studies, the time required to travel the distance between two locations on a map is proportional to the actual distance to be travelled. Nevertheless, the interpretation of these data has not gone unchallenged (Mitchell & Richman, 1980; Richman, Mitchell, & Reznick, 1979), and it has been argued that the results may reflect the subject's perception of task demands.

The current status of the debate on imagery is that there is general agreement on the importance of it and acceptance of the wide range of empirical findings. The disagreement lies in the theoretical explanation of imagery findings and in any necessity to posit an image code. For more information on the imagery debate, the reader should consult books by Block (1981) and Kosslyn (1983).

There are a variety of classroom demonstrations of imagery that instructors may use. My favorite, because it is convenient and because the effect is strong, is to instruct half the class in imagery procedures in learning paired associates, with a control group learning the list without imagery instructions. Subjects display the usual superiority in recall following imagery instructions, which leads to a good discussion of how imagery works.

Retrieval

Retrieval is the process of accessing information from memory. Psychologists acknowledge that information may be encoded and stored in one's memory and yet the person may not have ready access to all the information stored. Thus the understanding of retrieval has interested cognitive psychologists as part of the larger task of understanding memory.

Retrieval from Short-Term Memory

Retrieval from short-term memory involves a search of the contents of active memory, also commonly referred to as a memory scan. Not all information in short-term memory is immediately available and some search processing can occur in short-term memory. Sternberg (1966) first showed clearly that people do search for items of information in short-term memory, in a task now known as the Sternberg paradigm. His subjects were given a series of digits (the memory set), which varied in size from one to six digits. Shortly afterwards the subjects were given a probe digit and asked to indicate whether or not the probe had been presented in the memory set. On some test trials the probe had been presented in the memory set (positive trials) and on others it had not been presented (negative trials). The interesting finding was that the reaction time of the subjects varied as a function of the size of the memory set. As the memory set size increased, so did the reaction time to locate the probe item. Each additional item in the memory set added about 38 milliseconds to the time it required the subject to make a response.

Retrieval from Long-Term Memory

Retrieval from long-term memory is more complex than retrieval from short-term memory. Information in long-term memory is usually not directly available nor is it limited to a few items. From the perspective of information-processing, the process of retrieval can be seen as a three-stage affair involving searching, holding in working memory, and response programming. The first stage is a search through storage to locate information relevant to a query. This may be fairly direct and immediate or it may take on a more complex, problem-solving character. As relevant information is located, it is collected together and held in active memory. Finally, the information in active memory guides and directs an appropriate verbal or motor response. The first stage of retrieval, the search process, may be preceded by an even more general verification process, in which a decision is made as to whether or not to search for information. People seem to know whether or not the relevant information is available in long-term memory and will initiate a search only if the information is thought to be present (see Norman, 1973, 1976). If the preliminary decision is positive, then a search is initiated. The search does not appear to be random, but is usually guided by some sort of strategy that involves trying to obtain a general scenario or package of information. Afterwards, a great deal of specific information may become available.

In discussing retrieval in class, I like to illustrate it with a demonstration of the tip-of-the-tongue phenomenon as described by Brown and McNeill (1966). Subjects are given dictionary definitions of unfamiliar words and are asked to produce the word. They sometimes recall the word, but sometimes they recall only part of the word, the first letter of the word, or no word prior to subsequently recalling the entire word. This usually leads to a good discussion of how people retrieve information and the orderly search process they frequently use. One additional point about retrieval is that people sometimes know a good deal, or know at least something, about what they know about some topic. For example, people who play memory games, such as Trivial Pursuit, frequently have a good idea about whether or not they know the answer to some query. Similarly, students, upon completing a test, contend that they have a good idea about how well they did. This knowledge of one's own knowledge is called metamemory (cf. Flavell & Wellman, 1977). A good review of this literature can be seen in Brown (1975) and useful suggestions for demonstrations are seen in Zechmeister and Nyberg (1982).

An interesting phenomenon in retrieval is retrieval inhibition, in which the act of retrieving some information inhibits retrieval of the remaining set of information (Roediger & Neely, 1982). This is a fairly common experience and it is as if the retrieval of well-learned items blocks the retrieval of weaker items.

Encoding Specificity and Retrieval

The process of retrieval is greatly dependent on the use of good cues, so the question arises as to what makes a good cue. In a series of papers, Tulving has provided evidence that an effective cue is one that is specifically encoded with the to-be-remembered information (Tulving & Thomson, 1973; Flexner & Tulving, 1982). In a classic demonstration of encoding specificity, Tulving and Thomson (1971) demonstrated that cues that were weakly associated with target words were far more effective than cues that were associated strongly but not present during the encoding.

The encoding specificity idea has been applied to the effects of context and instructions. For example, Leonard and Whitten (1983) demonstrated that subjects' knowledge of a retrieval task influenced the way they encoded the material. Subjects were given a list of words to study; half were instructed to expect a recognition test and half expected a recall test. However, all subjects were given a recognition test, enabling the effects of encoding instructions to be examined. When the target item was embedded in a semantically related context, subjects who had been given recognition expectation instructions showed a decrement in performance compared to the recall expectation group.

Context Effects in Memory

Encoding specificity is directly related to the general issue of context effects in recall. Numerous researchers have shown that memory for information is greatest when the training and retrieval context remains the same. As a general rule, the greater the similarity between cues present at encoding and retrieval, the greater the recall (e.g., Eich, 1985; Hunt & Ellis, 1974; Nelson & McEvoy, 1979; Smith, 1986; Smith, Glenberg, & Bjork, 1978; Summers, Horton, & Diehl, 1985).

The effects of context are widespread. Not only is verbal context important, but the physical context in which something is learned has also been shown to be important. For example, studying in the same classroom that one will be tested in leads to a modest improvement in recall. Similarly Geiselman and Bjork (1980) have shown that having subjects imagine printed words being spoken in the same voices in which they were initially spoken can facilitate recognition memory of the words. Recently Smith (1986) has demonstrated context effects in recognition memory, a task in which environmental context effects have been difficult to obtain in earlier studies.

Because verbal context effects are usually strong, they can make a good demonstration in class. For example, this can be usually done by having subjects learn a set of words with a context word for each target item. At the testing stage, you might cue half of the target words with the old items (same context) and half with new items (new context) to show the facilitative effects of context. This can be easily accomplished in a group presentation with an overhead projector.

Cue-Dependent Retrieval and Forgetting

The ideas just discussed, which emphasize the importance of retrieval cues, are also applicable to the understanding of forgetting. The failure to remember stored information may be due to the failure to access information, and one important reason that information is not accessed is that the cues for retrieval are ineffective. From this perspective, forgetting becomes a matter of retrieval failure due to poor cues. This idea was proposed by Tulving (1974) and is directly related to the idea of encoding specificity.

Decay and Interference

The classical views of forgetting include those of decay and interference theory. Perhaps the oldest view of forgetting is that memories fade over time. According to decay theory, when some new fact or event is learned, a memory trace is formed. With the passage of time, this trace gradually decays. Thus forgetting occurs because of trace decay. How has this theory fared? The basic problem with this theory is that natural events, such as forgetting, are thought by many to be caused by factors other than the mere passage of time. Decay theory has been used to explain our transient sensory and short-term memories and has also been used to explain forgetting in long-term memory. Its use appears to arise when no obvious alternative explanation of forgetting is evident (e.g., Peterson & Peterson, 1959). The current status of decay theory is that of a possible explanation of some forgetting, but it is not the most popular or generally accepted theory of forgetting.

Many theorists contend that in order to account for the full range of findings about forgetting there must be an additional set of principles that are summarized by interference theory. Theorists on the subject of interference contend that forgetting occurs because of retroactive interference, in which new learning interferes with memory for old learning, or because of proactive interference, in which prior learning gets in the way of memory for new material. Research supporting interference mechanisms in memory has a long history (Postman & Underwood, 1973) and therefore I do not review it in this chapter. Perhaps the most important feature to note is the growing belief that a full explanation of forgetting will require both decay and interference principles.

State-Dependent Retrieval

Memory is dependent upon both internal and external cues. State-dependent memory is the idea that the states, or internal conditions, under which information is learned may be strong and important cues in retrieving particular information. Eich (1980) has thoroughly reviewed the literature on pharmacological state dependency and notes the effects of alcohol and drugs in producing state-dependent effects. Eich also argued that state-dependent effects are not observed when subjects are given explicit cues as in free recall and recognition memory.

There is also some evidence for mood-state dependency. Bower (1981) reported mood-state dependency in a variety of tasks ranging from free recall to memory of early childhood experiences. My colleague and I (Leight & Ellis, 1981) have reported limited evidence for mood-state dependency in recognition memory of letter sequences. In this instance, we studied 24-hour delayed recall, which would minimize the effect, and found the effect in only one of four recognition conditions. Thus mood-state dependent effects in recognition can be obtained under conditions in which the items are low in meaningfulness. The reader should be cautioned that researchers (e.g., Bower & Mayer, 1985) more recently have reported difficulty in obtaining mood-state dependency in memory studies. At this point I conclude that mood-state dependency is not a robust effect.

Emotion and Memory

Studies of mood-state dependency are related to the more general issue of the relation between emotion or affect and memory processes. The role of emotional states in memory and other cognitive processes has been of considerable interest in recent years. The research on the interface of cognition and emotion is an important development and already a wide range of research topics have been explored. Studies of arousal effects of affect on memory (e.g., Clark, Milberg, & Ross, 1983), mood effects on comprehension of prose (e.g., Hasher, Rose, Zacks, Sanft, & Doren, 1985), mood and encoding effort (Ellis, Thomas, & Rodriguez, 1984), clinical studies (e.g., Cohen, Weingartner, Smallberg, Pickar, & Murphy, 1982), mood congruence (e.g., Bower, 1981; Teasdale & Russell, 1983), and mood effects on retrieval (e.g., Ellis, Thomas, McFarland, & Lane, 1985) have been conducted.

Having established the importance of emotional variables, the current focus of research is on boundary conditions or the limits of mood effects, the role of task demands, dependence on task characteristics such as prose versus less organized materials, affective character of the material to be learned, mood intensity, and mood congruence effects. I have noted the effects produced by the induction of a depressed mood on a wide range of memory processes including encoding, retrieval, organization, and memory integration (Ellis, 1986b). This procedure involved testing predictions from my resource allocation theory in a variety of test situations (cf. Ellis et al., 1984, 1985; Ellis & Ashbrook, in press). We can expect to see continued interest in this new research area relating emotion and memory.

Memory and Awareness

Memory research has usually involved situations in which subjects are explicitly instructed to learn some laboratory task and told that their memory will be tested. In the past 10 or so years, researchers have turned their attention to the study of memory as it relates to various conditions of awareness. Some of this work has been summarized by Klatzky (1984) who examined the relation between three types of awareness and memory. One type of awareness is experiencing the here-and-now and is often called consciousness. A second type of awareness is the awareness of the contents of memory, that is, the cognizance of past experiences that are stored in memory. The third type of awareness is one's own cognizance of memory as a general human capacity.

I note only two examples of the research on memory and awareness in order to capture its flavor, but I emphasize that this is a rapidly growing area of research. An exciting line of research is the work of Johnson and her colleagues who have looked at the source of information, internal or external, as it affects the retrieval of information from memory (Johnson, 1983; Johnson & Raye, 1981; Johnson, Raye, Foley, & Foley, 1981). In these studies, interest has been in the ability of people to distinguish between internally generated information for memory, which is the result of imagination, and externally generated information, which is the result of perception or reality monitoring. Johnson and Raye (1981) note that information in memory stems from both perception and imagination, and raise the interesting question as to how they can be distinguished. Their approach to this question is to study the differences in the features of the retrieved information from the two sources of input. For example, the memory of an event or object actually experienced, as distinct from being imagined, should be richer and contain more detail. In a series of experiments, Johnson has begun to delineate these differences in memory features.

A different line of research in this area considers the distinction between *explicit* and *implicit* memory. Explicit memory requires conscious recollection, whereas with implicit memory, performance can be facilitated without conscious recollection (cf. Graf, Mandler, & Haden, 1982; Schacter & Graf, 1986). It has been argued that recent research on implicit and explicit memory suggests a fundamental difference between the two in terms of the variables that are relevant in the two situations (Schacter & Graf, 1986). For example, Jacoby and Dallas (1981) have suggested that performance on implicit memory tasks does not benefit from elaborative processing, in contrast to studies of explicit memory. Continuing this line of research, Schacter and Graf (1986) present new evidence showing that normal elaboration can play a role in both implicit and explicit memory, whereas procedures that provide for more extensive elaboration benefit explicit but not implicit memory.

Amnesia

Up to this point my comments have focused on the functioning of normal memories. During the past 25 years, researchers have become extensively involved in issues of memory pathology. Disorders of memory can arise from brain damage due to concussions or other physical injury, alcohol and other drugs, biochemical changes and disease conditions produced by invading organisms; disorders can also arise from psychogenic causes such as severe stress. One of the most significant of these disorders is amnesia, a condition in which a person has difficulty in remembering old events or difficulty in learning new material. One type of amnesia is *retrograde* amnesia in which a person suffers a memory loss for some period prior to an injury. Alternatively, *anterograde* amnesia refers to difficulties in learning new information following some injury. Such amnesia is seen in patients who suffer from Korsakoff's syndrome, a disorder of chronic alcoholic patients whose memory loss results from brain lesions due to excessive alcohol consumption.

In describing amnesia to introductory psychology students, I find it useful to cite the famous example of H. M., who received neurosurgery in order to minimize the effects of epileptic seizures; surgery resulted in a hippocampal lesion. Following surgery, H. M. was observed to suffer from selective memory loss. For example, he had a normal memory span but was apparently unable to add any new information to his long-term memory. He could not recognize anyone he had met after the surgery and had difficulty in finding his way around in new locations. In contrast, H. M.'s memories prior to surgery remained essentially intact, particularly for events that occurred a year or so before the surgery. For some, this distinction seems to support the idea of two distinct memory systems, short- and long-term memory, but others have questioned this interpretation.

Although it was earlier thought that amnesics were unable to learn new material, more recent studies have indicated that they can learn certain skills and that they show improvement with practice. Even though they improve, amnesic patients will say that they remember little or nothing of their learning experience. Several explanations of this discrepancy between actual performance and awareness of one's performance have been offered. One explanation is the distinction between procedural knowledge and verbal knowledge, the distinction between how to do something and being knowledgeable and aware of something (e.g., Squire, 1982). Another distinction that is generally agreed upon is that amnesia appears to be more susceptible to disruption in direct memory tasks, involving instructions to recall or recognize past events, than in indirect memory tasks such as mirror reading (e.g., Squire, Shimamura, & Graf, 1985). Finally, recent studies have indicated that amnesia is a selective and not a global defect. For example, Hirst, Johnson, Kim, Phelps, Risse, and Volpe (1986) have shown that recall and recognition are differentially affected by amnesia. When the recognition memory of amnesics and non-amnesic control subjects were the same, control subjects still showed between 200% and 1,200% greater recall than did amnesic subjects! These results clearly establish the point that amnesia affects recall more than it affects recognition.

Comprehension, Knowledge, and Schemas

In the past 15 years or so there has been a dramatic shift in memory research to sentences and stories as distinct from more traditional materials such as words. Interest has shifted toward how people extract meaning from texts, how comprehension develops, how current knowledge enables people to learn new information, and how schemas are used in encoding and retrieval of information. This is a rich and exciting development in memory research and is extended to materials that are more ecologically valid, as well as to more complex issues. Some of this work has its origin in Bartlett's (1932) studies of how people remember stories and in his ideas about the reconstructive nature of memory (Cofer, 1975). But many of these researchers have gone in new directions and many of the advances in this area are based upon relatively recent and sophisticated methodological–conceptual developments (e.g., Bower, Black, & Turner, 1979; Graesser, 1981; Kieras & Just, 1984; Kintsch & van Dijk, 1978; Mandler, 1984).

Themes and Prior Knowledge

One line of research in comprehension that has been focused on is the role of themes in comprehension. A theme may be the title of a passage or the lead sentence in a story, and thus may be presented experimentally, or a theme may be the abstracted general idea of a passage (e.g., Ellis & Hunt, 1983). The role of themes in facilitating memory and comprehension has been illustrated by Bransford and Johnson (1973). They demonstrated that providing subjects with titles for to-be-remembered passages facilitated memory. Similarly Sulin and Dooling (1974) demonstrated how prior knowledge could influence the retention of passages. Many other experiments have shown how relevant prior knowledge can provide a coherent framework in which a person can interpret stories (e.g., Morris, Bransford, & Franks, 1977) and the outcome of fictional baseball games (Spilich, Vesonder, Chiesi, & Voss, 1979).

The role of prior knowledge in influencing comprehension and memory can be readily demonstrated in the classroom in a variety of ways. One of my favorites, that is convenient and effective, is to adopt the passages from Bransford and Johnson (1973) and present subjects with either relevant titles or no titles in the control conditions. A good demonstration of the effects of prior knowledge on recall is given in Zechmeister and Nyberg (1982).

Presuppositions and Memory Distortions

Some materials can be understood only if certain other things are presupposed to be true. Therefore comprehension clearly is an active process, involving the interaction of a person's knowledge and presuppositions with the new material being processed. The role of presuppositions in eyewitness identification research has been nicely demonstrated by Loftus and her students (e.g., Loftus, Miller, & Burns, 1978; Loftus & Palmer, 1974). For instance, Loftus and Palmer (1974) were able to demonstrate that subjects who saw the film of an automobile accident could be influenced in their judgments of the speed of the car by how questions about the speed of the car were phrased: When asked how fast the cars were going when they (hit/smashed) each other, higher estimates of speed were given with the question loaded with the term *smashed*. In other words, the less neutral word *smashed* led to estimates of higher speed because it biased the subject's judgment. Loftus, Miller and Burns (1978) have argued that a semantic integration process, in which visual and verbal information became integrated, took place in these studies. Although the findings of Loftus's studies on the effects of misleading information are clearly replicable, some questions as to the interpretation of these findings have arisen (Bekerian & Bowers, 1983; McCloskey & Zaragoza, 1985).

Eyewitness Testimony and Identification

An interesting extension of the work on memory distortion has been the research on eyewitness identification, which has burgeoned in the past 10 years. Much of this work had been initially focused on inaccuracies in testimony and identification and on biasing effects in memory. A number of recent books have been entirely devoted to the topic (e.g., Lloyd-Bostock & Clifford, 1982; Loftus, 1979; Shepard, Ellis, & Davies, 1982; Wells & Loftus, 1984; Yarmey, 1979). Although subjects in experimental studies showed high rates of false identification, there is some question as to what extent this is true in the real world. Wells and Turtle (1986), however, argued persuasively that the rate of false identifications obtained in the laboratory is a fair estimate of identifications that would occur in real-world cases.

The range of research issues in eyewitness testimony and identification is quite extensive and includes such topics as bias in photo line-ups, the role of suggestion in identification, the use of misleading questions, the influence of previous knowledge about the culprit, cross-racial identification, the role of witness certainty, the role of stress and emotional factors, the effects of different types of photo arrays and line-ups. Demonstrations of the unreliability of eyewitness identification have long been standard fare in the classroom (see Loftus, 1979; Yarmey, 1979). These demonstrations can be interesting and can generate good discussions on how people make errors in identification.

Inferences and Memory

When people process information for memory they also make inferences about the material being processed, and these become part of what is remembered. Inference making is part of their efforts to develop a more coherent and meaningful representation of their world. Inferences may be logical, which are those demanded by the material (e.g., Bransford, Barclay, & Franks, 1972). They may also be pragmatic, which are inferences that are reasonably based on the information given but do not follow from rigorous logic (e.g., Johnson, Bransford, & Solomon, 1973). Finally, inferences may be invalid or misleading, as illustrated by Harris (1977, 1981). Harris has shown how misleading advertisements can lead people to draw inappropriate or invalid inferences. The study of inference making and memory for inferences is an important and exciting development in cognitive psychology, because the importance of how people construct a working model of their world is emphasized. From the perspective of teaching, materials on inference can be easily adapted for classroom use. The items used by Harris (1977) on misleading information in advertising are quite readily adapted and are interesting to students.

Constructive Processes in Memory

The fact that inferences are made at the time of encoding provides evidence for constructive processes in memory, that is, people construct part of what becomes represented in memory. Evidence of constructive processes that occur at encoding is available (Bower, Black, & Turner, 1979; Brewer & Treyens, 1981; Kintsch, 1974; Spiro, 1980). In contrast, the idea that memory can be *reconstructive* at the time of recall has been more difficult to support. While some researchers have supported the reconstructive view of memory, others (Hasher & Griffin, 1978; Spiro, 1980) have questioned this view.

Schemas and Memory

Much of what I have already described is consistent with and leads up to my discussion of schemas and memory. A schema is a large set of organized information, or knowledge domain, people have about various concepts or events. Given that a schema is an organized body of knowledge about something, then it becomes clear that a schema can serve to facilitate the encoding of new information, to aid in making inferences about material being processed, and to affect the manner in which information relevant to a given schema is retrieved. The organization of schemas is not necessarily hierarchical, but may be organized temporally or spatially (Mandler, 1979, 1984; Rabinowitz & Mandler, 1983). For example, event sequences, such as taking a vacation or going to a baseball game, can be organized into temporally ordered sequences of events. Such schemas have been labeled scripts by Schank and Abelson (1977). For example, a restaurant script is a description of the typical sequence of events one expects to occur when going to a restaurant.

The power of schemas has been demonstrated in a study by Brewer and Treyens (1981). Subjects were brought into a room and told that it was the *office* of the experimenter where they were to wait. Shortly afterwards, subjects were taken from the room and then asked to write down everything they could remember about it. It was expected that subjects would do well in remembering items that related to their schema of an office, and would do less well with respect to other items, which was precisely what happened. For example, virtually all subjects recalled that the office had a desk, chair, and walls. But far fewer recalled that it had other items, such as a skull. Interestingly, one third of the subjects reported that the office contained books, which it did not! In another study, Bower, Black, and Turner (1979) demonstrated that subjects tended to fill in the gaps in scripts with actions that were implied by the script.

It is possible to demonstrate the effects of a schema in organizing information in memory. Zechmeister and Nyberg (1982) have described several possible demonstrations, which I think are particularly good. Overall, work in comprehension and schemas is one of the most exciting developments in memory. Alba and Hasher (1983) provide a useful review of the recent work in schema theory.

Memory Strategies and Mnemonics

Interest in improving memory and in mnemonic techniques has existed for centuries. Since the days of the ancient Greeks and Romans (Yates, 1966) there has been interest in ways to improve memory. Today there are many popular books on these topics (e.g., Lorayne & Lucas, 1974) and psychologists have turned their attention to the serious study of memory strategies in the past 15–20 years. In this section I call attention to a few highlights of this development. There is now a vast amount of literature on memory strategies and mnemonics; however, I can touch on only a few aspects of this work. Bower (1970), Bellezza (1981), and McDaniel and Pressley (in press) provide excellent reviews of the entire literature on mnemonic devices. These are three of the most comprehensive reviews available and any instructor wishing to illustrate mnemonic devices in class will find these references invaluable. I also find the volume by Higbee (1977) and the examples given in Zechmeister and Nyberg (1982) especially helpful. In addition, there are a number of papers that deal with special techniques including the key-word method (Pressley, Levin, & Delaney, 1982), first-letter mnemonics (Nelson & Archer, 1972), and imagery mnemonics (Einstein & McDaniel, in press; Lesgold & Goldman, 1973; McDaniel & Einstein, 1986).

Imagery Mnemonics

One important class of mnemonics involves the use of imagery. One classic imagery technique is the *method of loci,* initially used by ancient Greek orators. The method of loci consists of the association of certain ideas or a speech with certain parts of a room in which a speech is to be made (Bower, 1972; Paivio, 1971). Another imagery mnemonic is the *peg-word* system (Bellezza, 1981), which requires knowledge of a series (for example, beginning with "one is a bun") in which the key words are used as pegs on which other items can be learned. Various elaborations of the peg-word system based on the phonetic alphabet (Higbee, 1977) have been developed, so the procedure can be modified in several ways. The key-word method has been extensively studied by Pressley and his colleagues (Pressley, Levin, & Delaney, 1982) and by Atkinson (1975) in foreign-language learning.

Classroom demonstrations of the effectiveness of imagery are particularly useful. Virtually any type of imagery mnemonic will demonstrate strong effects, which has the dual advantages of not only teaching students about imagery but also teaching them a mnemonic device which they may use in other settings.

Memory Strategies and the ARESIDORI System

One general approach in teaching memory strategies is to teach specific techniques or procedures, such as the method of loci. This is a perfectly appropriate approach, and typically it places emphasis on how to improve one's memory for specific events, such as names, dates, or faces.

A somewhat different strategy, that I have found useful, is to begin with a review of the processes or activities that are known to facilitate memory. After the set of important processes in memory is described, it then becomes useful to apply these to the subject of memory improvement. I call my own version of this approach the ARESIDORI System (Ellis, 1986a), which is a simple mnemonic code for the important processes that aid memory. These are:

1. *A*ttention
2. *R*ehearsal
3. *E*laboration
4. *S*emantic Processing
5. *I*magery
6. *D*istinctiveness
7. *O*rganization
8. *R*etrieval
9. *I*nterest

The first eight processes are drawn directly from my earlier discussion of encoding and retrieval. I begin with selective attention and end with retrieval, adding the importance of interest at the end, because it makes for a pronounceable code. (Strictly speaking, interest might be properly placed at the beginning of the list.) My teaching method is to get each student to review his or her own study habits and then judge his or her effectiveness in applying these principles or strategies. Frequently, students are able to identify a particular deficiency, such as a failure to practice retrieval or a failure to make concepts distinctive. In addition, I require students to develop particular techniques based on a given strategy. For example, students are asked how they would specifically go about improving their organization of the material in a particular course. I usually illustrate how this can be done with one or two examples, and then require students to generate one application of their own. More generally, the usefulness of this approach is at least threefold: First, it serves as a convenient review of the important processes in memory; second, it gets students to examine their own memory processes; and third, it gets them to develop and implement one or more specific techniques that are derived from a principle of memory.

A Framework for Mnemonic Devices

Bellezza (1981) has described a framework for studying and understanding mnemonic devices. He regards a mnemonic device as a strategy for organizing and encoding information with the purpose of making it more memorable. According to Bellezza, these encoding and organizing operations are the ones that help people to create and use *cognitive cuing structures*. These cuing structures are developed by the learner who then uses them to recall the information learned. Bellezza classifies mnemonics into two types: organizational and encoding. Organizational mnemonics include such categories as peg-type and chain-type mnemonics, whereas encoding mnemonics include the encoding of abstract words and the encoding of numbers. Finally, Bellezza suggests a set of useful criteria for evaluating mnemonic devices.

Individual Differences and Memory

I will briefly mention the topic of individual differences in memory, and it is appropriate to do so in this section because much of the research on individual differences in memory has focused on memory strategies. There has been a resurgence of interest in individual differences in memory and cognition in recent years, stimulated in part by Luria's (1968) intensive study of a newspaper reporter's memory. This research has included examinations of the performance of memory experts, the role of individual differences in information processing (e.g., Hunt, 1978), aging and memory (e.g., Craik & Simon, 1980), personality and memory (e.g., Ellis & Franklin, 1983), and clinical factors in memory. The literature in this area is massive and all that can be done in the space allowed in this chapter is to briefly note its importance.

One interesting feature of the research on individual differences in memory is that it calls attention to attribute-by-treatment interactions (Delaney, 1978). Delaney notes that much research in individual differences involves the manipulation of measured characteristics of subjects (attributes) and manipulated variables (treatments). In his work, for example, he shows that various individual-difference variables interact with visual and verbal elaboration instructions. Similarly my colleague and I (Ellis & Franklin, 1983) have highlighted the importance of locus-of-control personality variables (internal and external) in the way subjects organize a categorized list in free recall. Internally oriented subjects use conceptual information in organizing a list whereas externally oriented subjects are easily attracted to nonsemantic, perceptual features in organizing the list.

Study Systems

A variety of study skills systems have been developed over the years. Most of these are fairly similar and are based upon generally accepted principles of learning and memory. A classic in this field is the SQ3R system proposed by Robinson (1961). This method, which is focused on how to study textbooks and notes, is widely used in college and university programs that are designed to assist students with study techniques. Other systems focus on getting the best out of lectures. The PQ4R system proposed by Thomas and Robinson (1972), is a modification of the SQ3R system and refers to six steps in studying: preview, question, read, reflect, recite, and review. In general, the concrete recommendations of the PQ4R system can be directly related to the principles outlined in the ARESIDORI system; that is, they are derivable from general memory principles.

Concluding Remarks

In this chapter I have portrayed some of the major issues and developments in human memory. The overall structure of this area has been outlined and a number of specific features have been described. Although some of the research effort in memory will continue to involve filling in knowledge gaps and testing the boundary conditions of our generalizations, I anticipate that the next decade will see the rapid emergence of new areas, new developments, and new conceptual frameworks. The information-processing framework has served us reasonably well over the past 25 years but we can certainly expect modifications of this framework as well as new challenges to it.

A brief glance at current research in human memory already reflects the rapid developments in the area. Research in schemas, prototype formation, implicit and explicit memory, emotion and memory, memory and awareness, aging and memory, context effects, reality monitoring, the role of effort and generation, memory and comprehension, natural memories, spatial memory, amnesia, metamemory, memory for faces, and practical aspects and applications of memory represent a sample of the exciting range of work in memory.

The study of memory continues to be a central issue in cognitive psychology. The nature of memory representation, how events are interpreted and retrieved, and how our comprehension of events relates to other behaviors, such as problem solving, continues to be of major interest.

A second aspect of current research on memory is its considerable breadth. The study of memory has become, in many ways, truly interdisciplinary. Research on memory makes contact with and interacts with a variety of areas of psychology, including clinical, social, and developmental psychology. And work on the biological bases of memory, not reviewed here, continues to accelerate. A growing class of research in memory is clearly tied to clinical psychology. For example, recent work on mood and memory, affect and cognition in general, amnesia, and other memory pathologies attests to the growing interaction between cognitive and clinical psychology. Similarly, research in social cognition, person memory, and other areas reflect the growing interaction between cognitive and social psychology. Considerable work in cognitive development focuses on childrens' memory. This kind of interaction promises to enrich cognitive psychology and our understanding of human memory.

A third characteristic of current research in memory is the ease with which new methodologies are developed. Memory researchers are not wedded to one technique, method, or paradigm. Indeed the pluralism of methodology is a hallmark of current research.

Lastly, the pervasive influence of contextualist views is still present. This simply means that memory researchers are usually quick to accept the idea that experimental findings are frequently dependent upon a range of variables in the situation including task, instructional, and subject characteristics.

I anticipate that the study of memory will continue to be exciting, that it will increasingly involve a number of areas of psychology, and that there will be the emergence of new theoretical approaches. Those of us who work in the field of memory research will continue to be challenged.

References

Alba, J. W., & Hasher, L. (1983). Is memory schematic? *Psychological Bulletin, 93*, 203–231.

Anderson, J. R. (1976). *Language, memory and thought.* Hillsdale, NJ: Erlbaum.

Anderson, J. R. (1978). Arguments concerning representations for mental imagery. *Psychological Review, 85*, 249–277.

Anderson, J. R. (1983). A spreading activation theory of memory. *Journal of Verbal Learning and Verbal Behavior, 22*, 261–295.

Anderson, J. R. (1985). *Cognitive psychology & its implications.* New York: W. H. Freeman & Co.

Anderson, J. R., & Bower, G. H. (1973). *Human associative memory.* Hillsdale, NJ: Erlbaum.

Anderson, J. R., & Ross, B. H. (1980). Evidence against a semantic–episodic distinction. *Journal of Experimental Psychology: Human Learning and Memory, 6*, 441–465.

Atkinson, R. C. (1975). Mnemotechnic in second-language learning. *American Psychologist, 30*, 821–828.

Atkinson, R. C., & Shiffrin, R. M. (1968). Human memory: A proposed system and its control processes. In K. W. Spence & J. T. Spence (Eds.), *The psychology of learning and motivation* (Vol. 2, pp. 89–195) New York: Academic Press.

Averbach, E., & Coriell, A. S. (1961). Short-term memory in vision. *Bell System Technical Journal, 40*, 309–328.

Baddeley, A. D. (1976). *The psychology of memory.* New York: Basic Books.

Baddeley, A. D. (1978). The trouble with levels: A reexamination of Craik and Lockhart's framework. *Psychological Review, 85*, 139–152.

Baddeley, A. D., & Wilkins, A. (1984). Taking memory out of the laboratory.

In J. E. Harris & P. E. Morris (Eds.), *Everyday memory, actions, and absent-mindedness*. London: Academic Press.

Bahrick, H. P. (1984). Semantic memory content in permastore: Fifty years of memory for Spanish learned in school. *Journal of Experimental Psychology: General, 113,* 1–29.

Bartlett, F. C. (1932). *Remembering: A study in experimental and social psychology.* New York: Cambridge University Press.

Battig, W. F. (1979). The flexibility of human memory. In L. S. Cermak & F. I. M. Craik (Eds.), *Levels of processing in human memory.* Hillsdale, NJ: Erlbaum.

Bekerian, D. A., & Bowers, J. M. (1983). Eyewitness testimony: Were we mislead? *Journal of Experimental Psychology: Learning, Memory, and Cognition, 9,* 139–143.

Bellezza, F. S. (1981). Mnemonic devices: Classification, characteristics, and criteria. *Review of Educational Research, 51,* 247–275.

Best, J. B. (1986). *Cognitive psychology.* St. Paul, MN: West.

Block, N. (Ed.) (1981). *Imagery.* Cambridge, MA: MIT Press.

Bower, G. H. (1970). Analysis of a mnemonic device. *American Scientist, 58,* 496–501.

Bower, G. H. (1972). Mental imagery and associative learning. In L. Gregg (Ed.), *Cognition in learning and memory* (pp. 51–87). New York: Wiley.

Bower, G. H. (1981). Mood and memory. *American Psychologist, 36,* 129–148.

Bower, G. H., Black, J. B., & Turner, T. J. (1979). Scripts in memory for text. *Cognitive Psychology, 11,* 177–220.

Bower, G. H., & Karlin, M. B. (1974). Depth of processing pictures of faces and recognition memory. *Journal of Experimental Psychology, 103,* 751–757.

Bower, G. H., & Mayer, J. D. (1985). Failure to replicate mood-dependent retrieval. *Bulletin of the Psychonomic Society, 23,* 39–42.

Bransford, J. D., Barclay, J. R., & Franks, J. J. (1972). Sentence memory: A constructive versus interpretative approach. *Cognitive Psychology, 3,* 193–209.

Bransford, J. D., & Johnson, M. K. (1973). Contextual prerequisites for understanding: Some investigations of comprehension and recall. *Journal of Verbal Learning and Verbal Behavior, 11,* 717–726.

Brewer, W. F., & Treyens, J. C. (1981). Role of schemata in memory for places. *Cognitive Psychology, 13,* 207–230.

Brown, A. L. (1975). The development of memory: Knowing, knowing about knowing, and knowing how to know. In H. W. Reese (Ed.), *Advances in child behavior and development* (Vol. 10). New York: Academic Press.

Brown, R., & McNeill, D. (1966). The "tip of the tongue" phenomenon. *Journal of Verbal Learning and Verbal Behavior, 5,* 325–337.

Bruce, D. (1985). The how and why of ecological memory. *Journal of Experimental Psychology: General, 114,* 78–90.

Chase, W. G., & Ericsson, K. A. (1982). Skill and working memory. In G. H. Bower (Ed.), *Psychology of learning and motivation* (Vol. 16, pp. 1–58). New York: Academic Press.

Clark, M. S., Milberg, S., & Ross, J. (1983). Arousal cues arousal-related material in memory: Implications for understanding effects of mood on memory. *Journal of Verbal Learning and Verbal Behavior, 22,* 633–649.

Cofer, C. N. (Ed.). (1975). *The structure of human memory.* San Francisco: Freeman.

Cohen, R. M., Weingartner, H., Smallberg, S. A., Pickar, D., & Murphy, D. L. (1982). Effort and cognition in depression. *Archives of General Psychiatry, 39,* 593–597.

Collins, A. M., & Loftus, E. F. (1975). A spreading activation theory of semantic processing. *Psychological Review, 82,* 407–428.

Collins, A. M., & Quillian, M. R. (1969). Retrieval time from semantic memory. *Journal of Verbal Learning and Verbal Behavior, 8,* 240–247.

Coltheart, M. (1980). Iconic memory and visual persistence. *Perception and Psychophysics, 27,* 183–228.

Conrad, C. (1972). Cognitive economy in semantic memory. *Journal of Experimental Psychology, 92,* 149–154.

Craik, F. I. M., & Lockhart, R. S. (1972). Levels of processing: A framework for memory research. *Journal of Verbal Learning and Verbal Behavior, 11,* 671–684.

Craik, F. I. M., & Simon, E. (1980). Age differences in memory: The roles of attention and depth of processing. In L. W. Poon, J. L. Fozard, L. S. Cermak, D. Arenberg, & L. W. Thompson (Eds.), *New directions in memory and aging: Proceedings of the George Talland memorial conference.* Hillsdale, NJ: Erlbaum.

Craik, F. I. M., & Tulving, E. (1975). Depth of processing and the retention of words in episodic memory. *Journal of Experimental Psychology: General, 104,* 268–294.

Craik. F. I. M., & Watkins, M. J. (1973). The role of rehearsal in short-term memory. *Journal of Verbal Learning and Verbal Behavior, 12,* 559–607.

Delaney, H. D. (1978). Interactions of individual differences with visual and verbal elaboration instructions. *Journal of Educational Psychology, 70,* 306–318.

Didner, R., & Sperling, G. (1980). Perceptual delay: A consequence of metacontrast and apparent motion. *Journal of Experimental Psychology: Human Perception and Performance, 6,* 235–243.

Drewnowski, A., & Murdock, B. B., Jr. (1980). The role of auditory features in memory span for words. *Journal of Experimental Psychology: Human Learning and Memory, 6,* 319–332.

Eich, J. E. (1980). The cue-dependent nature of state-dependent retrieval. *Memory and Cognition, 8,* 157–183.

Eich, J. E. (1985). Context, memory, and integrated item/context imagery. *Journal of Experimental Psychology: Learning, Memory, and Cognition, 11,* 771–779.

Einstein, G. O., & Hunt, R. R. (1980). Levels of processing and organization: Additive effects of individual item and relational processing. *Journal of Experimental Psychology: Human Learning and Memory, 6,* 588–598.

Einstein, G. O., & McDaniel, M. A. (in press). A framework for understanding the mnemonic benefits of bizarre imagery. In M. A. McDaniel & M. Pressley (Eds.), *Imaginal and mnemonic processes.* New York: Springer-Verlag.

Einstein, G. O., McDaniel, M. A., Dunay, D. T., & Stevens, D. T. (1984). Memory for prose: The influence of relational and proposition-specific processing. *Journal of Experimental Psychology: Learning, Memory, and Cognition, 10,* 133–143.

Ellis, H. C. (1973). Stimulus encoding processes in human learning and memory. In G. H. Bower (Ed.), *The psychology of learning and motivation* (Vol. 7, pp. 123–182). New York: Academic Press.

Ellis, H. C. (1986a, March). *The ARESIDORI system: A guide for facilitating and improving your memory.* Unpublished talk presented at the University of New Mexico.

Ellis, H. C. (1986b, August). *Emotional states and memory.* Presidential address to the Division of Experimental Psychology at the annual meeting of the American Psychological Association, Washington, DC.

Ellis, H. C., & Asbrook, P. W. (in press). Resource allocation model of the effects of depressed mood states on memory. In K. Fiedler & J. Forgas (Eds.), *Affect, cognition and social behavior.* Toronto, Canada, and West Germany: Hogrefe.

Ellis, H. C., & Franklin, J. B. (1983). Memory and personality: External versus internal locus of control and superficial organization in free recall. *Journal of Verbal Learning and Verbal Behavior, 22,* 61–74.

Ellis, H. C., & Hunt, R. R. (1983). *Fundamentals of human memory and cognition.* Dubuque, IA: Wm. C. Brown.

Ellis, H. C., Thomas, R. L., McFarland, A. D., & Lane, J. W. (1985). Emotional states and retrieval in episodic memory. *Journal of Experimental Psychology: Learning, Memory, and Cognition, 11,* 363–370.

Ellis, H. C., Thomas, R. L., & Rodriguez, I. A. (1984). Emotional mood states and memory: Elaborative encoding, semantic processing, and cognitive effort. *Journal of Experimental Psychology: Learning, Memory, and Cognition, 10,* 470–482.

Ericsson, K. A., & Chase, W. G. (1982). Exceptional memory. *American Scientist, 10,* 607–614.

Eriksen, C. W., & Collins, J. F. (1967). Some temporal characteristics of visual pattern perception. *Journal of Experimental Psychology, 74,* 476–484.

Flavell, J. H., & Wellman, H. M. (1977). Metamemory. In R. V. Kail, Jr. & J. W. Hagen (Eds.), *Perspectives on the development of memory and cognition* (pp. 3–33). Hillsdale, NJ: Erlbaum.

Flexner, A. J., & Tulving, E. (1982). Priming and recognition failure. *Journal of Verbal Learning and Verbal Behavior, 21,* 260–281.

Geiselman, R. E., & Bjork, R. A. (1980). Primary versus secondary rehearsal in imagined voices: Differential effects on recognition. *Cognitive Psychology, 12,* 188–205.

Graesser, A. C. (1981). *Prose comprehension beyond the word.* New York: Springer-Verlag.

Graf, P., Mandler, G., & Haden, P. (1982). Stimulating amnesic symptoms in normal subjects. *Science, 218,* 1243–1244.

Haber, R. N. (1983). The impending demise of the icon: A critique of the concept of iconic storage in visual information processing. *The Behavioral and Brain Sciences, 6,* 1–54.

Harris, J. E. (1984). Remembering to do things: A forgotten topic. In J. E. Harris & P. E. Morris (Eds.), *Everyday memory, actions, and absentmindedness.* London: Academic Press.

Harris, J. E., & Morris, P. E. (Eds.). (1984). *Everyday memory, actions, and absentmindedness.* London: Academic Press.

Harris, R. J. (1977). Comprehension of pragmatic implications in advertising. *Journal of Applied Psychology, 62,* 603–608.

Harris, R. J. (1981). Inferences in information processing. In G. H. Bower (Ed.), *The psychology of learning and motivation* (Vol. 15, pp. 81–128). New York: Academic Press.

Hasher, L., & Griffin, M. (1978). Reconstructive and reproductive processes in memory. *Journal of Experimental Psychology: Human Learning and Memory, 4,* 318–330.

Hasher, L., Rose, K. C., Zacks, R. T., Sanft, H., & Doren, B. (1985). Mood, recall, and selectivity effects in normal college students. *Journal of Experimental Psychology: General, 114,* 104–118.

Hasher, L., & Zacks, R. T. (1979). Automatic and effortful processes in memory. *Journal of Experimental Psychology: General, 108,* 356–388.

Higbee, K. L. (1977). *Your memory: How it works and how to improve it.* Englewood Cliffs, NJ: Prentice-Hall.

Hirst, W., Johnson, M. K., Kim, J. K., Phelps, E. A., Risse, G., & Volpe, B. T. (1986). Recognition and recall in amnesics. *Journal of Experimental Psychology: Learning, Memory, and Cognition, 12,* 445–451.

Horton, D. L., & Mills, C. B. (1984). Human learning and memory. In M. R. Rosenzweig & L. M. Porter (Eds.), *Annual Review of Psychology, 35,* 361–394.

Hunt, E. (1978). Mechanics of verbal ability. *Psychological Review, 85,* 109–130.

Hunt, R. R., & Einstein, G. O. (1981). Relational and item specific information in memory. *Journal of Verbal Learning and Verbal Behavior, 20,* 497–514.

Hunt, R. R., & Ellis, H. C. (1974). Recognition memory and degree of semantic contextual change. *Journal of Experimental Psychology, 103,* 1153–1159.

Hunt, R. R., & Elliott, J. M. (1980). The role of nonsemantic information in memory: Orthographic distinctiveness effects upon retention. *Journal of Experimental Psychology: General, 109,* 49–74.

Hunt, R. R., Elliott, J. M., & Spence, M. J. (1979). Independent effects of process and structure on encoding. *Journal of Experimental Psychology: Human Learning and Memory, 5,* 339–347.

Hunt, R. R., & Mitchell, D. B. (1982). Independent effects of semantic and nonsemantic distinctiveness. *Journal of Experimental Psychology: Learning, Memory, and Cognition, 8,* 81–87.

Hyde, T. S., & Jenkins, J. J. (1969). Differential effects of incidental tasks on the organization of recall of a list of highly associated words. *Journal of Experimental Psychology, 82,* 472–481.

Jacoby, L. L. (1978). On interpreting the effects of repetition: Solving a problem versus remembering a solution. *Journal of Verbal Learning and Verbal Behavior, 17,* 649–667.

Jacoby, L. L., Craik, F. I. M., & Begg, I. (1979). Effects of decision difficulty on recognition and recall. *Journal of Verbal Learning and Verbal Behavior, 18,* 585–600.

Jacoby, L. L., & Dallas, M. (1981). On the relationship between autobiographical memory and perceptual learning. *Journal of Experimental Psychology: General, 110,* 306–340.

James, W. (1890). *Principles of psychology.* New York: Holt.

Johnson, M. K. (1983). A multiple-entry, modular memory system. In G. H. Bower (Ed.), *The psychology of learning and motivation* (Vol. 17, pp. 81–123). New York: Academic Press.

Johnson, M. K., Bransford, J. D., & Solomon, S. K. (1973). Memory for tacit implications of sentences. *Journal of Experimental Psychology, 98,* 203–205.

Johnson, M. K., & Raye, C. L. (1981). Reality monitoring. *Psychological Review, 88,* 67–85.

Johnson, M. K., Raye, C. L., Foley, H. J., & Foley, M. A. (1981). Cognitive operations and decision bias in reality monitoring. *American Journal of Psychology, 94,* 37–64.

Johnston, W. A., & Heinz, S. P. (1978). Flexibility and capacity demands of attention. *Journal of Experimental Psychology: General, 107,* 420–435.

Kahneman, D. (1973). *Attention and effort.* Englewood Cliffs, NJ: Prentice-Hall.

Kieras, D. E., & Just, M. A. (1984). *New methods in reading comprehension research.* Hillsdale, NJ: Erlbaum.

Kintsch, W. (1974). *The representation of meaning in memory.* Hillsdale, NJ: Erlbaum.

Kintsch, W., & van Dijk, T. A. (1978). Toward a model of text comprehension and production. *Psychological Review, 85,* 363–394.

Klatzky, R. L. (1980). *Human memory.* San Francisco: Freeman.

Klatzky, R. L. (1984). *Memory and awareness.* San Francisco: Freeman.

Kolers, P. (1983). Perception and representation. In M. R. Rosenzweig & L. W. Porter (Eds.), *Annual Review of Psychology, 34,* 129–166.

Kosslyn, S. M. (1981). The medium and message in mental imagery: A theory. *Psychological Review, 88,* 46–66.

Kosslyn, S. M. (1983). *Ghosts in the mind's machine.* New York: Norton.

Kosslyn, S. M., Ball, T. M., & Reiser, B. J. (1978). Visual images preserve metric spatial information: Evidence from studies of image scanning. *Journal of Experimental Psychology: Human Perception and Performance, 4,* 47–60.

Leight, K. A., & Ellis, H. C. (1981). Emotional mood states, strategies, and state-dependency in memory. *Journal of Verbal Learning and Verbal Behavior, 20,* 251–266.

Leonard, J. M., & Whitten, W. B. (1983). Information stored when expecting recall or recognition. *Journal of Experimental Psychology: Learning, Memory, and Cognition, 9,* 440–455.

Lesgold, A. M., & Goldman, S. R. (1973). Encoding uniqueness and the imagery mnemonic in associative learning. *Journal of Verbal Learning and Verbal Behavior, 12,* 193–202.

Lloyd-Bostock, S., & Clifford, B. R. (Eds.). (1982). *Evaluating witness evidence.* Chichester, England: Wiley.

Loftus, E. F. (1979). *Eyewitness testimony.* Cambridge, MA: Harvard University Press.

Loftus, E. F., & Loftus, G. R. (1980). On the permanence of stored information in the human brain. *American Psychologist, 35,* 409–420.

Loftus, E. F., Miller, D. G., & Burns, H. J. (1978). Semantic integration of verbal information into a visual memory. *Journal of Experimental Psychology: Human Learning and Memory, 4,* 19–31.

Loftus, E. F., & Palmer, J. C. (1974). Reconstruction of automobile destruction: An example of the interaction between language and memory. *Journal of Verbal Learning and Verbal Behavior, 13,* 585–589.

Lorayne, H., & Lucas, J. (1974). *The memory book.* New York: Stein & Day.

Luria, A. R. (1968). *The mind of a mnemonist.* New York: Basic Books.

Maki, R. H., & Schuler, J. (1980). Effects of rehearsal duration and level of processing on memory for words. *Journal of Verbal Learning and Verbal Behavior, 19,* 36–45.

Mandler, J. M. (1979). Categorical and schematic organization in memory. In C. R. Puff (Ed.), *Memory organization and structure.* New York: Academic Press.

Mandler, J. M. (1984). *Stories, scripts, and scenes: Aspects of schema theory.* Hillsdale, NJ: Erlbaum.

McCloskey, M., & Watkins, M. J. (1978). The seeing-more-than-is there phenomenon: Implications for the locus of iconic storage. *Journal of Experimental Psychology: Human Perception and Performance, 4,* 553–564.

McCloskey, M., & Zaragoza, M. (1985). Misleading postevent information and memory for events: Arguments and evidence against memory impairment hypotheses. *Journal of Experimental Psychology: General, 114,* 1–16.

McDaniel, M. A., & Einstein, G. O. (1986). Bizarre imagery as an effective mnemonic aid: The importance of distinctiveness. *Journal of Experimental Psychology: Learning, Memory, and Cognition, 12,* 54–65.

McDaniel, M. A., & Einstein, G. O., Dunay, P. K., & Cobb, R. C. (1986). Encoding difficulty and memory: Toward a unifying theory. *Journal of Memory and Language, 25,* 645–656.

McDaniel, M. A., & Pressley, M. (in press). *Imagery and mnemonic processes.* New York: Springer-Verlag.

McKoon, G., & Ratcliffe, R. (1979). Priming in episodic and semantic memory. *Journal of Verbal Learning and Verbal Behavior, 18,* 463–480.

McKoon, G., Ratcliffe, R., & Dell, G. S. (1986). A critical evaluation of the semantic–episodic distinction. *Journal of Experimental Psychology: Learning, Memory, and Cognition, 12,* 295–306.

Merikle, P. M. (1980). Selection from visual persistence by perceptual groups and category membership. *Journal of Experimental Psychology: General, 109,* 279–295.

Miller, G. A. (1966). The magical number seven, plus or minus two: Some limits on our capacity for information processing. *Psychological Review, 63,* 81–97.

Mitchell, D. B., & Richman, C. L. (1980). Confirmed reservations: Mental travel. *Journal of Experimental Psychology: Human Perception and Performance, 6,* 58–66.

Morris, C. D., Bransford, J. D., & Franks, J. J. (1977). Levels of processing versus test-appropriate strategies. *Journal of Verbal Learning and Verbal Behavior, 16,* 519–533.

Neisser, U. (1976). *Cognition and reality: Principles and Implications of Cognitive Psychology.* New York: Freeman.

Neisser, U. (1982). *Memory observed.* San Francisco: Freeman.

Nelson, D. L., & Archer, C. S. (1972). The first-letter mnemonic. *Journal of Educational Psychology, 63,* 482–486.

Nelson, D. L., & McEvoy, C. L. (1979). Encoding context and set size. *Journal of Experimental Psychology: Human Learning and Memory, 5,* 292–314.

Nelson, D. L., Walling, J. R., & McEvoy, C. L. (1979). Doubts about depth. *Journal of Experimental Psychology: Human Learning and Memory, 5,* 24–44.

Norman, D. A. (1973). Memory, knowledge, and the answering of questions. In R. L. Solso (Ed.), *Contemporary issues in cognitive psychology: The Loyola symposium.* Washington, DC: Winston.

Norman, D. A. (1976). *Memory and attention.* New York: Wiley.

Norman, D. A., & Rumelhart, D. E. (1975). *Explorations in cognition.* New York: Freeman.

O'Brien, E. J., & Myers, J. L. (1985). When comprehension difficulty improves memory for text. *Journal of Experimental Psychology: Learning, Memory, and Cognition, 11,* 12–21.

Paivio, A. (1969). Mental imagery in associative learning and memory. *Psychological Review, 76,* 241–263.

Paivio, A. (1971). *Imagery and verbal processes.* New York: Holt, Rinehart & Winston.

Paivio, A. (1974). Language and knowledge of the world. *Educational Researcher, 3,* 5–12.

Palmer, S. E. (1978). Fundamental aspects of cognition representation. In E. Rosch & B. Lloyd (Eds.), *Cognition and categorization.* Hillsdale, NJ: Erlbaum.

Parkin, A. J. (1984). Levels of processing, context, and facilitation of pronunciation. *Acta Psychologia, 55,* 19–29.

Peterson, L. R., & Peterson, M. J. (1959). Short-term retention of individual verbal items. *Journal of Experimental Psychology, 58,* 193–198.

Postman, L. J., & Underwood, B. J. (1973). Critical issues in interference theory. *Memory and Cognition, 1,* 19–40.

Pressley, M., Levin, J. R., & Delaney, H. D. (1982). The mnemonic keyword method. *Review of Educational Research, 52,* 61–91.

Pylyshyn, Z. W. (1973). What the mind's eye tells the mind's brain: A critique of mental imagery. *Psychological Bulletin, 80,* 1–24.

Rabinowitz, M., & Mandler, J. M. (1983). Organization and information retrieval. *Journal of Experimental Psychology: Learning, Memory, and Cognition, 9,* 430–439.

Ratcliffe, R., & McKoon, G. (1986). More on the distinction between episodic and semantic memories. *Journal of Experimental Psychology: Learning, Memory, and Cognition, 12,* 312–313.

Reed, S. K. (1982). *Cognition.* Monterey, CA: Brooks/Cole.

Richman, C. L., Mitchell, D. B., & Reznick, J. S. (1979). Mental travel: Some reservations. *Journal of Experimental Psychology: Human Perception and Performance, 5,* 13–18.

Rips, L. J., Shoben, E. J., & Smith, E. E. (1973). Semantic distance and the verification of semantic relations. *Journal of Verbal Learning and Verbal Behavior, 12,* 1–20.

Ritchey, G. H., & Beal, C. R. (1980). Image detail and recall: Evidence for within-item elaboration. *Journal of Experimental Psychology: Human Learning and Memory, 6,* 66–76.

Robinson, F. P. (1961). *Effective study.* New York: Harper & Row.

Roediger, H. L., & Neely, J. H. (1982). Retrieval blocks in episodic and semantic memory. *Canadian Journal of Psychology, 36,* 213–423.

Rundus, D. (1980). Maintenance rehearsal and long-term recency. *Memory and Cognition, 8,* 226–230.

Schacter, D. L., & Graf, P. (1986). Effects of elaborative processing on implicit and explicit memory for new associations. *Journal of Experimental Psychology: Learning, Memory, and Cognition, 12,* 432–444.

Schank, R., & Abelson, R. (1977). *Scripts, plans, goals, & understanding.* Hillsdale, NJ: Erlbaum.

Shepard, R. N., & Metzler, J. (1971). Mental rotation of three-dimensional objects. *Science, 171,* 701–703.

Shepherd, J. W., Ellis, H. D., & Davies, G. M. (1982). *Identification evidence: A psychological evaluation.* Aberdeen, Scotland: Aberdeen University Press.

Slamecka, N. J., & Fevreiski, J. (1983). The generation effect when generation fails. *Journal of Verbal Learning and Verbal Behavior, 22,* 153–163.

Slamecka, N. J., & Graf, P. (1978). The generation effect: Delineation of a phenomenon. *Journal of Experimental Psychology: Human Learning and Memory, 4,* 592–604.

Smith, E. E., Shoben, E. J., & Rips, L. J. (1974). Structure and processes in semantic memory: A featural model for semantic decision. *Psychological Review, 81,* 214–241.

Smith, S. M. (1986). Environmental context-dependent recognition memory using a short-term memory task for input. *Memory and Cognition, 14,* 347–354.

Smith, S. M., Glenberg, A., & Bjork, R. A. (1978). Environmental context and human memory. *Memory and Cognition, 6,* 342–353.

Sperling, G. (1960). The information available in brief visual presentations. *Psychological Monographs, 74* (Whole No. 498).

Spilich, G. J., Vesonder, G. T., Chiesi, H. L., & Voss, J. F. (1979). Text processing of domain-related information for individuals with high- and low-domain knowledge. *Journal of Verbal Learning and Verbal Behavior, 18,* 275–290.

Spiro, R. J. (1980). Accommodative reconstruction in prose recall. *Journal of Verbal Learning and Verbal Behavior, 19,* 84–95.

Squire, L. R. (1982). The neuropsychology of human memory. *Annual Review of Neuroscience, 5,* 241–273.

Squire, L. R., Shimamura, A. P., & Graf, P. (1985). Independence of recognition memory and priming effects: A neuropsychological analysis. *Journal of Experimental Psychology: Learning, Memory, and Cognition, 11,* 37–44.

Stein, B. S. (1978). Depth of processing reexamined: The effects of precision of encoding and test appropriateness. *Journal of Verbal Learning and Verbal Behavior, 17,* 165–174.

Stern, L. (1985). *The structures and strategies of human memory.* Homewood, IL: Dorsey Press.

Sternberg, S. (1966). High-speed scanning in human memory. *Science, 153,* 652–654.

Sulin, R. A., & Dooling, D. J. (1974). Intrusions of a thematic idea in retention of prose. *Journal of Experimental Psychology, 103,* 255–262.

Summers, W. V., Horton, D. L., & Diehl, V. A. (1985). Contextual knowledge during encoding influences sentence recognition. *Journal of Experimental Psychology: Learning, Memory, and Cognition, 11,* 771–779.

Swanson, H. L. (1984). Effects of cognitive effort and word distinctiveness on learning disabled and nondisabled readers' recall. *Journal of Educational Psychology, 76,* 894–908.

Teasdale, J. D., & Russell, M. L. (1983). Differential effects of induced mood on the recall of positive, negative and neutral words. *British Journal of Clinical Psychology, 22,* 163–172.

Thomas, E. L., & Robinson, H. A. (1972). *Improving reading in every class: A sourcebook for teachers.* Boston: Allyn & Bacon.

Tulving, E. (1962). Subjective organization in free recall of "unrelated" words. *Psychological Review, 69,* 344–354.

Tulving, E. (1974). Cue-dependent forgetting. *American Scientist, 62,* 78–82.

Tulving, E. (1983). *Elements of episodic memory.* Oxford: Oxford University Press.

Tulving, E. (1986). What kind of a hypothesis is the distinction between episodic and semantic memory? *Journal of Experimental Psychology: Learning, Memory, and Cognition, 12,* 307–311.

Tulving, E., & Thomson, D. M. (1971). Retrieval processes in recognition memory: Effects of associative context. *Journal of Experimental Psychology, 87,* 116–124.

Tulving, E., & Thomson, D. M. (1973). Encoding specificity and retrieval processes in episodic memory. *Psychological Review, 80,* 352–373.

Turvey, M. T. (1973). On peripheral and central processes in vision: Inferences from an information processing analysis of masking with patterned stimuli. *Psychological Review, 80,* 1–52.

Turvey, M. T. (1977). Contrasting orientations to the theory of visual information-processing. *Psychological Review, 80,* 67–88.

Tyler, S. W., Hertel, P. T., McCallum, M. C., & Ellis, H. C. (1979). Cognitive effort and memory. *Journal of Experimental Psychology: Human Learning and Memory, 5,* 607–617.

Waugh, N. C., & Norman, D. A. (1965). Primary memory. *Psychological Review, 72,* 89–104.

Wells, G. L., & Loftus, E. F. (Eds.). (1984). *Eyewitness testimony: Psychological perspectives.* New York: Cambridge University Press.

Wells, G. L., & Turtle, J. W. (1986). Eyewitness identification: The importance of lineup models. *Psychological Bulletin, 3,* 320–329.

Wessells, M. G. (1982). *Cognitive psychology.* New York: Harper & Row.

Wickelgren, W. A. (1973). The long and the short of memory. *Psychological Bulletin, 80,* 425–438.

Wood, G., & Underwood, B. J. (1967). Implicit verbal responses and conceptual similarity. *Journal of Verbal Learning and Verbal Behavior, 6,* 1–10.

Yarmey, A. D. (1979). *The psychology of eyewitness testimony.* New York: Free Press.

Yates, F. A. (1966). *The art of memory.* Chicago: University of Chicago Press.

Zacks, R. T., Hasher, L., Sanft, H. S., & Rose, K. C. (1983). Encoding effort and recall: A cautionary note. *Journal of Experimental Psychology: Learning, Memory, and Cognition, 9,* 747–756.

Zechmeister, E. B., & Nyberg, S. E. (1982). *Human memory.* Monterey, CA: Brooks/Cole.